WHERE THE WILD GRAPE GROWS

# Where the Wild Grape Grows

SELECTED WRITINGS, 1930–1950

DOROTHY WEST

Edited by Verner D. Mitchell and Cynthia Davis

UNIVERSITY OF MASSACHUSETTS PRESS    AMHERST AND BOSTON

LC 2004020329
ISBN 1-55849-471-5

Designed by Mary Mendell
Set in Quadraat by Graphic Composition, Inc.
Printed and bound by The Maple-Vail Book Manufacturing Group

Library of Congress Cataloging-in-Publication Data

West, Dorothy, 1909–
   Where the wild grape grows : selected writings, 1930–1950 /
Dorothy West ; edited by Verner D. Mitchell and Cynthia Davis.
      p. cm.
   ISBN 1-55849-471-5 (cloth : alk. paper)
   1. African Americans—Fiction. 2. West, Dorothy, 1909–
Correspondence. 3. Authors, American—20th century—
Correspondence. 4. African American authors—Correspondence.
5. Harlem Renaissance—Sources. I. Mitchell, Verner D., 1957–
II. Davis, Cynthia J., 1964– III. Title.
   PS3545.E82794W48 2004
   813'.54 dc22

                                        2004020329


British Library Cataloguing in Publication data are available.

For our parents
Mary and Willie Mitchell Sr.
and
Mary and Russell Davis

and to Veronica and Robert
with love

# CONTENTS

## ACKNOWLEDGMENTS

THIS BOOK would not have been possible without the generosity, kindness, and scholarship of a number of very important persons. Barbara and Courtney Franklin offered valuable perspectives on Dorothy West's family life. Abigail McGrath shared her memories of her mother, Helene Johnson, and of Edna and Lloyd Thomas and Olivia Wyndham. We are indebted to Michael Henry Adams for his groundbreaking research on queer Harlem. Isabel Washington Powell and Adelaide Cromwell gave generously of their time and memories in personal interviews.

The unsung heroes of academic research are, of course, librarians, and we were fortunate in working with some of the very best. We gratefully acknowledge Ruth Caruth, Beinecke Rare Book and Manuscript Library, Yale University; Karen Jefferson and Cathy Lynn Mundale, Atlanta University Center Archives; Janet Sims-Wood, Moorland-Spingarn Research Center, Howard University; Beth Madison Howse, Franklin Library, Fisk University; JC Johnson, Mugar Memorial Library, Boston University; Brenda B. Square, Amistad Research Center, Tulane University; Sylvia McDowell, Ellen Shea, and Jacalyn Blume, Schlesinger Library, Radcliffe Institute, Harvard University; Perida A. Mitchell, Thomas County (Georgia) Public Library; Dave Proulx, Family History Center, Plantation, Florida; Nishani Frazier, Carlos Torres, and Sarah Starr, Western Reserve Historical Society, Cleveland, Ohio; and the staff of the Library of Congress, Manuscript Division, WPA Federal Writers' Project Collection.

We also thank Dawn Jackson for helping to recover West's *Daily News* stories; Edward Hawthorne for his photographs of West's family homes; Theodies Mitchell and Susie and Kumar Shah for generously opening their homes to us during research trips; Michelle Banks, Equal Employment Office, University of Memphis, for vital help securing research funding; and Joan E. Kolligian of McGrath and Kane for assistance with permissions.

We are deeply indebted to Cheryl A. Wall, whose pioneering work on black women writers provided the inspiration for work on Helene Johnson and Dorothy West. Tom Wirth's book *Richard Bruce Nugent: Gay Rebel of the Harlem*

*Renaissance* was helpful in validating the important contribution of the gay artistic community. Warm thanks to our colleagues who read and commented on various parts of the manuscript: Amritjit Singh, Pearlie Peters, Maryemma Graham, Ethel Young-Minor, DoVeanna Fulton, Carol-Rae Sodano, Ladrica Menson-Furr, and Loretta McBride. For his commitment to African American literature, his consummate professionalism, and his encouragement, warmth, and generosity, we especially thank Dolan Hubbard. Finally, we thank our editors, Paul Wright, Carol Betsch, and Amanda Heller, and the staff at the University of Massachusetts Press.

# PREFACE
## Toward a Reappraisal of Dorothy West's Work

WHEN DOROTHY WEST died in 1998 at age ninety-one, she left, in addition to two published novels and many anthologized short stories, a body of writing that had never been published or collected. The essays West wrote for the Works Progress Administration (WPA), her articles in the *Vineyard Gazette*, and an unpublished novella—*Where the Wild Grape Grows*—offer a unique insight into the milieu of Boston's black upper-middle class as well as into the personal and intellectual life of one of its daughters. These pieces, along with West's letters, provide a hitherto unavailable perspective on the life and work of a community of African American women writers in the mid-twentieth century and should, we believe, contribute to the reappraisal of West's work.

We have organized this book into three main sections. First is a general introduction, where we provide a sociocultural analysis of West's family as representative members of the black Bostonian middle class, offer a critical overview of her writing, and trace the influence of a number of important individuals on her life. We make available, in section two, the best of West's uncollected and unpublished short stories, WPA essays, and her novella *Where the Wild Grape Grows*. And in part three we offer a selection of her correspondence with other artists, in an effort to contextualize her position in the Harlem Renaissance.

Like her cousin Helene Johnson, Dorothy West was an extremely private person. While Johnson, however, refused interviews and effectively made herself invisible, West employed what her friend Zora Hurston called "feather-bed resistance." She allowed the probes of inquisitive interviewers in—but they never came out. Despite her witty and vivacious personality, she maintained a discreet silence around her personal life; rarely did she disclose information other than that which she had already shaped and honed in her public writing. Her many interviews, masterpieces of diplomacy and evasion, served largely to mythologize her Bostonian family and her precocious, privileged childhood. Over the years, she repeated the identical anecdotes, sometimes launching into a well-rehearsed story even before the visitor asked the first question. Interviews typically included a description of her mother, Rachel

Benson, the much younger, very beautiful golden-skinned wife of Isaac West, one of the first black wholesale merchants in Boston's Faneuil Hall market. Rachel eventually brought her father and several of her eighteen siblings from the family home in Camden, South Carolina, to her large, four-story house on Brookline Avenue, which Grampa Benson always compared to the nearby Boston Museum of Fine Arts. Other stories in West's interview repertoire involved her extraordinary maturity and exceptional talent for writing: the family called her "a little sawed-off woman" (Dalsgård 30). While she enjoyed recounting how she and Helene Johnson traveled to New York City for the 1926 Literary Awards Dinner hosted by *Opportunity* magazine, won prizes there, and became the youngest members of the Harlem Renaissance, she downplayed the fact that Helene's work had been published in *Opportunity* the previous year.

With the exception of her father, Isaac, men rarely figured in West's conversations, though she often concluded by mentioning proposals of marriage from Countee Cullen, Henry Moon, and Langston Hughes, and by alluding vaguely to reasons why she chose never to marry: she would not have been a good wife; her parents' marriage had been dysfunctional; she could not make decisions; she did not want a sexual relationship; one could not combine art with a family, as indeed proved to be the case with Helene Johnson.

Although her stories were fundamentally true, West left much unsaid. She often teased interviewers by adopting a free-associative style, switching topics in midstream, uttering non sequiturs, ignoring direct questions, and practicing her mother's dictum that "speech was given man to hide his thoughts" (West, *The Richer* 169). Like Rachel, West never told the whole story. She rarely discussed the years between 1945 and her "rediscovery" in the 1980s, or her important friendships with Marian Minus and Elizabeth White. Seldom, moreover, did she address those issues of particular interest to literary historians and critics. Specifically, how did family stories transmute into literature? Where did she receive her education? Which writers had influenced her? With whom did she establish emotional, sexual, and intellectual connections? In making available to the public a selection of West's work, we hope to answer some of these questions.

Dorothy West wrote throughout her long life, but the need to support herself, her commitment to a large extended family, and her sensitivity to possible critical rebuff limited her output. Before moving back to Massachusetts in 1945, she worked in New York as an actress, a WPA writer, a social worker, and an editor of two literary magazines. Her family required a great deal of her time, and this was a double-edged sword. On the one hand, they inspired her best novels and short stories: the Benson-West history offers a unique perspective on the first wave of black Southerners who migrated north around the turn of the century and achieved middle-class status. On the other hand, the demands of her widowed mother and the obligation to care for a number of elderly relatives interrupted what should have been the most productive years of her life. Perhaps, too, West's reluctance to submit her work reflected her extreme sensitivity; she admitted to being temperamental about her writing. When she began work on The Wedding, her second novel, the outspoken contempt for the black middle class among the Black Arts Movement of the 1960s discouraged her, and she suspended the project for many years. She finally published it in 1995, at age eighty-eight, with the support of her fellow Martha's Vineyard resident and editor Jacqueline Kennedy Onassis, to whom it is dedicated.

Although she spent considerable time in Europe, West set few of her stories abroad. Rather than search for exotic locations or unusual material, she worked and reworked certain themes and topics, grounded in her social milieu, which resonated with her in a powerful way. These themes are reflected in this volume: the bonds of work and cooperation among women ("Blackberrying" and "Quilting"); the constraints of race, class, color, and gender ("Elephant's Dance," "Mammy," "Mrs. Marlowe," and "The Black Dress"); dysfunctional marriages ("Hannah Byde" and "Prologue to a Life"); children's vulnerability and loss of innocence ("Pluto" and "My Baby"); the courage and loneliness of the elderly ("The Stairs," "The Inroads of Time," and Where the Wild Grape Grows); the arresting beauty and power of nature ("Winter on Martha's Vineyard" and "Carolina"). West's nature writing is rarely addressed, yet much of her work includes lyrical descriptions of plants, animals, and the changing seasons. Her column for the Vineyard Gazette, "The Water Boy," recorded her bird watching and the subtle interplay of people and nature on the island of Martha's Vineyard.

Also included is at least one selection that will perhaps seem out of character. "The House Across the Way" is a gothic tale of repressed passion and domestic sacrifice, reminiscent of Edith Wharton's Ethan Frome. Although it is unlike anything else West ever wrote, it does reflect her interest in the supernatural: as a child she had several psychic experiences and believed she had "healing hands" (Roses 49). The story also suggests West's psychological reasons for not marrying and for devoting herself to ailing relatives, animals, and children.

Central to all her writing, however, is the powerful influence of her mother, Rachel Benson. Rachel's artistic talent, intelligence, wit, and irrepressible personality are reflected in dozens of fictional characters, ranging in age from eleven to sixty-three. Rachel's progress from childhood to old age becomes for West the journey of the black female artist whose talent, thwarted by racial, class, and gender oppression, sometimes expresses itself vicariously through her children's success, and sometimes festers in domestic discontent. Husbands are cheated, lied to, and thrown out of the bedroom primarily because, although black men's lives are certainly no "crystal stair," men are perceived as enjoying more independence and opportunities than women. Children, by contrast, represent the future and merit limitless sacrifice. West's Rachelesque characters are never merely one-dimensional shrews, however, because of her compassion for the tragedy of wasted feminine ability. In investigating the "real" Rachel Benson, we explore black women's struggle for recognition and validation in the early part of the twentieth century.

Rachel not only inspired the subject matter of West's fiction but also taught her daughter much of the craft of storytelling. From her mother, West learned how to exaggerate—to shape or change details in order to make her point. She learned that a good storyteller never reveals everything, and she was able to employ suspense, irony, and understatement in her work.

In addition to Rachel, West was deeply influenced and inspired by many creative and talented individuals. She was close to most of the important Harlem Renaissance writers, including Helene Johnson, Wallace Thurman, Zora Neale Hurston, Countee Cullen, Arna Bontemps, Claude McKay, Langston Hughes, and Marian Minus. Members of West's artistic circle included Edna Lewis Thomas, Alberta Hunter, Augusta Savage, Richmond Barthé, Henry and Mollie Moon, and Lois Mailou Jones. Since West never married or had children, her friends were an important source of intellectual and emotional support. Over the years, they cooked and ate together, traveled, and critiqued and promoted one another's work.

Among the many critics who have called for sustained study of Dorothy West's fiction is Patricia Liggins Hill, who writes in *Call & Response* (1998), "Of good use would be a definitive collection of West's short stories introduced by a very perceptive scholar" (Hill 1272). *Where the Wild Grape Grows* answers, in part, Hill's call. Although we include some of West's later writings, we generally limit our collection to pieces written between 1930 and 1950, the decades of West's most prolific and critically praised work.

WHERE THE WILD GRAPE GROWS

# INTRODUCTION
## Dorothy West and Her Circle

DOROTHY WEST discovered the style and themes of her work at an early age. Her first extant written words, composed at the age of five on scraps of lined paper, were, "money book dear send please loving." A subsequent draft read: "Dear Father, Send me a box please of rose ribbon and put some money in the box. Put love in the box too. With love."[1] Because other practice words included "sand" and "sea," and the date is given as August 19, 1912, it seems likely that Rachel Benson West and her daughter were summering at their cottage on Martha's Vineyard and that Rachel was combining Dorothy's penmanship lesson with one of her frequent, oblique requests for money.

Rachel's need for money was a fraught subject in the household. According to West, her mother always resented the fact that "my father was quite well-to-do, but he never gave [her] any money" (Guinier 157). Isaac prided himself on being a good provider and had given Rachel the Vineyard cottage on her twenty-first birthday. Nevertheless, his childhood in slavery and the need for liquidity in a volatile business made him frugal, while Rachel's assistance to her many siblings in South Carolina and her social aspirations required a great deal of cash. Frustrated by her financial dependence and her lack of real power in the household, Rachel engaged in constant sub rosa warfare with Isaac over access to the family income. She had no qualms about lying to her husband or using her daughter as a pawn in her convoluted schemes.

Even when Dorothy was a very young child, her moral sense told her it was wrong to use people for one's own ends. She was precocious; she saw clearly how adults manipulated the truth, and even their children, in the struggle for domestic control, and was "fascinated by the power that parents have over their children" (McDowell 277). In stories such as "Funeral," West's young characters feel betrayed and vulnerable. "My mummy tells lies," says Judy sadly. "It's wicked to lie to your little girl" (72). The children in West's stories,

---

1. Dorothy West Papers, box 1, folder 3, Schlesinger Library, Radcliffe Institute, Harvard University. Subsequent references to this collection are cited in the text, abbreviated DWP, followed by the box number and folder number.

notes Margaret Perry, are innocent and incorruptible; "it is only in the child's confrontation with the adult world that . . . ruination begins" (132). At the age of seven, West had found a focus for her writing. She began transmuting family dramas into little sketches. Always sensitive to hypocrisy and suspicious of hierarchies of power—whether between parents and children, men and women, or the state and the individual—West explored these issues in her short stories, essays, and two novels, The Living Is Easy (1948) and The Wedding (1995).

As Dorothy later recognized, her mother's intrigues were not completely selfish. Although she pawned everything to raise cash, much of her ambition was driven by a desire for racial uplift, particularly for her daughter and for Helene Johnson and Eugenia Rickson, the two nieces whom she and Isaac supported. She and her husband had suffered poverty and humiliation in the rural South, and she was determined that the next generation would never know the deprivations from which they had escaped to Boston. Toward this goal, she lobbied Isaac to move the family to increasingly upscale neighborhoods. In 1914 the family left the South End for predominantly Irish and Jewish Brookline Avenue, on the edge of Back Bay. According to West's cousin Abigail McGrath, however, the version of the family finances presented in The Living Is Easy was much exaggerated. Although the façade of "real Boston Brahmins" was preserved, in reality "all of the sisters pitched in together . . . in order to maintain a lifestyle" in which the girls "went to the theater, joined writing clubs, did all of the cultural things that young ladies of privilege did" (124).

## The Black Bostonians

It is not surprising that Dorothy West became a novelist; after all, both her parents possessed the vivid imagination and intelligence that enabled them to construct their own narratives of American success and to evade the paralyzing constrictions of race and class. In writing down her family's stories, West demonstrated the rise of the black middle class through hard work and persistence against almost overwhelming obstacles. In this context, it is difficult to overestimate the importance of the city of Boston in the family narrative and in the sense of identity of the Wests. Whether Isaac and Rachel met in Springfield or Boston,[2] the point remains that both moved north at the turn of the century. For each, the city offered different but complementary advantages: for Isaac, the opportunities were in business; for Rachel, in education, culture, and the advancement of her family.

Isaac West, a generation older than his wife, was born in 1860 on a planta-

2. West often claimed that she had written so many versions of her parents' meeting, she was not sure which was the true one.

tion in Henrico County, Virginia, where his father was probably a preacher and his mother a cook. The family appears to have been stable and close-knit. After Emancipation, his widowed mother, Mary, moved her five sons to Richmond, where she cooked in a boardinghouse. Isaac, whose job was to accompany his mother's employer to the market, loved the excitement of haggling, the rapid-fire calculations, and the exchange of fresh foods and money. Despite the lack of models or mentors for young black entrepreneurs, Isaac knew that he wanted his own business. On October 20, 1871, Isaac's eldest brother, Christopher, escorted Mary, Isaac, and brothers Winston, John, and Warner from their home on Richmond's Eighth Street to the Freedman's Bank, where he opened accounts for all of them.[3] Isaac was eleven years old.

According to West, her father was a disciplined and frugal child who habitually denied himself treats in order to save, in an old cigar box, the pennies he earned doing chores. He and his mother combined their savings and by 1880 had opened a popular boardinghouse and restaurant, where Mary cooked and Isaac, Winston, and John waited on customers.[4] Although he had no formal education, Isaac purchased lessons from educated individuals; he "taught himself to write in a Spencerian hand, to read whatever was set before him, to talk with a totally literate tongue, and . . . to figure like a wizard" (West, *The Richer* 183).

The city of Richmond could not contain Isaac's ambition; eventually, he and Mary sold the boardinghouse and moved to Springfield, Massachusetts. The Freedman's Bank of Virginia encouraged settlement in the industrial Massachusetts cities of Springfield, Worcester, New Bedford, and Boston, and perhaps it was at the bank where he deposited his childhood savings that Isaac learned about his future home. He apprenticed himself to a fruit wholesaler and a few years later opened his own retail fruit store and ice cream parlor on Springfield's main street. His courage and entrepreneurship are particularly impressive, considering that free black businessmen had always faced obstacles in the North. According to an observer from France in 1788, "the whites . . . like not to give them credit to enable them to undertake any extensive commerce nor even to give them means of a common education by receiving them into their counting houses" (Piersen 46). Isaac's difficulties in getting credit from a bank probably inspired West's description of his namesake in *The Wedding*. It is unclear why Isaac left Springfield, but West suggests in *The Living Is Easy* that his partner had embezzled funds from the business.

Undeterred, Isaac arrived in Boston with five dollars in his pocket and sought work in the Faneuil Hall wholesale district. When he opened his own

3. Freedman Bank records and U.S. Bureau of the Census, 1880, Richmond, Henrico County, Virginia, National Archives film T9-1371, 164C.
4. Ibid.

fruit business, his skills at calculating accounts, anticipating the market, and ripening fruit earned the respect of his employees, his competitors, his bankers, and his adopted city. A distributor for the Boston Fruit Company (which became United Fruit in 1899), he was nicknamed "The Black Banana King." According to West's cousin Barbara Franklin, the city of Boston presented him with several tokens of appreciation, including the gold charms of a banana and a pineapple that Dorothy always wore for good luck.

There were a number of reasons why Massachusetts at the turn of the century was the destination of choice for black Southerners like Isaac and Rachel West. First, Boston had long been associated with opportunity and social justice. In 1656, "Bostion" Ken became the first African American to purchase property when he acquired a house in Dorchester and four acres of wheat. Second, alliances between free blacks and abolitionists were long-standing. Frederick Douglass and David Walker both began their freedom-fighting activities in Massachusetts. Walker, in fact, deliberately selected Boston as his base because of "the opportunity [it] afforded him to work to free his shackled brothers and sisters. . . . Within months of his entrance into Massachusetts, Walker was actively engaged in organized resistance" (Mitchell, "David Walker" 96). He was undoubtedly familiar with the work of the abolitionist John Kenrick, a white horticulturalist, the owner of one of the finest fruit tree nurseries in America, and probably a supplier to Thomas Jefferson. Kenrick's fifty-nine-page pamphlet "Horrors of Slavery," which predated the work of William Lloyd Garrison and Wendell Phillips, warned that "Americans stand exposed to the righteous rebukes of Providence for this glaring inconsistency and inhumanity" (qtd. in Marchione 2). Finally, prospective emigrants would have been aware that the 2,000 soldiers in the famous Fifty-fourth and Fifty-fifth Infantry and the Fifth Cavalry had trained at Camp Meigs in Hyde Park, a suburb of Boston, and that many veterans, like James Trotter, had settled in the area after the Civil War.

The written word was particularly instrumental in publicizing Massachusetts as a desirable location. The state had figured prominently not only in Douglass's freedom narratives and Walker's *Appeal in Four Articles* (1830) but also in *A Black Woman's Civil War Memoirs* by Susie King Taylor. In fact, Taylor's 1902 autobiography provided a detailed guide for newcomers to Boston. Her precise description of how she claimed her husband's military pension, left Savannah by steamboat, acquired work in Boston, and became an advocate for black veterans was clearly intended to facilitate the migration of others. She even provided the addresses of potential employers.

Employment, as would be expected, was the most compelling draw of Massachusetts for Isaac West and his contemporaries. Although free persons of color in New England had always faced many challenges—in the eighteenth century, whites twice drove William Grimes of Connecticut out of business, used the courts against him, and warned him out of town—the North provided relatively more opportunity than the postwar South for both employment and education (Piersen 46). Between 1890 and 1900, African Americans worked in 96 of the 123 vocations listed in the census. They found jobs on the docks and in mills and factories, and were hired as ostlers, drivers, masons, tailors, carpenters, undertakers, milliners, grocery clerks, and domestics. Heads of household in Everett, where many of Rachel West's friends lived, worked as customhouse officials, barbers, chefs, brakemen, steelworkers, machinists, dry goods salesmen, granite cutters, seamen, and pastry cooks. A number of black merchants, such as Henry C. Turner, Phoebe Whitehurst Glover, J. H. Lewis, Joseph Lee, John C. Coburn, and eventually Isaac West, owned prosperous businesses in desirable locations on Boston's Washington, Market, and Newbury streets. By 1914, one-eighth of Boston's African American residents owned their own homes.[5] Their children attended either the free public schools or private academies, and some, such as Richard Greener (class of 1870), Clement Morgan ('90), and Alberta Scott ('98), graduated from Harvard and Radcliffe. Boston was also the destination of brilliant men like Roland Hayes, who had graduated from prominent black universities such as Atlanta and Fisk.

Black-owned publications connected the community and publicized Boston's advantages. Archibald Grimké's journal *The Hub* (whose audience was interracial) advised young people on proper deportment and protested any form of discrimination in public facilities. In the 1890s Julia Coston created the *Afro-American Journal of Fashion* and solicited articles from Mary Church Terrell. Josephine Ruffin's *Woman's Era*, an organ of the Woman's Era Club, had an explicitly political, suffragist, anti-lynching platform. After Monroe Trotter and George Forbes launched the Boston *Guardian* in 1910, an anti-Trotter faction published the *Chronicle* in order to promote Booker T. Washington's philosophy, and Washington also secretly underwrote Pauline Hopkins's *Colored American Magazine*, although this affiliation resulted in Hopkins resigning her position as editor in 1904.

Housing was not segregated, and unlike in Southern cities, which provided services based on racially determined neighborhoods, Boston's "public agencies pursued a policy of service without regard to ethnic background. . . . Sewer, water, gas, and electric utilities were . . . as available in the immigrant North End as in the native Back Bay" (Warner 32). Isaac West readily found lodgings in the predominantly Irish and African American South End. The original black community was located in the West End, on the north slope of Beacon Hill, where the first school for black children was established on May Street in 1798. A few blocks away on Smith Court, in 1806, free blacks raised

---

5. U.S. Bureau of the Census, 1900, Middlesex County, Massachusetts; Daniels 329, 371.

$7,000 and black craftsmen and laborers built the African Meeting House. Under the spiritual direction of the Reverend Thomas Paul, an ancestor of Pauline Hopkins, "the Meeting House performed many social and religious functions and served as an anchor for African American settlement" (Sichel 25).[6] Before the Civil War, Irish, Italians, Russian Jews, and other immigrants lived together in the West End, but "while African American residents . . . often lived in the same buildings as whites . . . black Boston maintained a separate cultural presence which revolved around its own schools, churches, mutual aid and fraternal organizations" (Sichel 25).

As the West End became overcrowded and public transport improved, African American and Irish families followed the old Yankees into the newly created South End, with its redbrick town houses, modeled on London squares. In the 1830s the marshy, polluted wastelands south of the city, inhabited by the so-called shanty Irish, were filled in, and by 1880 seventy-three acres of new land had been developed and were completely built up (Warner 17). The planned community, laid out by Charles Bulfinch, boasted bow-fronted houses with brick façades, fountains, green spaces, and wrought iron decorative detail. Originally, Boston Brahmin families had bought the properties, but, as William Dean Howells showed in *The Rise of Silas Lapham*, as the neighborhood became associated with the new post–Civil War industrial millionaires, the Brahmins quickly decamped to the Back Bay. The South End maintained its prestige until the depression of 1873, when banks collapsed (including the Freedman's Bank), developers went bankrupt, and the elegant redbrick squares were rapidly converted to flats and boardinghouses. Low rents, good public transportation, and proximity to jobs made the South End especially appealing to newcomers like Isaac West.

West was a well-established businessman in Faneuil Hall when he met Rachel Pease Benson, whose mother had sent her to Massachusetts as a companion to a genteel spinster around 1894. Unlettered herself, and born into slavery near Camden, South Carolina, Helen Pease Benson was ambitious for her children and sacrificed to enable them to attend a private elementary school staffed by Northern teachers. Rachel left for Massachusetts believing that she was to attend night school; when that failed to materialize, she embarked on a strenuous program of self-education. According to West's portrait of her mother in *The Living Is Easy*, Rachel read voraciously, learned Shakespeare by heart, eliminated her Southern accent, took singing lessons, and planned a career in the theater. Shortly after meeting Isaac, who was eighteen

6. The abolitionist Massachusetts General Colored Association and New England Anti-Slavery Society were organized at the African Meeting House in 1826 and 1832, respectively. Among the activists who lectured at the Meeting House were William Lloyd Garrison, Maria W. Stewart, Angelina Grimké, David Walker, and Frederick Douglass. Today the African Meeting House is a National Park Service site and the oldest standing black church building in the United States.

years her senior, Rachel borrowed a large sum of money from him and took it to South Carolina for a family emergency. When she returned, she had no way of repaying him, and thus reluctantly acquiesced to his proposal of marriage (Dalsgård 40).

Although Rachel never again lived in South Carolina, the landscape of her childhood left its mark on her consciousness, particularly in her passionate connection to nature and her womanist worldview. With Rachel, as with other nostalgic emigrants from the South, "what lingered was not the harshness of its whites . . . but the beauty of its land, the abundance of its beauty" (West, *The Wedding* 139). The chapter included here from *The Living Is Easy* depicts Rachel's childhood as a time of unfettered freedom and limitless potential, symbolized by the girl's friendship with the Colonel's daughter and her fearless encounters with his horse and a neighborhood boy. In the usual negative reading of Cleo/Rachel's character, critics rarely mention this chapter, although it contextualizes her future behavior. Just a few years later, as Cleo becomes well aware that her opportunities are constrained by race, class, and gender, her eyes have turned "sea-green from her sullen anger at working in the white folks' kitchen" (West, *The Living* 24). In a sense, she is "driven to . . . madness by the springs of creativity in [her] for which there [is] no release" (Walker, *In Search* 233).

Another important element of Rachel's South Carolina background was the emotional intimacy and the support that rural women offered one another in the domestic pursuits of cooking, sewing, and child care. Rachel and her sisters often accompanied their mother to quilting bees and to berrying and canning parties. When West was working for the Works Progress Administration (WPA), she interviewed several of her aunts and recorded their memories in two of the selections included here, "Quilting" and "Blackberrying." The pride expressed by the women in their work beautifully reflects Alice Walker's belief that, in the absence of other outlets, genius can be expressed through domestic skills, and an unlettered woman could become "an artist who left her mark in the only materials she could afford, and in the only medium her position in society allowed her to use" (239).

A womanist environment continued to surround Rachel after she moved to Boston with her elderly, unmarried guardian. Her admiration for strong, brave, uncompromising women was to influence her daughter's choice of both friends and subjects for her fiction. Rachel's first inspiration was her own foremothers, "Great-aunt Fanny who hung herself in the hay loft where her master left her running blood after he gave her her first whipping for stepping on the tail of his valuable hunting hound . . . and Great-grandmother Patsy [who] walked out of that kitchen and down to the river. When they fished her out by her long black hair, her soul had got free and she didn't have to listen to anybody's lip forever after" (West, *The Living* 90–91). In addition to her courageous family, Rachel always admired women who earned their own living in the theater, and she was close to the African American actresses Inez Clough and Edna Lewis Thomas. She also loved fashionable high society and avidly read the *Boston Globe*'s rotogravure section, which chronicled the lives of the Boston Brahmins; a particular favorite was Eleanora Sears, a legendary beauty who never married and was famous for being able to walk forty miles in a single day. West always remembered her mother calling her to watch Sears striding purposefully past the house (Guinier 194). As West makes clear in *The Living Is Easy*, Rachel's preference for women manifested itself in an aversion to sex and wariness toward men. Perhaps, as Mary Helen Washington suggests, Rachel "connect[ed] sexuality to women's repression," and in repudiating it she asserted a modicum of control over her life (37). At the same time, as a woman without a profession or family connections, she needed the financial security of marriage.

The relationship between Lila/Rachel and Jude/Isaac in West's unpublished and incomplete novel *Jude* suggests that Rachel married her husband not only for economic reasons but also because she recognized in him a sort of kindred unconventionality and felt that he would not constrain her independent, androgynous nature. She evidently misread Isaac, who, contemptuous of social pretension, insisted on conventional behavior in his wife. Their mutual misunderstanding is anticipated in the chapter that we title "At the Swan Boats."

When Lila meets Jude in the Public Gardens, her childish outfit, long braid, and bicycle proclaim her unwillingness to grow up. Jude, remembering her the night before in formal dress, is baffled and upset; instead of a stunning woman whose appearance on his arm would publicly confirm his superior taste, he confronts a little girl and is uncomfortably aware that his attentions to her could be misconstrued as child molestation. The scene in which Lila then asserts her dominance by teaching him how to ride her bicycle prefigures the sexual and emotional battlefield of their marriage, one of the many unhappy marital relationships in West's writing.

By the time Rachel and Isaac married and moved to his flat in Boston's South End, the racial tolerance that had attracted so many Southerners to the area was changing. The black political base centered in the West End was disappearing because of redistricting and the availability of housing throughout the city. The perspicacious but unorthodox Monroe Trotter believed that African and Irish Americans should join forces against the Boston Brahmins. Trotter campaigned for James Curley in the 1914 mayoral race against "Honey Fitz" Fitzgerald (the father of Rose Kennedy) because Curley also "encouraged alliances between Boston's Irish and black working class against the old Yankee 'codfish aristocracy'" (Alexander 508). African Americans, however, identified more closely with the Protestant Republicans, who had helped them achieve emancipation. They felt betrayed when "the warm afterglow of the tradition of abolition gradually burned out as the old leaders died and their sons moved from the Boston area . . . or became preoccupied with the problems caused by the Irish influx" (Cromwell 63). West captures this situation in *The Living Is Easy*, when the elderly Yankee, Mr. Van Ruyper, tells Cleo/Rachel, his prospective tenant, that he is leaving the city because, while still sympathetic to Negroes, he is "distinctly prejudiced against the Irish" (47).[7]

Cleo wants to rent Mr. Van Ruyper's house in Brookline because she has observed that in the South End, the "once fine houses of the rich were fast emptying of middle-class whites and filling up with lower-class blacks. The street was becoming another big road, with rough-looking loungers leaning in the doorways of decaying houses and dingy stores" (37). She sees that her race is being squeezed into "the narrow geographical strip bounded by Columbus Ave., Washington St., Dartmouth St., and Dudley St.," and she refuses to let such de facto segregation limit her own ambitions (Sichel 25). In real life, the West family moved to 478 Brookline Avenue, where the children could receive a better education and Rachel could socialize with the black elite.

Rachel arranged that the three little girls (Dorothy and her cousins Helene and Eugenia)[8] attend Georgine Glover Brown's exclusive dancing class and learn music, deportment, and reading from Bessie Trotter, whose family was a leader in black Boston. Bessie's father, James Trotter, had been one of the first African American commissioned officers in the Fifty-fifth Massachusetts Infantry. He held a supervisory position at the post office and had written a book on black musicians. His controversial son Monroe, the first black member of Phi Beta Kappa at Harvard, edited the African American newspaper the *Guardian* and strenuously opposed Booker T. Washington's politics of accommodationism.

That Rachel successfully joined this exclusive set is clear not only from her portrait in *The Living Is Easy* but also from her letters, which contain references to prominent Bostonians such as Mrs. Ruffin, Edna Lewis Thomas, the Trotters, the Turners, and the composer Harry T. Burleigh. Once ensconced in the right neighborhood, Rachel found a social and cultural milieu to satisfy even her discriminating tastes. The "Other Brahmins," as the black aristocracy was called, "summered [in] Saratoga, Newport, and Oak Bluffs . . . went regularly to Friday Symphony and the Metropolitan Opera during its Boston season . . . and attended all open events at Harvard" (Cromwell 57). They would have applauded tenors Roland Hayes and Sidney Woodward and admired the work of sculptors Edmonia Lewis and Meta Warrick Vaux Fuller. In fact, Fuller's

7. For more on the rift between African Americans and Irish immigrants, see Ignatiev.
8. Helene Johnson's given name was Helen. Her aunt Rachel suggested that she use "Helene," as it was more glamorous.

famous sculpture *Emancipation*, commissioned by W. E. B. Du Bois, "underscored Boston's place as a cultural, educational and political center in dialogue with other black communities throughout the United States" (Gaither 20).

Given her passion for the arts, Rachel would undoubtedly have attended the lectures and recitals sponsored by the two important black cultural groups, the Boston Literary and Historical Association and the St. Mark Musical and Literary Union, especially since her friend Maud Trotter served as Executive Committee member of the former, and president of the latter. Rachel probably also enjoyed events sponsored by the Negro Artist Club, the Allied Arts Center (directed by her friend Maud Cuney Hare), and the Boston Players (directed by playwright Ralf M. Coleman, a neighbor on Martha's Vineyard). The Lafayette Players (1915–1932), the longest-running African American stock company, appeared frequently and Rachel would have attended their performances with her friend Edna Lewis, who eventually joined the company. Even before her marriage, Rachel would have attended black revues such as *The Octoroon* (1895) and *Oriental America* (1896) at the Old Howard in Scollay Square. It was perhaps then that she decided on a career in the theater, and envisioned herself "singing and kicking her heels on a stage in a swirl of lace petticoats," although "that would be wickeder than anything she had ever done" (West, *The Living* 29).

The black Bostonians considered themselves not only culturally sophisticated but also "progressive and nationally important," with a history that allied them to "such racially crucial struggles as emancipation and social justice" (Gaither 19). They attended Boston's Trinity Church and supported philanthropies such as the Harriet Tubman House, the Plymouth Hospital, and St. Monica's Home. Some joined the first chapter of the NAACP, which was organized in Boston in 1910, while others lent support the following year to Monroe Trotter's Equal Rights League.

At the same time, as West's ironic treatment of the group clearly shows in *Living*, they were capable of the most blatant snobbery and intraracial prejudice. "Who are her people?" was the watchword for inclusion, as membership was predicated on "nonenslaved ancestry . . . education . . . a white-collar job; manners; dress; precise verbal syntax; affiliation with organizations like the National Negro Business League . . . appropriate church affiliation . . . and military service." Deterrents would include a parent's "enslavement, illiteracy, rural Southern background, menial employment . . . recent arrival in Boston, absence of distinguished forbears . . . [and] dark skin" (Alexander 230). Considering that all of these "negative" criteria except the last applied to Rachel, it is a testimony to her ambition that she managed to gain acceptance at all. Of course, as Adele Logan Alexander points out, "some recent immigrants from the South—light-skinned and beautiful—qualified at least as provisional members," assuming, one suspects, that a husband's money went along with the complexion (231).

Perhaps because her satiric tone has been misread and the character of Cleo taken at face value, some critics have objected to West's selection of this milieu for her work. In fact, West attributed the long hiatus between her two novels to fear of a hostile reception in the black community. Although Cleo's materialism, social climbing, and racist sneers are reprehensible, the moral center of the book is not Cleo/Rachel but her daughter Judy/Dorothy, through whose eyes we see not only the compromises, denials, and hypocrisies of the black Bostonians but also their courage and determination to survive in a hostile environment.

## At Home with Rachel: 1916–1925

All of Rachel's efforts seemed to have paid off when, at the age of ten, Dorothy passed the examination for Girls' Latin, Boston's premier public school, where her cousin Helene Johnson was already a student. Rachel's pride in her daughter can be seen in the sketch she drew of Dorothy and herself as they walked from 478 Brookline Avenue to the imposing school building on Huntington Avenue in the spring of 1916. Dorothy wore a white dotted swiss frock trimmed with black ribbons, white silk hose, and a matching black tam (DWP 2:37). Rachel had paid the exorbitant sum of ten dollars for the dress, but always recalled it as one of her favorites. The affirmation of one's social position through discreet and elegant clothing was important to both women, and through the years Dorothy wrote her mother detailed descriptions of her outfits, from the green organdy she wore at a shipboard dinner en route to London in 1929 to the winter suits she and her friend Marian Minus designed for themselves in 1938.

Although they shared an interest in fashion and the arts, Dorothy's desire for independence from her dominating mother provoked a lifelong tension. In the sketch described above, Dorothy asks to be dropped near the school, but Rachel, possibly wishing to protect Dorothy from the racist taunts of the rough Irish children, responds, "Come on Dorothy I know what I'm doing." West often recalled her mother's consternation the first time she asked to have her door closed so she could concentrate on writing. She told Rachel that in order to write a story she had to think very hard to "get it right." Another time, when her parents were arguing about her future career, she told them, "I don't belong to either of you. . . . I belong to myself" (McDowell 266). The problem was that Rachel wished to live vicariously through Dorothy and "was thoroughly disconcerted by the fact that her child was a separate being with independent emotions" (West, The Living 86).

Despite their conflicts, Rachel (or Ray as she was known in the family) was an overwhelming influence on West's life and a major source of material for her fiction. In a piece of juvenilia, probably written in 1918, the protagonist,

Lily, is an intense, emotional visionary whose mother has died in childbirth. "[Lily] was as passionately beautiful as ever her mother had been. And she was sadder in her darkness and more mysterious." To the suggestion by her grandmother that she run outside and play, the child responds: "I do play sometimes. But I'd rather read. And I try so hard to write. Sometimes my thoughts are words so beautiful that I tremble and cry, and my head feels light and my body is burning" (DWP 1:26). In this fantasy, West recognizes both Rachel's emotional power over her and her own destiny as a writer. At the same time, she often feared that Rachel herself, out of frustration with the confines of domesticity, might abandon the family. Her mother had a volatile temper, and when she became angry with Dorothy she would say: "I don't know why I'm putting up with you. . . . I am so beautiful that I can just walk out of here and never come back. Then what will you do?" (Dalsgård 29).

Rachel's golden-skinned beauty and the fact that West was so much darker than her mother—she was the darkest in the family and quite unlike Jude/Isaac's fantasy of a fair, "soft-haired child"—were sources of insecurity for Dorothy. Her complexion exposed her to insensitive remarks by both whites and blacks and made her very aware of color prejudice. A few years before her death, speaking to the Reverend Calvin Butts of Harlem's Abyssinian Baptist Church, West recalled: "My mother was much lighter than I and she had a place in the Jewish section [of Boston]. They told her all winter long, 'But you're not black.' They said she did not look colored. They told me all winter that I was not my mother's daughter. 'She adopted you.'"[9] Another time, in the black community of Oak Bluffs on Martha's Vineyard, a newcomer described a gorgeous woman she had seen; when West said it was her mother, the neighbor could not conceal her disbelief (Guinier 191). In her defense, Rachel abhorred compliments on her complexion. Her niece Katherine Benson Washington, who spent summers in Oak Bluffs, recalled that "she was a very beautiful woman, but whenever anyone told her this she would blush feverishly, tell them they were silly and quickly change the subject." With whites whom she suspected of prejudice, Rachel was more confrontational. West recalled that "she was always maneuvering white people into a position to ask her what she was, and she would say 'I'm a nigger.' And they didn't know what to say" (Guinier 187).

No one of any race or class could intimidate Rachel, and she strove to instill the same confidence in the children of the family. West has described her as a genius and a Renaissance woman who loved opera, film, and literature and

9. Dorothy West Collection, Special Collections at Boston University. The Jewish section of Boston is on the border with Brookline. When West was a child, her home on Brookline Avenue was in the Irish section of Back Bay; the other side of the street was Brookline. By the time she was a young adult, that area had all become Jewish.

who always encouraged her daughter's writing. After her death, those who had most strenuously resisted her influence asked, "Have you noticed that those of us who sound just like her are the ones who laugh a lot, love children a lot, don't have any hang-ups about race or color, and never give up without trying?" (West, *The Richer* 168).

Given her outsized personality, it is not surprising that the theater was Rachel's particular passion. Although her dream of the stage was thwarted by marriage, she made sure that Dorothy and her cousins took advantage of Boston's position as a major theatrical center. They would have seen not only vaudeville stars such as George Walker, Bert Williams, and Sissle and Blake, but also the dramatic actors Charles Gilpin, Leigh Whipper, and Rose McClendon. Competing with the legitimate stage, Boston's movie houses showed early motion pictures, or "photoplays," starring Laura Bowman, Paul Robeson, Robert Earl Jones (father of James Earl Jones), and Lorenzo Tucker ("the black Valentino"), all of whom later appeared in the race movies of Oscar Michaux. The family's favorite white actresses were Tallulah Bankhead, Greta Garbo, Helen Hayes, and Irene Bordoni, with whom Dorothy and Helene Johnson corresponded for many years.

With these influences, one sees why Dorothy first thought of becoming a playwright. In an essay written in her senior year at Brighton High School,[10] she compared the play and the novel and concluded that although "books by well-versed authors present the keys to the world . . . no matter how vivid a novel may be it cannot compare with a play which to me offers the truest representation of life. . . . There is nothing in all the world more fascinating to me than the play" (DWP 2:41). Dorothy, like her mother, read voraciously. Her favorite dramatists were Eugene O'Neill and J. M. Barrie (the author of *Peter Pan*); her favorite novelist was Dostoyevsky, but she also liked Edith Wharton, Sinclair Lewis, Booth Tarkington, and Mary Roberts Rinehart. As a teenager she enjoyed Fanny Hurst but in later years withdrew her approval. Oddly, West recalled no black writers who influenced her early work until much later, when she herself became an advocate for Arna Bontemps, Zora Neale Hurston, Countee Cullen, Wallace Thurman, and Richard Wright. Drama and literature were sources of much family activity and entertainment. According to Helene Johnson's daughter Abigail McGrath, "at night [West and her cousins] would write pieces and read them aloud" (124).

The girls did not lack for literary models. In addition to reading Goethe, Schiller, and Shakespeare, they subscribed to *Cosmopolitan* (which, under the editorship of Ray Long, published critically acclaimed writers) and to *Theater*

10. Although West implied in interviews that she graduated from Girls' Latin, there is no record. According to her cousin Barbara Franklin, the family was quarantined for illness and West missed too much school. Thus she later completed her senior year at Brighton High School.

*Magazine.* Sydney Rosenfeld offered in that magazine to critique unpublished manuscripts for a fee of twenty-five dollars, and in 1925 Dorothy sent him a play titled *The Emergence of Eleanor*. Rosenfeld thought that the dialogue and atmosphere were excellent but found the technical directions limited and noted that Dorothy tended to "tell not show action." He also questioned the "unsavory, unappetizing environment" and the trite plot, which he summarized as: "the mother is fast—the daughter arrives and becomes fast—the mother becomes contrite." Dorothy apparently objected to his comments, but Rosenfeld held his ground, conceding only that her play was "a clever novelistic narrative" (DWP 1:19).

Perhaps discouraged with drama, West then sent a story to Cosmo Hamilton, a popular British playwright and screenwriter, and received a favorable response. She also sent a few stories to George H. Doran, the publisher of the magazine *The Bookman.* In addition, she submitted a multigenerational novel set on Martha's Vineyard. The main character is a strong-minded, nature-loving, androgynous young woman named Step, who clearly resembles Ray. West received a kind rejection in which the editor suggested that her best writing described the older members of the family. This surprised her, as "I had no interest in writing about people of forty . . . but perhaps it was the beginning of me writing about people past the years of youthful dreams" (DWP 1:19). West came to believe that her strength lay in writing about the underdog—children, animals, the poor, and the elderly—those who are vulnerable to the abuse of power by others.

Nineteen twenty-five was an important year in the literary development of both Dorothy West and Helene Johnson. On the strength of Johnson's poems in the *Boston Guardian* and West's stories in the *Boston Post*, they were invited to join the Saturday Evening Quill Club, hosted by the journalist Eugene Gordon and his wife, Edythe Mae. Like Zora Neale Hurston, Gordon hailed from a small town in central Florida, attended Howard University, and was an outspoken iconoclast. In 1919, after serving as a second lieutenant in the army, Gordon was hired as an editor at the *Boston Post*, where he was in charge of the short story contest in which West won so many prizes.

Gordon held the race to the strictest standards while refusing to be limited or stereotyped by color: in 1924 his frank articles in *Opportunity* on the mediocrity of the black press had infuriated the community. When he won an award in an *Opportunity* contest, his anger over discrimination is reflected in his remark that "I was born colored in Oviedo, Florida, and have remained more or less so since. I honestly admit I am not proud of being known everywhere I go and by everything I do as a colored man. I [am] less annoyed in this respect, however, in Massachusetts than [in] Washington, D.C., or Oviedo, or New Orleans."[11] Dis-

11. *Opportunity* 5.7 (July 1927): 204.

gusted with racism in the United States, Gordon joined the Communist Party. He eventually moved to New York and, like his friends Richard Wright and Ralph Ellison, was a member of the party's League of American Writers. Margaret Walker recalls dining with the three men at the organization's 1939 congress (128).

Gordon clearly set the bar high for his literary club, and West and Johnson would have benefited from his insistence on technical excellence. He described the group as "an organization of Boston writers. Most of these men and women are unprofessionals, and all, incidentally, are Negroes, although anybody is eligible to become a member." Gordon published three numbers of the club's annual and included, in addition to the work of West and Johnson, that of Waring Cuney, Florida Ruffin Ridley, Alvira Hazzard, Gertrude Schalk, and Edythe Mae Gordon. The publication was favorably reviewed by the *Boston Herald*, the *Amsterdam News*, and *Commonweal*, and was praised by both W. E .B. Du Bois, who deemed it the best of the black literary journals, and Alice Dunbar Nelson, who appreciated its judicious editing and "seventy-two pages of very excellent material."[12] Eventually, stories by both the Gordons and Schalk, as well as West's story "An Unimportant Man," were listed under favorable headings in Edward J. O'Brien's *Best Short Stories of 1928* and in the *O. Henry Memorial Award Prize Stories of 1928*.

That Gordon mentored and influenced West's work can be seen in the similarities between the two writers in theme and style. His work, like West's, is naturalistic and grounded in the urban environment of Boston; streetcars rattle down Huntington Avenue, Albany Street, and other thoroughfares that divide the city along ethnic and economic lines. He too wrote about dysfunctional marriages based on hegemonic definitions of beauty and success, and he explored the existential loneliness of the black man's confrontation with racism and prejudice. Although West, in one of her oft-repeated anecdotes, attributed her literary debut to an aunt bringing home a copy of *Opportunity* in which the second contest was announced, it seems more likely that it was Gordon, already a regular contributor to the magazine, who encouraged Helene Johnson to send "Trees at Night" to the first contest in 1925. The following year, several Saturday Evening Quill members, including Gordon, West, and Johnson, submitted their work.

*The New York Years: 1926–1932*

On May 4, 1926, Charles S. Johnson, the editor of *Opportunity*, wrote to inform West that she and Zora Neale Hurston had each won half of the second prize in

---

12. The quotes appear in the April 1929 issue of the *Saturday Evening Quill*, in a section titled "Excerpts from Comments on the First Number of The *Saturday Evening Quill*."

the short story contest. Helene Johnson won three honorable mentions; her poem "Magula" was admired by Robert Frost, one of the judges, as a "macabresque fantasy mingled with living emotion."[13] Charles Johnson promised, in addition to the prize money, publication in the magazine as well as "in some other medium that will bring [you] to the attention of the public."[14] The editor did not exaggerate: at the awards dinner, the two young Bostonians met not only members of the white establishment who would help them professionally, such as Fanny Hurst, Carl Van Vechten, and Blanche Colton Williams, but also talented black writers destined to become longtime friends— Langston Hughes, Countee Cullen, Wallace Thurman, Eric Walrond, and Zora Neale Hurston. Before West left New York in 1945, she was to know almost every black artist and intellectual in the city.

In her prize-winning story, "The Typewriter," West describes a middle-aged man in a bleak urban setting. The story particularizes a black emigrant to the North who has been excluded from the "American dream," while it interrogates the broader social and economic forces that crush the human spirit. The story's "proletarian aesthetic . . . documents the complex manner in which race, class and gender often militate against individuals in a racist, sexist and elitist environment" (Jones 156). "The Typewriter" is similar to other stories West wrote at this time, including "An Unimportant Man" and "Prologue to a Life," which appeared in the Saturday Evening Quill Club's 1928 and 1929 annuals, respectively, and to "Hannah Byde," which she published in The Messenger in 1926.

The four stories, West's first important publications, are thematically related in that they depict "unachieving, disappointed [men] who still have retained a measure of innocence," but who are unable to satisfy their frigid, bitter wives (Perry 133). The men are partially at fault for the marital discord because, internalizing racist standards of beauty, each has chosen a wife on the basis of her fair skin rather than on "the content of her character." As Margaret Perry indicates, the influence of Dostoyevsky can be seen not only in the claustrophobic apartments that suggest the couples' confinement in prisons of bourgeois respectability, but also in West's preoccupation with the "incorruptible nature of children" (132). Spurned by their wives, the men identify closely with their children, and in the end, by protecting or supporting the children, they achieve a sort of redemption through suffering. In contrast to the men, the women are acutely aware of the limitations imposed by race, class, and gender, and are ultimately too angry and bitter to nurture their children.

Because the issues and themes addressed in these stories—the dialectic of race and gender, sexual dysfunction, the abuse of domestic power, emotional

13. *Opportunity* 4.42 (June 1926): 174.
14. See the opening letter in this volume.

cruelty—reflect a cynical imagination unusual in a young woman in her late teens, one looks for their inspiration in West's own experience, especially since she often told interviewers that her stories were all based on her family (Dalsgård 37; Guinier 206). Although ostensibly her secure existence with a successful father was far from the sad lives she describes, it does seem likely that the frustrated and angry women are based on her mother: certainly they all resemble her physically. According to her grandniece Abigail McGrath, Rachel was "formidable . . . extremely intelligent . . . [but] her bitterness clouded all of her actions" (125). West recalls that she rather insensitively said to her mother as she and Helene were leaving for New York, "Well, your beauty was certainly wasted on you. All you did with it was raise children and run your sisters' lives" (The Richer 168). It was not until later that West realized "my mother had done what she felt she had to do, knowing the risks, knowing there would be no rewards, but determined to build a foundation for the generations unborn" (168).

In the spring of 1926, the two young women left their family in Boston and moved to the YWCA on 137th Street in Harlem. Several of their friends left contemporary accounts of the city they encountered. According to James Weldon Johnson, Harlem was "exotic, colourful, and sensuous." In the wide streets there were "gay crowds skipping from one place of amusement to another, lines of taxicabs and limousines standing under the sparkling lights of . . . famous night-clubs" (160–61). There was something for everyone; those who could not afford or were not welcome in the essentially whites-only clubs enjoyed the public dance halls. Wallace Thurman described the Savoy Ballroom on Lenox Avenue, where Dorothy often went dancing with Countee Cullen, as "an elaborate ensemble with a Chinese garden . . . two orchestras that work in relays . . . and hostesses . . . for partnerless young men." He wrote, "One can spend twelve hours in this jazz palace for sixty-five cents, and the price of a . . . sandwich and drink" (79–80). Even without that modest price of admission, one could still enjoy the "lost art of strolling" and attend church functions and fraternal organizations (Johnson 162). Close to the YWCA was the famous Harlem branch of the New York Public Library, which sponsored poetry readings and cultural events. "Nordics" were fascinated by Harlem; the sophisticated New Yorker listed places to go, and British aristocrats such as Lady Mountbatten and Nancy Cunard were frequent visitors. Dorothy and Helene soon made friends with a coterie of handsome, witty, and talented young men, most of whom were homosexual. Their busy social life included Countee Cullen, Ed Perry, Bruce Nugent, Eric Walrond, Alexander Gumby, and Alonzo (Al) Thayer. Thayer, a gregarious actor who appeared in Green Pastures, recalled that "it was a soft living for all young writers, artists, musicians and pseudo intellectuals [who had] a passable wardrobe, a smooth line of chatter and a flair for the latest dances"

Rachel West as a young woman.
(Schlesinger Library, Radcliffe
Institute, Harvard University.)

Dorothy West at Oak Bluffs, circa
1924. (This and all photographs not
otherwise credited courtesy of Mrs.
B. L. Franklin.)

Helene Johnson and her mother, Ella Benson Johnson, circa 1924.

Benjamin Benson, Rachel
West's brother, Worcester,
circa 1940.

Rachel's sister Sarah
Benson (*right*) with
her husband and her
niece Katherine
Benson, Boston,
1940s.

Dorothy spent her early childhood in this apartment, second doorway, at 10 Cedar Street, Roxbury. (Photograph by Edward Hawthorne, 2002.)

Rachel West's house at 23 Worthington Street, Roxbury. (Photograph by Edward Hawthorne, 2002.)

Edna Lewis Thomas, June 18, 1932. (Yale Collection of American Literature, Beinecke Rare Book and Manuscript Library. Photograph by Carl Van Vechten. By permission of the Van Vechten Trust.)

En route to Moscow, June 1932.
(*First row, left to right*) Louise Thompson, Dorothy West;
(*second row*) Mildred Jones, Constance White,
Katherine Jenkins, Sylvia Garner, Mollie Lewis;
(*third row*) Wayland Rudd, Frank Montero, Matt
Crawford, George Sample, Laurence Alberga,
Langston Hughes, Juanita Lewis, Alan McKenzie;
(*back row*) Ted Poston, Henry Lee Moon, Thurston
McNairy Lewis, Lloyd Patterson, Loren Miller. (Yale
Collection of American Literature, Beinecke Rare
Book and Manuscript Library.)

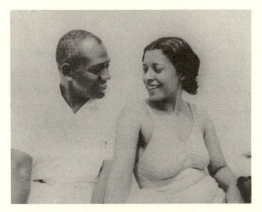

Henry and Mollie Moon the year after their marriage, Long Island, July 2, 1939. (The Western Reserve Historical Society, Cleveland, Ohio.)

Dorothy West in her apartment in Harlem, circa 1938. (Schlesinger Library, Radcliffe Institute, Harvard University.)

Barbara Washington Franklin and
Marian Minus at Oak Bluffs, 1940.

Dorothy, Marian Minus, and Snowball at Oak Bluffs, 1955.

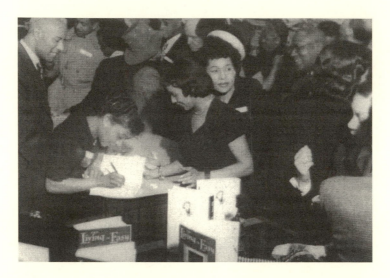

Dorothy West at a book signing for *The Living Is Easy*, May 13, 1948. Harold Jackman standing at left; Mollie and Henry Moon at right. (Countee Cullen–Harold Jackman Memorial Collection, Atlanta University Center, Robert W. Woodruff Library.)

*The Living Is Easy* book signing. Fredi Washington at left next to Dorothy West; Grace Nail Johnson at far right. (Schlesinger Library, Radcliffe Institute, Harvard University.)

Harold Jackman Memorial Committee Meeting at
Playboy Club, New York City, April 12, 1964.
(First row, seated on floor, left to right) Glenn Carrington,
Ernest Hembey, Embry Bonner, Cynthia Barrow,
Martin Turbee; (second row, standing) Beryl Edelen,
Margaret Bonds, Ivie A. Jackman, Edna Pemberton,
Marian Minus, Louise Jefferson, Helen Harden;
(back row) Roberta Bosley Hubert, Pearl M. Fisher,
Conrad Ferrari, Charles Miles, Lionel Barrow,
Clinton Oliver, Vernell Oliver. (Countee Cullen–
Harold Jackman Memorial Collection, Atlanta
University Center, Robert W. Woodruff Library.
Photograph by Bill Anderson.)

Dorothy West and Barbara Washington Franklin at Oak Bluffs, 1995.

Dorothy West and Courtney Franklin at Oak Bluffs, 1995.

Dorothy West at her writing desk, Oak Bluffs, 1996.

(Byrd). After witnessing a mob-related murder, however, he became aware of the area's violent underside and moved to California.

Like Thayer, West eventually became disenchanted with the self-indulgent life she and her friends led in New York; but during her years there she also became involved, personally and professionally, with several independent, strong-minded women who resembled her mother in many ways and who were to affect profoundly her intellectual, artistic, emotional, and sexual development. For various reasons, West aligned herself with Zora Neale Hurston, Edna Lewis Thomas, Blanche Colton Williams, Dorothy Scarborough, Mildred Jones, and Marian Minus, each of whom made a unique contribution to her life and work.

*Literary Mentors: Blanche Colton Williams and Dorothy Scarborough*

Blanche Colton Williams (1879–1944) was one of the first contacts Dorothy made in New York. A graduate of Mississippi University for Women, she was a judge of the 1925 and 1926 *Opportunity* contests, a professor at Columbia University, and the first series editor of the O. Henry Memorial Awards. Her interests included mystery and detective writing and American philology and dialect. She pioneered the teaching of university rhetoric and composition courses, and published several books on the short story. Williams and West liked several of the same writers, including Edith Wharton, Mary Roberts Rinehart, and Booth Tarkington.

A friend of many intellectuals of the Harlem Renaissance, Williams was particularly encouraging to young black writers. It was she who enabled West to enroll in creative writing classes in Columbia University's Extension Division.[15] Williams may also have encouraged her colleague Angus Burrell to reprint "An Unimportant Man" in *Copy*, the university's literary magazine, in 1929. Since she felt that "the short story is the literary medium that supersedes all others in America," she undoubtedly contributed to West's opinion that it is "the most perfect literary form" (Williams ii; McDowell 281). Today, Williams's preference for linear narrative and privileged point of view seems old-fashioned. She believed that stories should be accessible and "popular"; she liked writers who "mastered the art of surprise" and "emotionally moved" their audience. While she disdained melodrama, she also objected to "subtle shades of emotion" and obscure language (Williams 202). She was a regionalist and praised the winners of the *Opportunity* contest for "sticking to their people, to the subjects about which they should be familiar."[16] Her devotion to O. Henry seems particularly out-

15. *Vineyard Gazette*, March 12, 1948.
16. *Opportunity* 3.29 (May 1925): 130.

dated, and though she clearly validated West's desire to write about the black bourgeoisie, she may also have been responsible for the trite, O. Henry-esque quality of some of West's *New York Daily News* stories, which feature sentimental and contrived plots, summarized action, and one-dimensional characters.[17]

Through Williams, West met other professors at Columbia, including the writer Erskine Caldwell and Dorothy Scarborough (1878–1935), a teacher, novelist, journalist, and folklorist. Born in Smith County, Texas, Scarborough received her doctorate in literature in 1917 from Columbia, where she later taught creative writing in the Extension Division. Like Williams, Scarborough came from a progressive, liberal Southern family. Her interests included the supernatural and African American folklore, specifically the oral tradition, "hoodoo," and the blues. She interviewed a number of musicians, including the composer and bandleader W. C. Handy (Dougan 346). She was close to Charles Johnson (who published her work on folk songs) and, like Williams, was a judge of the first *Opportunity* contest.

Scarborough clearly recognized West's talent and was instrumental in nurturing her first novel. It is likely that it was Scarborough who taught West to write concisely, to minimize adjectives, and to "tell a novel in one sentence." Scarborough may also have worked with West on character development and taught her that "the best character . . . makes the greatest change." It was probably in Scarborough's class that West read Lajos Egri's *Art of Dramatic Writing*, which was "everybody's bible" at the time (Guinier 156, 159). She may also have encouraged West's interest in the supernatural, in gender and class issues, and in the vulnerability of women and children. Scarborough's controversial novel *The Wind* (1925), which was made into a silent movie starring Lillian Gish, depicts a sensitive woman driven mad by the incessant wind and bleak environment of a Texas cattle ranch. Scarborough wrote critically about women's rights, child exploitation in cotton sharecropping, and agricultural reform, and she edited two books of ghost stories. Her best-known work is *On the Trail of Negro Folksongs* (1925).

For reasons that are unclear but were probably financial, West dropped out of Columbia in 1928 but remained in touch with Scarborough as she worked on the novel she had begun in the summer of 1927. This was probably the one to which the composer Harry T. Burleigh referred when he wrote to West: "The news about your novel is wonderful. . . . What is it about?"[18] Although Scarborough scolded her in February 1928 for a "weakness for procrastination," she sympathized with West's withdrawal from school and suggested

17. See, for example, "The Puppy," *Daily News*, May 9, 1942, and "Wives and Women," *Daily News*, March 7, 1947.
18. West Collection, Boston University.

she complete the work out of class. She put West on a writing schedule and promised to help place the novel for publication (DWP 1:12). West did not follow through with Scarborough at this time, although she did show Wallace Thurman a manuscript in the summer of 1929. He guessed at the inspiration for some of the characters, including Edna Thomas and Cheryl Crawford, suggested publishers, and wrote in her support "most eloquently to Mr. Furman at Macaulay's damning the easily published and untalented Fausets and Larsens and pleading for recognition of potential talent from a newer . . . generation" (Mitchell, *This Waiting* 105–6).

The following December, Helene Johnson wrote that "anyone with your nerve [West had written to the actress Irene Bordoni, whom they both admired] has got to accomplish a simple little thing like selling a novel." West was still working on the book in October 1930, when Helene again encouraged her to "hurry up and finish the old novel" (Mitchell, *This Waiting* 108, 110). In 1931, West contacted Scarborough, who responded, "I shall be glad to read it and to criticize it—if you can send it on right away, and there will not be any charge for you paid enough before. . . . I am glad to take an interest in an interesting story begun in my class" (DWP 1:11). In March, Dorothy met with Scarborough, who felt the book, now titled *Five Sheaves*, needed "only minor changes."[19] West also received an encouraging call from Grace Nail Johnson (wife of James Weldon Johnson), which "rekindle[d] the spark. . . . Just when I was beginning to think, oh dear, I shall never finish this wretched novel, and certainly it will never be published, your . . . voice came over the telephone, and I am actually inspired."[20]

West submitted *Five Sheaves* to the literary agent John Trounstine in the spring of 1931, but she heard nothing until the following October, when Trounstine, apparently unable to place it, dropped the manuscript off with Countee Cullen. Cullen reread it and was "enthusiastic about everything except the ending which seems too much of a slow down. The conversation is good, and much of the straight writing is quite biblical. Something must come of it." In May 1932 the novel was "finally and completely revised," and Cullen apparently suggested that West approach Trounstine again (DWP 1:6). By September, however, she had put the novel aside and decided to go "back to the short story, my best and favorite form."[21] There is no record of further correspondence with Scarborough, who died suddenly of influenza in 1935. Clearly, however, she believed in West's talent and expected her to succeed. The manuscript is not among West's papers and may have disap-

19. West to Countee Cullen, March 1931, Cullen Papers, box 6, folder 12, Amistad Research Center, Tulane University.
20. See West's letter of March 8, 1931.
21. See West's letter of September 9, 1933.

peared in a mysterious robbery at Zora Neale Hurston's apartment in the mid-1930s.

*Literary Sisters:*
*Dorothy West, Helene Johnson, and Zora Neale Hurston*

Zora Neale Hurston was a brilliant, multifaceted woman who had a great impact on the lives and the creative work of both West and Helene Johnson. Although Hurston differed from the Boston cousins in temperament and background, the three women were close for many years. On a professional level, Hurston definitely broadened West's style and subject matter to include an appreciation of her Southern folk roots. When Hurston left New York for Florida in February 1927, she offered West and Johnson, who were still living at the YWCA, the sublet of her apartment at 43 West Sixty-sixth Street. At the time, West was working at the Labor Temple on East Fourteenth Street, the center for the city's labor community and an employment bureau for poor immigrants on the Lower East Side. According to Benson family lore, Hurston had assured the women that her rent was paid up, but when they arrived, the landlady appeared at the door saying that Hurston was two months in arrears (Franklin, personal interview). This episode may have been the "trick" that West later said Zora had played on them (Guinier 171).

Hurston was a complex woman, and she may have had an ulterior motive for offering the apartment to Dorothy and Helene. Before going south to collect folklore, she had signed an iron-bound contract with Mrs. Osgood Mason, a wealthy white patron she called "Godmother," in which Hurston promised to relinquish all rights to her research and to send the material to Mason. "Given the terms of this Faustian compact," Cheryl Wall points out, Hurston "devised what loopholes she could" (155). In addition to seeking the advice of Franz Boas, she began sending Dorothy and Helene manuscripts from New Orleans marked "Top Secret" with instructions that they were either to place them in storage or mail them back. "PLEASE," she wrote, "DONT LET ANYONE KNOW THAT YOU HAVE HEARD FROM ME OR SEE MY PAPERS." Perhaps Hurston intended to reserve some of the raw material for her own writing and did not feel that she could trust her friend Langston Hughes, who was also helped by Mason, or other members of their circle. She told West and Johnson that she trusted them more than anyone else in New York and promised, in return for their loyalty, that she had "a lot in store" for them (Kaplan 130).

It seems likely that Hurston's interest in the folk tradition may have sensitized West to the richness of her culture. West certainly would have read the "classified" material that Hurston sent her, which included games, love letters, work songs, sympathetic magic, conjure ceremonies, religious symbolism, and sermons. A few years later, West's WPA essays drew on her own family's folk material on children's games, ghost stories, and rural customs, as well as on "urban messiahs" like Daddy Grace.

West's fiction also shows Hurston's influence. Cleo's rebellious Southern childhood in The Living Is Easy recalls episodes in both Dust Tracks on a Road, Hurston's autobiography, and Their Eyes Were Watching God. Even West's last novel, The Wedding, which includes the tall tale of how Isaac fooled the white folks, suggests stories Hurston collected in Mules and Men.

In addition to an interest in the folk roots of black life and literature, the two women shared a distaste for writing that sacrificed art to polemic, although this approach made their work less appealing to critics such as Richard Wright. Hurston, for example, admired Rudolph Fisher, whom West planned to include in Challenge, her 1934 literary journal. She considered him "greater than the Negroes rate him generally . . . because he is too honest to pander to our inferiority complex and write 'race' propaganda" (Kaplan 297).[22] Similarly, West worried that The Living Is Easy, which she submitted for a Rosenwald grant in 1945, would not be accepted (it wasn't) because "it is not a 'race' novel—I'm more concerned with character."[23]

There was a great deal of social and intellectual exchange among West, Hurston, and Helene Johnson. According to Verner Mitchell, the trio formed an "intimate literary community [that provided] warmly affirmative support for each other's writings . . . and worked out ideas" (This Waiting 90). They all shared a literary agent, Elisabeth Marbury, and were friendly with the same influential whites, such as Carl Van Vechten and Fannie Hurst. West called Hurston "Sister" and mailed her books and materials from New York, while the latter sent gifts of Florida pecans and promoted Helene Johnson's work in poetry readings throughout the South. Their collaboration is evident in a letter Hurston wrote in 1928 promising to help them on Harlem, the literary magazine started by Wallace Thurman, and saying that she had "lots of things for you to help me work out" (Kaplan 133). In 1929, when West went to England with Porgy and Helene went on the road with Thurman's play Harlem, Rachel and other family members moved into Hurston's Sixty-sixth Street apartment. A few years later, West wrote to Rachel that she was taking her meals with Hurston and introducing her to society people like Judge and Mrs. James Watson.[24] Hurston knew all of West's family, and, according to Johnson, her "eligible" brother Everett was madly in love with West and had broken off his engagement because of her (Mitchell, This Waiting 110).

Despite their initial closeness, the two women drifted apart. Zora Neale

22. Rudolph Fisher died of cancer in December 1934, which likely accounts for West's failure to publish him in Challenge.
23. West to Countee Cullen, January 26, 1945, Cullen Papers, box 6, folder 12, Amistad Research Center.
24. See West's letter to her mother of October 3, 1935.

Hurston was a powerful personality, accustomed to dominating rooms and relationships and to commanding friends to "come a running" when she wanted to see them (Kaplan 395). She was also, according to West, a "snoop" who listened at friends' doors and threatened them with voodoo spells (Guinier 220). By 1930, Helene Johnson was begging her cousin to "write to Zora sometimes, she thinks of you as her more or less wilfull baby" (Mitchell, *This Waiting* 110). West, however, who may have felt that Hurston was using her for her own purposes, was adept at eluding anyone's control, having been, as she said, "bossed by a real boss"—her mother, Rachel (Guinier 222).

Other events came between them. Hurston could be witty and sarcastic at her friends' expense. She joked about the twenty-two African Americans who went to Russia in 1932 to make a movie on racism in America, and was probably referring to Dorothy when she remarked on the irony that among the whole group "only two in the crowd look anything like Negroes" (Kaplan 263). After West returned from the Soviet Union in the summer of 1933, she stored her new fur coat at Zora's; the storage area was burgled, and the coat and several boxes of West's papers disappeared. West always maintained that "Zora needed money . . . and staged the robbery, and took my little fur coat" (Guinier 173). Zora was chronically short of money and may have been trying to scrape together the tuition for graduate work at Columbia University. Although West was more distressed by the loss of her papers, the cost of replacing the coat was significant on her limited budget; she complained to Claude McKay that she could have been saving up for a trip to Paris "if that wretch hadn't walked off with my coat."[25] Coincidentally, in 1937 Zora wrote to Carl Van Vechten that she was "trying to find Helen Johnson who put a box of papers in storage for me," and gossiped, "I find that she has lost her job [and] broken up her home" (Kaplan 408). Her comment is surprising, considering that Helene's daughter Abigail was born in New York in 1940, and it was not until January 1941 that Helene left her husband.[26]

In 1934, however, West and Hurston were friendly enough for West to ask for a story for *Challenge*; Hurston responded with enthusiasm, comparing West's courage in starting the magazine to that of King Harold in the Battle of Hastings (Kaplan 296). Although there is no record of any communication between the two during Hurston's last sad years in Florida, West always professed to care for her. Her eyes would sometimes fill with tears when she thought about her friend "because she was a very gifted person" (Guinier 171).

Like Hurston, West was struggling financially in these years. She did receive some support from her father, but it was apparently not enough to pay both tuition at Columbia and her living expenses. According to West, "there were

25. See West's letter to McKay of September 13, 1935.
26. Dorothy West to Rachel West, January 1 and March 24, 1941, Schlesinger Library, box 1, folder 1.

some . . . traumatic things" that had occurred in the family; she had to will herself not "to be bitter about it," but she never revealed the details (Guinier 201). It is possible that Isaac, like his fictional counterpart in *Living*, lost his business after the First World War. When asked why she did not go to college, considering the intellectual tenor of the household, West simply said, "We were supposed to go to Columbia. We were very poor, so we didn't have much money" (Guinier 168).

The family finances had obviously destabilized around 1927, when Isaac left Boston and moved to Brooklyn and Rachel moved out of the big house at 478 Brookline Avenue and into a nearby flat. Dorothy never discussed her parents' separation, although she used it as the dramatic conclusion to *The Living Is Easy*. West's cousin Barbara Franklin recalls overhearing adults whispering that "Mr. West had left Rachel for another woman" and that "Rachel did not know where he was." In 1929, when West was in London, she wrote to her father at Rachel's address, which suggests she may indeed not have known where he was living. Rachel, however, wrote the following month from Hurston's apartment; she was staying on in New York, she said, because "Mr. West had such a bad cold, I just did not have the heart to leave him."[27]

In the absence of financial support from Isaac, West and Helene Johnson worked at a variety of jobs in New York. Dorothy had applied for a position at the Theater Guild, and thanks to Rachel's close friend Edna Lewis Thomas, she was hired as a supernumerary for the London cast of *Porgy*. Thomas, who starred in Orson Welles's all-black *Voodoo Macbeth* in 1936, and played the Spanish flower seller in *A Streetcar Named Desire* in both stage and film versions, was a nurturing, generous surrogate mother to West and Johnson. In addition, as a prominent member of the glamorous gay and bisexual subculture of Harlem, Thomas introduced West to a milieu that was to have a major impact on her but about which she had probably heard very little in Boston's staid Back Bay.

*A Mentor and Friend: Edna Lewis Thomas (1886–1974)*

Rachel West's close friend Edna Lewis Thomas was an exquisitely beautiful and cultivated woman and a leader of the black theater movement of the twenties and thirties. She was a precursor to Dorothy Dandridge in that, like other "fair-skinned, extraordinarily beautiful black female actresses, [she] ran into difficulty in securing roles because she was too fair to be considered black, and yet was not permitted to play 'white' roles" (Gill 67). The early years were painful. Her twelve-year-old mother, working as a nursemaid, had been raped

27. Letter to Isaac West, April 19, 1929; letter from Rachel West, May 9, 1929; Schlesinger Library, box 1, folders 2 and 3. For more on West and Hurston, see Davis.

by her white employer in Lawrenceville, Virginia. Shortly after Edna's birth, mother, child, and grandmother relocated to Boston's West End (Henry 563). At age sixteen, after completing two years of high school, Edna moved into what West called "brown society" when she married a son of J. H. Lewis, the black entrepreneur "whose tailoring establishment stood on the present site of Filene's department store. Lewis paid $10,000 a year in rent and employed more than fifty men and women" (Cromwell 359). The marriage was unhappy: her husband was an alcoholic and a compulsive gambler and eventually died of tuberculosis. Edna maintained a close relationship with her father-in-law; both were active in philanthropic organizations and dedicated themselves to racial uplift. Because she needed to support herself, she returned to school to study music. West may have drawn on Edna's history for the character of the Duchess in *The Living Is Easy*. Like Edna, the Duchess is able to pass for white and redeems her mother's tragic past by marrying into black Brahmin society.

Thomas's theatrical career, owing to her complicated personal life, began relatively late. Eventually she took a job as social secretary to Madame C. J. Walker, the self-made millionaire and founder of a hair care empire. In addition to her secretarial duties, Edna tutored Madame Walker in reading and etiquette. At this time she met and married Lloyd Thomas, who was the manager of Madame Walker's Harlem salon. Lloyd was extremely handsome and a homosexual, although that was not immediately apparent to Edna. She described him as "a dour, taciturn, indifferent man, also of light complexion. . . . I had never met a man like this before and his indifference fascinated me" (Henry 566). Lloyd fancied himself an aesthete and was fond of quoting the Chinese poet Li Po. Both Helene and Dorothy lived with the Thomases at various times, although they held differing opinions of Lloyd. Helene, like Edna, thought him one of the most intelligent men she had ever met, while Dorothy found him "trifling" and disliked seeing him drift around the house all day in his bathrobe.[28]

Edna was sexually attracted to both men and women, but found relationships with women to be more emotionally satisfying. Like a number of her friends, she combined a homosexual private life with a discreet, heterosexual public persona. Lloyd, although he never supported her, evidently cared for her and, according to Rachel, missed her when she was on tour. The marriage provided a useful façade; even when Edna fell in love with the hedonistic British aristocrat Olivia Wyndham, the three of them lived together. They purchased a large apartment on Seventh Avenue, where they also rented rooms to friends and where Dorothy and Helene often stayed. Edna's official explanation, even to Carl Van Vechten, who would scarcely have been shocked, was that Olivia was

28. Abigail McGrath, personal conversation, October 8, 2001; Dorothy West to Countee Cullen, March 13, 1931, Cullen Papers, box 6, folder 12, Amistad Research Center.

a "house guest" who "helped with expenses" (Gill 74). Lloyd apparently accepted the arrangement since the alternative was finding a job.

It was Lloyd, in fact, who introduced his wife to the eccentric young British aristocrat. Olivia's impeccable family tree included a number of distinguished military officers, three aunts who posed for John Singer Sargent's painting *The Three Graces*, and her first cousin Cynthia Asquith (daughter-in-law of the British prime minister). Always unconventional, Olivia flung herself into a decadent lifestyle after World War I and counted among her friends Frederick Ashton, Nancy Cunard, Tallulah Bankhead, Noel Coward, Adele Astaire, and the Prince of Wales. "Wantonly promiscuous, Olivia was unstoppable. . . . At King's Road parties, when [she] was not disappearing with one person after another, male or female, she was playing pander, 'dragging people upstairs and putting them on top of each other'" (Kavanagh 81–82). Olivia was considered one of the "bright young things," a group of self-indulgent and sophisticated socialites depicted in the novels of Evelyn Waugh, Aldous Huxley, and Anthony Powell. During the war she met Haywood Spencer, scion of an aristocratic New York family, a graduate of Annapolis, and an honorary captain in the British navy. Spencer was just as eccentric and sexually ambiguous as she, and the two apparently discussed marriage. Despite her flamboyant lifestyle, Olivia had many redeeming qualities. According to her half-brother Francis Wyndham, "she always showed extreme sensitivity to the sufferings of other creatures, animal as well as human. 'She was deeply upset by any manifestation of exclusion, of selectivity, of judgment—anything even faintly implying discrimination'" (Kavanagh 67).

Olivia came to New York to marry Spencer and became sidetracked by the beautiful but indifferent Edna. On May 14, 1930, despairing of her affections, Olivia abruptly went through with the marriage on Spencer's family estate just across the Hudson from Franklin Delano Roosevelt's Hyde Park. That evening, before sailing to England on their honeymoon, Olivia made one last attempt to see Edna. When the latter unexpectedly reciprocated her feelings, she apparently informed her husband that the marriage was over and sailed alone for England on the *Berengaria*. She later sued him for $4,000. Spencer, meanwhile, infuriated his neighbor FDR, first by changing the name of his estate to "Crum Elbow" (a name West borrowed for Jude's surname in an unpublished novel), and then by selling the estate to the evangelist Father Divine.

Once Olivia entered Edna's life, her money helped maintain the household. Some years earlier, when Madame Walker died suddenly in 1919, Edna had found herself out of work and in a precarious position. Despite the fact that she moved in the glamorous circle of Madame Walker's daughter A'Lelia and was referred to as "a well-known socialite" in the *New York Age*, she needed an income.[29]

---

29. *New York Age*, November 6, 1920, 6. All newspaper citations are from the vertical file on Edna Thomas at Howard University's Moorland-Spingarn Research Center.

Like many upper-middle-class women at the time, she frequently participated in amateur theatricals and fund-raisers. Her talent for singing spirituals was well known, and it was in a benefit performance for Rosamund Johnson's music school that she came to the attention of the Lafayette Players.[30] Her many admirers in Boston and New York were convinced of her "star quality," but when she broached the idea of the professional stage to Lloyd, he was "repulsed" and refused to allow her to consider it (Thompson 262).

In 1920, despite Lloyd's objections, she launched her career by accepting the lead in *Confidence*, a one-act play by Frank Wilson. The play was mounted by the Lafayette Players at the Putnam Theater in Brooklyn and later went on tour. Edna was an immediate success and "an emphatic hit" in Philadelphia, Washington, D.C., and Norfolk, Virginia.[31] Leonard de Paur remembers her as "lift[ing] her stage by reason of her own integrity and greatness as an actress. . . . She was one of the three great ladies of the theatre we had at that time. . . . [S]he, Rose McClendon, and Laura Bowman could have played any type of theatre that was ever staged" (qtd. in Gill 75). Thomas performed over one hundred roles with the Lafayette Players, and also played in Hall Johnson's *Run, Lil' Chillun* and *LuLu Belle*. In 1936 she received rave reviews as Lady Macbeth in Orson Welles's Federal Theater production. Welles was infatuated with her; after rehearsals he liked to take her out to nightclubs and recite poetry to her.

Thomas was politically active in the battle for civil rights and was a longtime proponent of a relief organization for actors. In 1939 she was appointed acting head supervisor for the WPA Negro Theater Productions, where she probably met Elizabeth Pope White, a friend of West's from Martha's Vineyard who was later to play an important role in West's life. Like White, Thomas believed that African Americans should write, direct, and star in plays that reflected their particular issues rather than imitate white Broadway productions.

Socially, Edna and Lloyd Thomas knew everyone in bohemian Harlem. In 1927 Lloyd and a partner opened the Club Ebony, a nightspot named after Gwendolyn Bennett's "Ebony Flute" column in *Opportunity*, and both were close friends of Carl Van Vechten and his flamboyant circle.[32] Edna, or "Tommy," as her friends called her, was a bon vivant who loved champagne, beautiful women, gourmet food, witty gossip, and poker. Given the lifelong friendship between Edna Thomas and Rachel West and the latter's undisguised preference for women, it is tempting to wonder what Rachel thought of her friend's lifestyle and to speculate whether the two may have been intimate

---

30. *New York Age*, May 20, 1939.
31. *New York Age*, November 6, 1920, 6.
32. Among the "many notables" present on Club Ebony's opening night, wrote Bennett, were "Carl Van Vechten, Madame A'Lelia Walker, Dr. W. E. B. Du Bois, Eric Walrond, Jessie Fauset and goodness knows who else." *Opportunity* (November 1927): 340.

when Rachel visited her in New York. Rachel seems not to have objected to Dorothy's living in a homosexual milieu. In fact, Edna and Olivia may have provided for Dorothy a domestic model that influenced her eventual choice of a partner.

In 1926 Thomas auditioned for the part of Bess in the Theater Guild's production of *Porgy*. Having been raised in Boston, she spoke like Katharine Hepburn and was unfamiliar with the Charleston dialect; nevertheless, she studied the poems of Paul Laurence Dunbar, won the part, and announced it to all her friends. When DuBose and Dorothy Heyward, the play's white authors, saw her, they objected to the casting: she was "too refined . . . too white." They wanted "a 'natural.'"[33] Tellingly, Wallace Thurman was also rejected by the Heywards as being too "supercilious." Edna was furious and refused the lesser part of Clara which was offered; instead, she understudied her friend Evelyn Preer in *Lulu Belle* and eventually took over the role.[34] In 1929, however, she reconsidered and agreed to portray Clara for the play's London run. When one of the play's supernumeraries backed out, she persuaded Cheryl Crawford to hire Dorothy.

Traveling with Edna was, as Dorothy wrote to her mother with typical understatement, "broadening." On shipboard Edna rented deck chairs for both of them, "enjoyed the almost continual meals as only she can enjoy them," won seven dollars at poker, and organized a champagne club every few nights, at which she, Georgette Harvey (who was also an avowed lesbian), and two other actresses drank four quarts of champagne and recited "glorious" poetry.[35] In London, Edna introduced her to many celebrities, including George Dewey Washington, Zaidee Jackson, the Paul Robesons, and John Payne, the baritone, choirmaster, and unofficial ambassador of the black expatriate community. At Payne's Sunday open house, recent arrivals from America networked in professional and entertainment circles. Payne knew everyone through his good friend Lady Mary Cook. Lady Mary, a descendent of Admiral Nelson, loved black entertainers and assisted many with money and public relations. She insisted they call her "Mother" and claimed that she had been married to John Payne in an earlier incarnation—except, interestingly, she was then the husband and he the wife (Taylor 99). It was probably through Payne's contacts at the BBC that Edna recorded some spirituals on a program with Marian Anderson, who boarded with Payne while in London. Countee Cullen was also in London in the summer of 1929, and his poem "A Song of Praise" was published in the BBC Radio Times to accompany the broadcast.

33. *Washington Afro-American*, February 11, 1939.
34. Ibid.
35. Dorothy West to Rachel West, March 29 and April 2, 1929, Schlesinger Library, box 1, folder 1.

West enjoyed her stay in London; the English, she wrote to her father, were "polite," and she had encountered no prejudice. To Rachel she confided that she was having "a great deal of fun with Countee" and his friend Edward Perry.[36] She makes no reference to Cullen's failed marriage to Yolande Du Bois, nor does she appear to be aware of any sexual chemistry between the two men. In 1929 West was still a virgin and very naïve about human sexuality; in fact, it was around this time that Wallace Thurman advised her not to write about sex since her inexperience prevented her from describing it authentically.

### Mildred Jones and Langston Hughes in Russia

When West returned from England in the summer of 1929, she and Helene joined the family on Martha's Vineyard, where Dorothy worked on *Five Sheaves* and Helene recuperated from a leg injury sustained while dancing in Wallace Thurman's play *Harlem*. West planned to return to Europe in the fall; Countee Cullen, Eric Walrond, and Augusta Savage were all in Paris, and Cullen reminded her that they had dreamed of setting up a "Utopian household"; it was to be an artistic colony with the two of them as "the guiding spirits of the venture."[37] Given Cullen's sexuality and West's innocence, however, the arrangement smacks more of J. M. Barrie's colony of "lost boys," with Cullen as Peter Pan and West as Wendy. Thurman, predictably, was skeptical when West invited him to join in: "Such things generally turn out to be stupid unless colorful personality abounds, and then it grows tedious and unproductive" (Mitchell, *This Waiting* 103).

Paris did not materialize; by December, West was back in Hurston's apartment in New York and working for Fanny Hurst. The following year she was living with Edna and Lloyd Thomas and Olivia Wyndham, and moving in literary circles. On Sundays she always attended Hurston's get-togethers, and she, Zora, and Countee Cullen hosted a reception for Arna Bontemps's new novel *God Sends Sunday*. As members of Harlem's artistic elite, Dorothy and Helene were regularly invited to parties hosted by Carl Van Vechten and other wealthy "Park Avenue" whites.

Socially, Dorothy was blossoming. She was not only intelligent but also popular and charming, and an excellent dancer. Harry T. Burleigh considered her one of the most beautiful girls in New York at the time, an opinion corroborated by photographs that show her "velvet skin, the dark hair like a cloud, the dark eyes like wells to drown in" (West, *The Wedding* 97). Perhaps because of Thurman's remarks, she wanted badly to lose her virginity but was ambivalent

36. Letters to Isaac West, April 19, 1929 and Rachel West, May 19, 1929, Schlesinger Library, box 1, folders 1 and 3.
37. Cullen to West, October 10, 1929, Schlesinger Library, box 1, folder 6.

about actually having sex. Dorothy recalled later that young women, no matter how intellectual, were preyed on by men in New York, particularly by powerful white men like Frank Crowninshield, the editor of Vanity Fair, who had made a pass at Helene in his office. Both women were repelled by such harassment (McDowell 273). Perhaps defensively, West established a pattern in which she gravitated toward asexual or homosexual artists with whom she hoped to have a child. The baby, she promised, would in no way compromise the father's freedom or artistic career.[38] In the early thirties she was seeing a "blonde boy," as well as Countee Cullen and Bruce Nugent. She evidently asked Helene's advice about marrying a gay man, for her cousin urged her to marry whomever she wanted "no matter what he is like." The only important function of the male, Helene believed, was procreation; after the baby was born, a separation could always be arranged. In terms of a man's "abnormality" (the then current term for homosexuality), Helene did not think it made any difference to the bond between husband and wife (Mitchell, This Waiting 111). Such an unconventional yet naïve approach to sexuality is not surprising, given that Helene and Dorothy had been raised in a household of women and their friends included such ambivalently gendered couples as Edna and Lloyd Thomas and the Van Vechtens.

One beau who was definitely not gay was Henry Moon, a young journalist at the Amsterdam News, and a cousin of the writer Chester Himes. Moon was in love with West and proposed marriage, but she refused because "if I married Henry I would be in bed with him, and I was just sick of all that" (Guinier 220). It is possible, however, that she became pregnant with his child; around this time she seems to have had a miscarriage and was then told by her doctor that she probably could not conceive again. According to West, the white doctor told her cruelly that "it was just as well because there were too many black children in the world as it was."[39]

It was Henry Moon who persuaded West in the summer of 1932 to join the group of African Americans who had been invited to make a film in the Soviet Union. Originally, professional actors had been approached, but none were willing to accept payment in the essentially worthless Russian currency. Moon was responsible for organizing the participants and publicizing the trip; those who signed on included Ted Poston, his colleague at the Amsterdam News; Louise Thompson; Mollie Lewis, a graduate of Meharry Medical College's Pharmacy School and an old friend of Zora Neale Hurston; Mildred Jones, an artist and graduate of the Hampton Institute; actors Sylvia Garner and Wayland Rudd; singer Juanita Lewis; two members of the American Communist Party, Thurston Lewis and Alan McKenzie; Laurence Alberga, a Jamaican ag-

38. See, for example, West's March 1931 letter to Countee Cullen, Cullen Collection, box 6, folder 12, Amistad Research Center.
39. Personal conversation with K. Courtney Franklin, June 2002.

riculturalist; attorney Loren Miller; social workers Constance White and Leonard Hill; and the most famous member of the group, Langston Hughes, a boyhood friend of Moon's from Cleveland.

Although Moon had paid West's passage in the hope of getting her to himself and away from the Harlem social scene, it was to Hughes that she was drawn almost immediately. After a champagne party the two "went out and looked at the stars. The moon was big and friendly. The sea was calm."[40] In Helsinki, Hughes took her for a carriage ride in the country and they stopped at an inn for tea. Perhaps because plans with West were not proceeding as anticipated, Moon was subdued and "strangely quiet," according to Louise Thompson (Rampersad 243).[41] West undoubtedly thought she had fallen in love with Hughes, but their experience and backgrounds were so different it is unlikely that she understood him or her own feelings. In contrast to her sheltered upbringing, his independent, peripatetic existence had made him conscious of Europe's precarious economic situation. West, for example, loved Berlin, which she described as "a thrilling and beautiful city. Marvellous buildings, night life, everything enchanting,"[42] while "Hughes found the slum-ridden, prostitute-infested city, wracked by years of economic depression, distressing in the scale of its misery" (Rampersad 244).

Under his suave, sociable demeanor, Hughes was serious and ambitious and had no intention of limiting his options by a commitment to an unworldly Bostonian. He was, however, quite flirtatious with women, and during his year in Russia he had affairs with Sylvia Chen, an exquisite Chinese-Jamaican dancer; Lydia Myrtseva, the group's tour guide; and a married Russian actress named Natasha. Although he was "awfully nice" to West, he was equally attentive to her beautiful roommate Mildred Jones, who typed up his poems after he had them translated into Russian and Chinese.[43]

Hughes's talent and prestige, good looks, and boyish charm made him exactly West's type of man. She described her view of their relationship in "Russian Correspondence," in which an American woman in Moscow commits her overwrought thoughts to a journal that she intends to share with her lover when they meet in Baku. Tack (read "Lang"), a free-spirited artist and the quintessential "lost boy," is supposed to be sending her a telegram arranging their

40. Dorothy West to Rachel West, June 18, 1932, Schlesinger Library, box 1, folder 1.
41. Louise Thompson was briefly married to Wallace Thurman in 1928. She wrote in June 1932 to her mother: "Henry seems about the most subdued person on the boat, for what reason I don't know. All the rest are so hilarious that it may be only the contrast which makes it seem so." Louise Thompson Patterson Collection, box 1, folder 24, Special Collections and Archives, Woodruff Library, Emory University.
42. Dorothy West to Rachel West, June 29, 1932, Schlesinger Library, box 1, folder 1.
43. Rampersad gives a detailed account of the Russian trip that corroborates what West told Guinier.

meeting; meanwhile she urges him to "laugh a lot and ride a camel in your brave boots. . . . Be a wild boy. Bruise yourself, but don't break any bones. . . . Be as noisy as you like. Go to bed very tired." She is not jealous, she insists, and invites him to seduce not only Nadya, the Russian guide, but also "the little French girl" with whom he is traveling (14–15). The "wild boy" theme is reinforced by the view outside the window of ragged street urchins, pressing close to a fire for warmth and gaily singing despite their bare feet and evident hunger. As the ironic title of the story implies, the rendezvous will not take place, and the "Russian correspondence" is thus completely one-sided. This is exactly what happened in real life: when West, who had stayed in Moscow to work in a film, joined the group in Baku, hoping to meet Hughes, she found that he had been left behind in Uzbekistan.

Although West has been portrayed by critics as apolitical, the year in the Soviet Union was germinal to her political development. Both "Russian Correspondence" and "Room in Red Square" show her awareness of the hypocrisies of Soviet life. While ordinary Russians stood in line for hours for sour cream or bread before returning to cramped lodgings, the party elite shopped at well-stocked stores and lived in six-room apartments. West praised many aspects of the Soviet Union, particularly the lack of institutionalized racism, but she chafed at the invisible and powerful bureaucracy that controlled every aspect of one's life. In "Russian Correspondence" she contrasts the vulnerable street children with the omnipotent Tartakoff, with whom the narrator has to beg and plead for permission to visit Baku. West also noted the weekly trials of "enemies of the state" and the mass deportations to Siberia. Unlike either Langston Hughes or Richard Wright, both of whom signed a statement in 1936 supporting Stalin's purges and the Moscow show trials, she always deplored the absolute power of the Soviet bureaucracy and the discrepancy between public policy and private reality (Rowley 126).

Other factors besides politics complicated the relationship between West and Hughes. Despite her belief that she loved Hughes, she had become involved with Mildred Jones. Their contrasting styles are revealed in a shipboard photograph: Jones reclines languorously in a deck chair, while West sits cross-legged on the ground like a little girl, her face shaded by her yachting cap. Dorothy wrote to her mother that Mildred was "a lovely kid . . . serious-minded, intelligent, very fine" and that she preferred her company to that of her other friend, Mollie Lewis.[44] Once Dorothy became intimate with Mildred, Hughes—out of either pique or relief—left the field to Jones, which is how matters stood when they both left Dorothy in Moscow and departed for Baku.

While they were away, West decided that what she really wanted was to

44. See West's letter of July 1932.

## CHALLENGE

*A Literary Quarterly*

DOROTHY WEST, Editor
HAROLD JACKMAN, Associate Editor

VOLUME I      MAY 1935      NUMBER 3

### CONTENTS

Published four times yearly by the Boston Chronicle, 794 Tremont St., Boston

Contents page for *Challenge: A Literary Quarterly*, May 1935, inscribed by Dorothy West to her favorite Aunt Carrie. (Schlesinger Library, Radcliffe Institute, Harvard University.)

marry Hughes and bear his child. She felt confident that he would understand her lapse and forgive her, but she was still unwilling to hurt Mildred because "her *feeling* for me is deep and sincere. I cannot wound her in any way. . . . It is simply that this is the first time I have had the stamina to admit to myself that I do not, and I do not now remember when I did, want her as she wants me."[45] West was apparently resisting her first lesbian relationship; a socially sanctioned marriage to Hughes would enable her to break with Mildred while protecting her friend's pride. West wrote to Hughes that she would go to Paris with Mollie Lewis since she and Mildred would continue to be intimate if she stayed ("And I could not torture her or myself by my nearness"), and then she would return to Moscow to wait for him. Hughes did not respond. Mildred's

---

45. See West's letter to Hughes of October 27, 1932.

feelings about the affair are not recorded, but many years later West did claim that a friend in Moscow had called her and threatened suicide (Guinier 213). In his biography of Hughes, Arnold Rampersad also mentions a lesbian affair and a "theatrical" suicide attempt in which "someone sipped potassium formaldehyde," but the individual remains nameless (246).

The sudden death of Isaac West in February 1933 altered all of Dorothy's plans. Although Mildred had moved out of the hotel and was being courted by a voluble Russian, she was still friendly with Hughes and West, and the three of them began to discuss returning home via China. West tried to persuade Hughes, who by now was involved with Sylvia Chen, to accompany her to Latvia to obtain their exit visas, but he managed to depart the week before she did. In May she made one more attempt to connect with him. In a passionate letter she asked him to marry her, saying that since her father's death she realized she wanted a baby; she even imagined their child's appearance: "a dark son . . . or a brown daughter." Most important, the child would not limit Hughes's freedom as a poet. Remembering her conversation with Helene the previous year, she assured him that all he had to do was get her pregnant and she would move back to Boston with Rachel. He could "be forever a boy" and continue to "have adventures to the last of [his] life."[46]

Although this letter might make sense in terms of West's family dynamics, it also reveals a conflict about her own sexuality. On the one hand, she seems really to have believed that Hughes loved her, despite the fact that they never had sex, since his hug told her "more than another man's passionate kiss." Yet the conclusion of the letter—in which it occurs to her *as she is writing* that she might be mistaken and begs him, if that is the case, never to acknowledge its receipt—suggests that, like the narrator of "Russian Correspondence," she recognizes that the relationship is a fantasy. When he again did not respond, she promptly left the Soviet Union with Mildred. En route to the United States, they stopped in London, where they were "so happy"; West took Mildred to see the apartment she had shared with Edna Thomas a few years earlier and was devastated to find it had become a gentlemen's club (Dalsgård 36).

Despite their passionate Russian interlude, West mentioned Mildred only obliquely, as "a woman whom I loved very much" (Dalsgård 36). In interviews she never acknowledged her women lovers, although she frequently boasted about the men in her life. Like her friend Alberta Hunter, the blues singer, who maintained a discreet lesbian lifestyle and never admitted she was gay, West had grown up in a household that frowned on all discussion of sexuality, let alone homosexuality; probably neither woman had the language with which to describe her orientation. For years West and Hunter socialized with the same coterie of gay men in New York, including Ed Perry, Caska Bonds, Bruce Nu-

46. See West's letter to Hughes of May 26, 1933.

gent, and Alex Gumby, and gave similarly evasive answers when asked why they never married. As Margaret Walker points out, at that time "polite society ostracized the individual known as 'queer,'" adding, "There was no such thing as a sexual revolution or gay rights or 'coming out of the closet'" (88). In addition to fearing public censure, West always resisted labels. As she told one interviewer, "You can't make a good Communist out of me. But then again you can't make a good anything out of me" (Dalsgård 38). Although West never wrote about homosexuality, the many unhappy couples in her work, who sacrifice love for marriages of convenience based on socially sanctioned attributes such as color and class, reflect a dynamic that West would certainly have understood in terms of the risks of "coming out" to family and friends. The Russian letters and stories are thus significant in that they represent the only time West committed to paper her romantic attachments to either men or women.

What is certain is that West was able to sublimate her emotions when it came to her work; she always maintained relationships with friends and former lovers that stood her in good stead when she needed professional favors. Claude McKay liked to say that when Dorothy approached with a charming smile, she wanted something. West managed to stay on good terms with both Jones and Hughes and to press them into assisting her with her literary magazine, *Challenge*. Jones designed all the covers and the layout over the next few years, while Hughes's pieces were a major coup for the young and heretofore unknown editor. Even Henry Moon (who eventually married Mollie Lewis) remained in the fold and contributed several articles.

*Partners in Life and Literature:*
*Dorothy West and Marian Minus (1913–1972)*

After her father's death, West moved to 23 Worthington Street in Boston, ostensibly to assist Rachel, but perhaps also because she knew that if she returned to Harlem, she would be caught up in the fast-paced life of cocktails and speakeasies and dancing at the Savoy from which Moon had sought to distract her. She may have been avoiding the temptation to continue the relationship with Mildred Jones, who had obtained a job in the New York Welfare Bureau, or to become involved with another woman. Instead, she chose to lead "a retiring life"[47] and to concentrate on establishing a journal devoted to young black writers that she initially funded with the three hundred dollars paid her by the Soviet government upon her departure.

West was only twenty-five, but the letters she wrote soliciting material and

47. West to Countee Cullen, December 1933, Cullen Collection, box 6, folder 12, Amistad Research Center.

arranging for publication show a mature and self-confident woman dedicated to the uplift of the race. The journal was "the most unselfish thing" she had ever done; she envisioned it as "a space for young dark throats to sing heard songs" and specifically hoped to reach students at black colleges.[48] By calling on her extensive network of friends and acquaintances, she eventually published work by Langston Hughes, Sterling Brown, Margaret Walker, Richard Wright, Alain Locke, Ralph Ellison, Bruce Nugent, Arna Bontemps, Alfred Mendes, Frank Yerby, Mae Cowdery, and Pauli Murray. Needless to say, the poetry of Helene Johnson—of whom Hughes wrote enthusiastically, "Somebody ought to bring out a book of hers"—also found a forum.[49] Almost immediately the journal was criticized for its apolitical stance, but West firmly editorialized that while she encouraged "proletarian" writing, she would not sacrifice aesthetics to propaganda. By the time the third issue was published in May 1935, Harold Jackman was on board as associate editor. The following year she added a business manager, Jimmie Daniels, but by the fall of 1937, the entire masthead had changed: the journal was now *New Challenge*; the associate editor was Richard Wright, while West and her friend Marian Minus were co-editors.

West probably met Marian Minus, with whom she was to live for over a decade, in New York in the early thirties. Marian was living with her mother, Laura Whitener Minus, who, like Rachel West, had been born in South Carolina. Marian's grandmother Laura Lyles Whitener was the "white grandmother" on whom West based the character of Gram in *The Wedding*, but she, unlike the fictional and aristocratic Gram, came from a poor white family from which she had escaped by marrying an educated, middle-class black man. Eventually she moved in with her daughter Laura, but she remained, like Gram, bitter about having to "live colored." She took her anger out on brown-skinned Marian, although on her deathbed she begged the child's forgiveness (Guinier 154–55). When Marian was around five, her parents left South Carolina for Ohio, where her father, Claude Wellington Minus, taught at Wilberforce University. Laura Minus seems to have been divorced or widowed by the time she and Marian met Dorothy West in New York.

Marian Minus was an exceptionally intelligent and accomplished woman. In 1935 she graduated magna cum laude from Fisk University, where she had majored in sociology. Sociable and extremely athletic, she played basketball and tennis and pledged the Delta Sigma Theta sorority. Upon graduation, she won a Rosenwald Fellowship to the University of Chicago and began graduate

48. Ibid., and in this volume West to James Weldon Johnson, October 23, 1933. Also see her letter to Langston Hughes of February 2, 1934.
49. Hughes to West, February 22, 1934. Johnson's book had to wait seventy years until her poetry was collected by Verner Mitchell in *This Waiting*.

work in social anthropology. Dorothy visited her in 1936, and they stayed near campus at the Partridge Inn; after she left, Minus wrote wistfully that her feet strayed of their own accord toward the inn, expecting Dorothy still to be there.[50] It is likely that the two became lovers at this time, or at least pledged a commitment to each other.

Minus was an aspiring writer and was committed to social justice. She joined the militant South Side Writers' Group, whose purpose was to explore the relation of the Negro writer to politics and social movements. There she met poets Bob Davis and Frank Marshall Davis, Margaret Walker, and the undisputed genius of the group, Richard Wright. Marian, an "intellectual" who "was always willing to help others," recalled West, edited Wright's stories and "did quite a bit" for him (Dalsgård 39).

In addition to literature, both Minus and Wright were involved with the Communist Party. Although Marian supported Earl Browder, the party's candidate for president in 1936, she was becoming disenchanted and told Wright that he was subordinating his talent to politics. Unaware that she was involved with West, Wright pursued her. He found her attractive and warmed to her "Negro smile full of Negro sunshine" (Rowley 122). His friends thought he was in love with her, and West herself always boasted that he wanted to marry Marian (Dalsgård 39). Surprisingly, Wright was unaware of Minus's sexual orientation and was apparently shocked when he discovered it. Everyone else knew that Marian was gay since, unlike West, she made no attempt to deny her sexuality. Margaret Walker remembers that Marian "dressed mannishly and looked lesbian in a male fashion" (91).

By 1937 Minus had moved to New York to be with West. Although she had completed all the course work for her doctorate, she never finished her dissertation or received her degree. The next fifteen years were significant ones for the two women on both personal and professional levels. A letter written to Rachel in January 1941 shows their comfortable intimacy: on New Year's Eve, West reported, "Matt[51] had two invitations for New Year's parties, but it was then so late—we had hoped to reach home by ten—that we simply went up to Gene's for a drink, then walked a little way through Harlem, where the celebrants were whooping it up, then came home, talked, turned on the radio, toasted the New Year again, ate eggs and bacon, and talked until past four" (DWP 1:1).

In addition to their personal connection, the two women were working together on a number of projects. Minus persuaded West that *Challenge* needed a more relevant, political focus if it were to survive, and suggested that Richard Wright guest-edit an issue devoted to the South Side Writers' Group.

50. See Minus's letter of October 21, 1936.
51. Her full name was Mattie Marian Minus.

Wright, who had been working for the WPA in Chicago, had also relocated to New York and was hoping to transfer to the Manhattan office. Meanwhile he was writing for the *Daily Worker*. Envisioning *Challenge* as the first black leftist periodical, he accepted the offer with enthusiasm. He not only secured the writers' contributions but also persuaded the *Daily Worker* to promote it and, with Ralph Ellison, actively canvassed for subscriptions. While he may have hoped to continue his personal relationship with Marian, he was eager to distance himself from the writing in the journal's previous six issues, which even the loyal Wallace Thurman had described as bourgeois and affected. Perhaps misunderstanding the extent to which West and Minus wanted him involved, he changed the publication's name to *New Challenge*. In his "Blueprint for Negro Writing," which was to be the publication's manifesto, he urged black writers to explore issues of social justice within a social realist style. The essay ridiculed the Harlem Renaissance writers as effete and decadent; they were "French poodles" that showed off and did parlor tricks for white patrons. In the same month he wrote a scathing review in the leftist magazine *New Masses* of Hurston's novel *Their Eyes Were Watching God*.[52] Hurston had no ideology, he said, and she pandered to white readers' desire for comical and entertaining black characters.

Chagrined and offended, West demoted him to associate editor and placed her own and Minus's names on the masthead as editors. Minus countered "Blueprint for Negro Writing" with a positive review of Hurston's novel in the same issue, although, perhaps to avoid confrontation, she signed the article with just her initials. Wright realized too late not only that the journal was in debt, and not solvent as he had been led to believe, but also that Minus had allied herself with West, and that the two women were intimate. He then insisted that West sign over the journal to him, undoubtedly to protect the copyright of his work. West, claiming to have been intimidated because she thought the Communist Party was behind his demand, complied.

Despite their disagreement, West never criticized Wright, except to complain about his politics and his penchant for white women. She admired his writing and may have used him, albeit not very accurately or successfully, as the model for Pierce Hunter in *Where the Wild Grape Grows*. Good-looking and personable, Hunter has published a book of short stories that graphically depicts racism and dispossession. He has also produced a novel about "the anguish and beauty of a black boy's spiritual growth in a stunted corner of the South, written with powerful cadence and clarity."[53] Despite his success, Hunter betrays his loyal and nurturing wife with other women. Although

---

52. See Wright, "Blueprint" and "Between Laughter and Tears."
53. "Where the Wild Grape Grows," unpublished manuscript, 85, Schlesinger Library, box 2, folders 35 and 36.

West treats Pierce with sympathy, his relationship with his wife does not ring true and flaws her otherwise lyrical and psychologically astute work. Other than the stories involving middle-aged men and modeled on her father, West probably should have followed Thurman's advice and avoided writing about males or heterosexual relationships at all. Her forte would always be the development of character and the portrayal of women, children, the elderly, and the dispossessed.

The *New Challenge* episode did not, apparently, mar the relationship between the two women, who continued to live and work together. Both were writing constantly, but Minus also typed and edited West's manuscripts. They mined each other's family sources for their fiction and may have collaborated on the unpublished novel *Jude*. During the early forties they were well known in the New York publishing world, thanks to their agent, George Bye, who worked hard to place their work in the "slick" magazines. Although he was not successful in that venue, in the years between 1938 and 1952 Minus published in *The Crisis*, *Opportunity*, and *Woman's Day*, while Dorothy's first story of many, "Jack in the Pot," was accepted by the *New York Daily News*.

The aesthetic of black writing that Minus propounded in "Present Trends of Negro Literature" was undoubtedly shared by West, since its tenets were reflected in her stories. Although they agreed with Wright that black writing must not be held hostage to middle-class values, they also objected to a narrow racialism. Citing Gertrude Stein, Minus argued for an African American literature that combined "universality of appeal" with "the immortalization of character and social situation" (9). Like Wright, she urged writers to find inspiration in "the earthy, burning, vital forces which typify the greater proportion of Negro existence," but also to set the particular truth of the black experience "against the background of the total configuration of world-wide human emotions, ideals and struggles" (10–11). Thus West's stories focused more on character development and the human condition than on the African American experience per se.

Like Zora Neale Hurston, Minus and West did not write exclusively about their own race. All three, for example, explored the erotic attraction of transgressive interracial relationships. Hurston wrote two novels with white male protagonists, the unpublished *Barney Turk* and *Seraph on the Suwanee*. In the latter, the lifelong relationship between white Jim Meserve and black Joe Kelsey is more intimate and fulfilling than that between Jim and his neurotic wife, Arvay, who is jealous of Joe. In addition to sharing a work ethic, an appreciation of the Florida environment, and an entrepreneurial spirit, the two men like each other "tremendously." Joe has "the best-looking smile that Jim had ever seen on a man. . . . Just seeing Joe put him into a playful mood," an effect Arvay never has on her husband (43). Similarly, in *The Wedding*, Gram becomes the virtual wife of her black son-in-law everywhere save the bedroom. Close to death, she realizes that, unlike her white family, only he knew and understood her. In her story "The Fine Line," Minus supplies an account of her grandmother's adolescence and the motivation for her interracial marriage. Cadie Culkey's mill job is the sole support of her family—a slatternly mother, unkempt siblings, and a bigoted, tubercular father who constantly invokes the Bible to justify his racism. One night, depressed by her environment and unable to eat a greasy, unappetizing dinner, she hears a young black man improvise a blues about the red Southern moon and she intuits an erotic, interracial connection. Cadie leaves her home and steals into the forbidden garden of a black family, hungry for the ripe figs that are "firm and full inside their rich, dark skins." After plucking the fruit she feels "the fig lying heavy in her hand, and in the moonlight she could see the thick white fluid where it smeared her fingertips" (336). Although the owner is angry at her trespass and apprehensive about its racial ramifications, his wife invites Cadie into the house, where she sees an order and harmony lacking in her own. Minus suggests that in rejecting both the racism and the spurious, patriarchal religion of the South, Cadie is destined to cross, at the very least, the color line.

During these years West and Minus struggled hard to support themselves with their writing. Apparently, to judge from a Christmas card sent by Mollie Lewis to "the Misses West and Minus," they moved in with Laura Minus on West 117th Street when Marian returned from Chicago (DWP 1:15). West had obtained a job as a home relief investigator, perhaps through Mollie, who was a social worker with the Bureau of Welfare, but Minus listed herself as unemployed on her social security application. In 1938 they moved to West 110th Street. Dorothy was laid off, but she soon found work with the Writers' Project, possibly through Laura Minus, who was employed by the WPA.

At the Writers' Project, West was in illustrious company; Zora Neale Hurston, Langston Hughes, Ralph Ellison, Chester Himes, Nelson Algren, Claude McKay, Richard Wright, Frank Byrd, and Ted Poston were all on the payroll. West produced crisp, ironic sketches on Harlem life such as "Cocktail Party" and "Amateur Night at the Apollo," as well as poignant stories of her welfare work in "Pluto" and "Mammy." She even interviewed Laura Minus for a piece about the ghosts in their Harlem apartment.

Marian was eventually hired as a correspondent for the Consumers Union in Mt. Vernon, New York, where Helene Johnson and Gwendolyn Bennett were also working. Her article "The Negro as a Consumer" drew on her experiences in Chicago, Harlem, and the South, where lack of consumer education in the black community contributed to the purchase of goods produced by child labor and disenfranchised workers, and to high mortality rates from misuse of patent medicines.

Rachel West was very much a part of Dorothy's and Marian's lives. After her daughter left Boston, Rachel moved around the less affluent sections of Roxbury, living sometimes alone and sometimes with her sisters. Her finances were precarious, and West sent money every month for the rent. It is unclear whether Rachel recognized the nature of Dorothy's relationship with Marian; in 1939 she sent birthday presents to both women, asking Dorothy to "tell Matt I love her and I want her always to stay close to you to be the sister you should have had" (DWP 1:2). In 1941 Dorothy, sounding discouraged about money, wrote to her mother: "I wish I knew how soon my ship was coming in. Of course, I realize that since the war many ships have been sunk. I hope mine wasn't." After speaking wistfully about Helene's baby daughter, Abigail, she adds unexpectedly: "Someday marriage may enter into the heads of both Matt and me. So far it hasn't, but in life nothing is certain, and everything is subject to change. You can depend upon it that if it happens, he will have a nice income." The letter ends with Matt sending "love to you and the whole tremendous family" (DWP 1:1).

Finances did not improve, and domestic change was inevitable. In August 1942, Minus wrote to West, who was staying with Rachel on Martha's Vineyard, that they were in danger of being evicted from the apartment on 110th Street. The landlord had threatened to put their furniture on the street, contact the *Daily News*, and garnish West's pay (DWP 1:15). That may have been the final straw, for the following year West moved back to the island, ostensibly to help Rachel take care of her ailing sister Carrie. She had never lost her passion for Martha's Vineyard and had once written her mother: "I wish I could fly thru the air to the island. . . . That is the one spot on earth that I want never to change. It is the closest to paradise I will ever come on earth" (DWP 1:1). In an unpublished draft of her essay "The Legend of Oak Bluffs," West was more specific: "Nowhere else in America was there a place so favorable to the condition of being colored" (DWP 2:39). Many years later West would tell interviewers that she moved back because she could not write with all the distractions of a busy social life, but according to Barbara and Courtney Franklin, the real reason was that she no longer wanted to struggle at making a living in New York.

West and Minus remained close, at least until 1950; Marian may have lived briefly on the island, and she was a constant visitor. Barbara Franklin remembers both women caring for her affectionately on her summer visits with Aunt Isabel. Among her other talents, Marian was an expert auto mechanic. Abigail McGrath recalls that a frequent sight in the neighborhood was Marian under the hood of a car, with Dorothy standing by, handing the requested wrenches. During one of these visits, Dorothy apparently got the idea for *The Living Is Easy*. She wrote it quickly, and in January 1945 she sent Countee Cullen six chapters, asking him to recommend it for a Rosenwald grant. Congratulating him on the possibility that Lena Horne might star in his musical *St. Louis Woman*, she added, "Both Marian and I wish you all the success in the world."[54]

*The Living Is Easy* was published in 1948 to immediate critical acclaim. Every black newspaper in the country reviewed it favorably, and it was well received in mainstream publications such as the *New York Times*, the *New Orleans Times-Picayune*, and Boston's *Commonweal*. Of Cleo/Rachel, Florence Codman wrote in *Commonweal*, "Miss West has created a . . . wholly plausible, tantalizing creature."[55] West was interviewed by the *Boston Herald* and logged her first appearance in the *Vineyard Gazette* in another interview. It was in these encounters with the press that West began the delicate revisions of history that she maintained throughout her career. For example, she claimed that she had graduated from Girls' Latin and attended Boston University, although neither institution could verify that information. She also said that she went to Russia not to make an anti-American film but because of her passion for Tolstoy and Dostoyevsky, and that "all the characters in my book were filtered through the creative process and are really not based on any living person."[56]

Minus may have joined West on the Vineyard for a while in 1948, for in October they received a birth announcement from Gail Jackson, the niece of Dorothy's close friend Elizabeth Pope White. Shortly thereafter, however, Minus returned to New York and, after eleven years of freelance writing, took a full-time job as an office supervisor. In 1957 she acquired a certificate from the Management Institute of New York University, and in 1958 she was appointed personnel director at Consumers Union, where she remained until her retirement. At some point she met or renewed her acquaintance with Edna Pemberton, and they moved to an apartment at 1925 Seventh Avenue, the same building in which Zora Neale Hurston had lived many years before.

Pemberton and Minus maintained their ties with literary and artistic Harlem. Their circle included Harold Jackman and his sister Ivie Jackman, Ida (Mrs. Countee) Cullen, Gwendolyn Bennett, the painter Romare Bearden and the art teacher Louise Jefferson, actress Juanita Hall, columnist Roberta Bosley Hubert, Hall Johnson, the Bruce Nugents, actress Vinnette Carroll, the Ossie Davises, lawyer Barbara Watson, and Urban League officers Helen Harden and Beryl Edelen. After Jackman's death, they became founding members of the Harold Jackman Memorial Committee. Carl Van Vechten served as honorary

---

54. West to Cullen, January 26, 1945, Cullen Collection, box 6, folder 12, Amistad Research Center. *St. Louis Woman* opened on Broadway on March 30, 1946, at New York's Martin Beck Theatre. Lena Horne decided not to play Della, the leading character, and as a result Ruby Hill got the role. Others in the opening night cast were Harold Nicholas, who played Little Augie, and a young Pearl Bailey, whose singing and dancing drew rave reviews.
55. *Commonweal*, June 25, 1948; all reviews of *The Living Is Easy* are from the Schlesinger Library's West Collection, box 3, folder 52.
56. Quoted by Rudolph Elie, *Boston Herald*, May 27, 1948.

chairman, and associate members included Arna Bontemps, Langston Hughes, the painter Jacob Lawrence, Arthur Spingarn, and Dorothy West. The parting between West and Minus was apparently amicable because family members remember visiting Marian in New York.

It is difficult, however, to determine who initiated the breakup, and whether or not it was a traumatic one. According to Adelaide Cromwell, West was always extremely private and not particularly close to anyone on the island; her main interests were her writing, her family, and her pets. Her neighbor Isabel Washington Powell maintains that while Rachel West was "lovely," Dorothy was downright difficult and insisted on feeding and attracting nuisance birds to their adjacent porches. Barbara Franklin recalls, however, that after Marian and Dorothy separated, Dorothy became very friendly with Elizabeth Pope White.

"Aunt Liz," as Barbara called her, was a childhood friend from the Vineyard; her grandfather, Bostonian Charles Shearer, had bought land in 1908, built a cottage, and founded the Baptist Tabernacle on the Vineyard. In fact, the Shearers, the Wests, and the family of artist Lois Mailou Jones were the original black property owners on the island. Because blacks were not welcome at island hotels, the Shearers opened a guest house, where, among other prominent African Americans, Adam Clayton Powell Sr. and his family enjoyed the summers. Other guests included Ethel Waters, Paul Robeson, the composer Harry T. Burleigh, and Martin Luther King Jr.

Liz was, according to West, an avid Shakespearian, and a talented dancer, actress, and costume designer (Saunders and Shackleford 105). She loved films about Shakespeare and period dramas, to which she was always dragging Dorothy (Guinier 207). In the 1930s she moved to New York, where she worked for the Federal Theatre Project with Edna Lewis Thomas. Like Thomas, however, she discovered that her fair complexion precluded black roles and her race excluded her from white ones. Although she could have "passed," she refused to do so. Liz married and lived in New York but returned in the summers to help her sister, Doris Pope Jackson, run the guest house.

In 1944 she conceived the idea of organizing a community theater on the family property. Her dynamic personality and her ability to blend professional and amateur actors with family members made for successful productions. In 1954 she purchased Twin Cottage, a double Victorian summer mansion built by a whaling captain for his two daughters. As a little girl, Liz had thought the deserted cottage was haunted, but she later saw a resemblance to Shakespeare's Globe Theatre, and set about renovating its ancient plumbing and wiring and transforming it into an open-air stage (Hayden and Hayden 99–100). Actors, darting in and out of the many porches and balconies, made full use of the unconventional space. It was not unusual on a given night for over two hundred people, of all races and nationalities, to attend one of her avant-garde productions.

In 1960 White decided to produce a film of *Othello* with an all-black cast and an Afro-Caribbean jazz score, a project that consumed her energy and re-sources for the next twenty years and eventually brought an end to the summer theater (Hayden and Hayden 101). West joined the project as location manager, although, with characteristic modesty, she described her job as "gopher," say-ing, "We were both healthy as horses with unlimited energy—it was fun for me—my station wagon standing ready to be packed with props, coolers, and whatever paraphernalia Liz was seeking" (Saunders and Shackleford 118). Eventually the film was completed and won several awards.

West's relationship with Liz White, though intense, was undoubtedly platonic; in fact, the historian Adelaide Cromwell flatly denies that West was ever interested in women sexually. On the contrary, she believes that West had a long-term affair with an older white man on the island. This may have been the "millionaire" who wanted to marry her when she was "about forty-five" (Roses 49). Given West's ro-mantic history, Cromwell's comments are surprising. Nevertheless, West was clearly mindful of her mother's teachings on decorum. "Social graces came as second nature," notes one family member, "and propriety ran through your veins as smoothly as did your blood" (Franklin, "Beloved Cousin" 11).

### Where the Wild Grape Grows

Just as The Living Is Easy described Rachel's life as a young woman, so West's next book, Where the Wild Grape Grows, was intended to examine Rachel's later years as she and her sisters grew older. Unfortunately, the melodramatic sub-plot involving the writer Pierce Hunter and his long-suffering wife detracts from the novel's autumnal mood. The novel was rejected, and West did not try to publish it again.

After the deaths of Rachel and her sister Carrie, West lived alone in the Vine-yard house. For over twenty years she wrote columns for the Vineyard Gazette and worked on The Wedding, a novel about the elite African American summer colony on Martha's Vineyard. Feeling out of tune with the times, she decided against publishing the book for fear it would be deprecated by the new militants, who had no interest in the black aristocracy. It was not until The Living Is Easy was re-published in 1982 that West's work was again given the attention it deserves. She was encouraged to finish The Wedding and invited to speak at colleges and universities as the last living member of the Harlem Renaissance. Well into her eighties she found herself so feted by celebrities and pursued by admirers that she was compelled to post a little sign on her cottage door: "Writer at work. Please call again. Trying to Make a Living." For her ninetieth birthday, West was treated to a lavish party, attended by first lady Hillary Clinton and televised in-ternationally. The awards, acclaim, and attention showered on her in her final years capped an exhilarating journey and proved a fitting tribute to the woman who was indeed the last member of the Harlem Renaissance.

## Works Cited

Alexander, Adele Logan. *Homelands and Waterways: The American Journey of the Bond Family, 1846–1926.* New York: Vintage, 2000.

Byrd, Frank. "Interview of Alonzo Thayer." Ca. 1938. Library of Congress, Manuscript Division, WPA Federal Writers' Project Collection.

Cromwell, Adelaide M. *The Other Brahmins: Boston's Black Upper Class, 1750–1950.* Fayetteville: University of Arkansas Press, 1994.

——. Personal interview. April 2003.

Dalsgård, Katrine. "Alive and Well and Living on the Island of Martha's Vineyard: An Interview with Dorothy West, October 29, 1988." *Langston Hughes Review* 12.2 (Fall 1993): 28–44.

Daniels, John. *In Freedom's Birthplace.* Boston: Houghton Mifflin, 1914.

Davis, Cynthia. "The Living Ain't Easy: Signifying on the American Dream." *Langston Hughes Review* 16.1, 2 (Fall/Spring 1999–2001): 12–18.

Dorothy West Papers (DWP). Schlesinger Library, Radcliffe Institute, Harvard University.

Dougan, Michael B. "Dorothy Scarborough." *American National Biography.* Ed. John Garraty and Mark Carnes. Vol. 19. New York: Oxford University Press, 1999. 345–46.

Franklin, Barbara L. Personal interviews. June 2002 and January 2003.

Franklin, K. Courtney. "Beloved Cousin Was 'Aunt Dorothy.'" *Vineyard Gazette,* August 25, 1998, 11.

——. Personal interview. June 2002.

Gaither, Barry. "Seeing Ourselves." In Sichel, 19–21.

Gill, Glenda E. *A Study of the Federal Theatre, 1935–1939.* New York: Peter Lang, 1989.

Gordon, Eugene. "Editor's Note." *Saturday Evening Quill* 1 (June 1928): 1.

Guinier, Genii. "Interview with Dorothy West, May 6, 1978." In *The Black Women Oral History Project.* Ed. Ruth Edmonds Hill. Vol. 10. Westport, Conn.: Meckler, 1991. 143–223.

Hayden, Karen, and Robert Hayden. *African-Americans on Martha's Vineyard and Nantucket: A History of People, Places and Events.* Boston: Select Publications, 1999.

Henry, George W. *Sex Variants: A Study of Homosexual Patterns.* New York: Paul Hoebber, 1948.

Hill, Patricia Liggins, ed. *Call and Response: The Riverside Anthology of the African American Literary Tradition.* New York: Houghton Mifflin, 1998.

Hurston, Zora Neale. *Seraph on the Suwanee.* 1948. New York: Harper Perennial, 1991.

Ignatiev, Noel. *How the Irish Became White.* New York: Routledge, 1995.

Johnson, James Weldon. *Black Manhattan.* 1930. New York: Da Capo, 1991.

Jones, Sharon. "Rereading the Harlem Renaissance: The 'Folk,' 'Bourgeois,' and 'Proletarian' Aesthetics in the Fiction of Jessie Fauset, Zora Neale Hurston, and Dorothy West." Ph.D. diss., University of Georgia, 1996.

Kaplan, Carla, ed. *Zora Neale Hurston: A Life in Letters.* New York: Doubleday, 2002.

Kavanagh, Julie. *Secret Muses: The Life of Frederick Ashton.* New York: Pantheon, 1997.

Marchione, William P. *Of Horticulture and Antislavery: The Kenricks of Newton.* Boston: Chandler Pond Preservation Society, 2001.

McDowell, Deborah E. "Conversations with Dorothy West." In *The Harlem Renaissance Reexamined.* Ed. Victor A. Kramer. New York: AMS Press, 1987. 265–82.

McGrath, Abigail. "A Daughter Reminisces." In Mitchell, *This Waiting,* 123–30.

Minus, Marian. "Present Trends of Negro Literature." *Challenge* 2.1 (April 1937): 9–11.

——. "The Fine Line." *Opportunity* 17.11 (November 1939): 333–37, 351.

——. "The Negro as a Consumer." *Opportunity* 16.9 (September 1938): 274–76.

Mitchell, Verner D. "David Walker, African Rights, and Liberty." In *Multiculturalism: Roots and Realities.* Ed. C. James Trotman. Bloomington: Indiana University Press, 2002. 94–107.

——. ed. *This Waiting for Love: Helene Johnson, Poet of the Harlem Renaissance.* Amherst: University of Massachusetts Press, 2000.

Perry, Margaret. *Silence to the Drums: A Survey of the Literature of the Harlem Renaissance.* Westport, Conn.: Greenwood, 1976.

Piersen, William D. *Black Yankees: The Development of an Afro-American Subculture in Eighteenth-Century New England.* Amherst: University of Massachusetts Press, 1988.

Powell, Isabel Washington. Personal interview. May 2003.

Rampersad, Arnold. *The Life of Langston Hughes.* Vol. 1. New York: Oxford University Press, 1986.

Roses, Lorraine Elena. "Dorothy West at Oak Bluffs, Massachusetts, July 1984." *SAGE* 2.1 (Spring 1985): 47–49.

Rowley, Hazel. *Richard Wright: The Life and Times.* New York: Henry Holt, 2001.

Saunders, James, and Renae Shackleford, eds. *The Dorothy West Martha's Vineyard.* Jefferson, N.C.: McFarland, 2001.

Sichel, Kim, ed. *Black Boston: Documentary Photography and the African American Experience.* Boston: Boston University Art Gallery and Philadelphia: University of Pennsylvania Press, 1995.

Sollors, Werner, Caldwell Titcomb, and Thomas A. Underwood. *Blacks at Harvard.* New York: New York University Press, 1993.

Taylor, Frank C. *Alberta Hunter: A Celebration in Blues.* New York: McGraw-Hill, 1987.

Taylor, Susie King. *A Black Woman's Civil War Memoirs.* New York: Markus Wiener, 1999.

Thompson, Sister Mary Francesca. "The Lafayette Players: 1915–1932." Ph.D. diss., University of Michigan, 1972.

Thurman, Wallace. "Negro Life in New York's Harlem." 1928. In *Speech and Power: The African-American Essay and Its Cultural Content from Polemics to Pulpit.* Ed. Gerald Early. Hopewell, N.J.: Ecco, 1992. 70–91.

Walker, Alice. *In Search of Our Mothers' Gardens.* New York: Harcourt Brace, 1983.

Walker, Margaret. *Richard Wright: Daemonic Genius.* New York: Amistad, 1988.

Wall, Cheryl A. *Women of the Harlem Renaissance.* Bloomington: Indiana University Press, 1995.

Warner Jr., Sam B. *Streetcar Suburbs: The Process of Growth in Boston, 1870–1900.* New York: Atheneum, 1972.

Washington, Katherine Benson. "My Aunt Rachel." N.p., [ca. 1985].

Washington, Mary Helen. "'The Darkened Eye Restored': Notes Toward a Literary History of Black Women." In *Reading Black, Reading Feminist: A Critical Anthology.* Ed. Henry Louis Gates Jr. New York: Meridian, 1990. 30–43.

West, Dorothy. "Funeral." 1930. In *The Richer,* 59–75.

—— [as Mary Christopher]. "Room in Red Square." *Challenge* 1.1 (March 1934): 10–15.

—— [as Mary Christopher]. "Russian Correspondence." *Challenge* 1.2 (September 1934): 14–20.

—— *The Living Is Easy.* 1948. New York: Feminist Press, 1982.

——. *The Richer, the Poorer: Stories, Sketches, and Reminiscences.* New York: Anchor, 1995.

——. *The Wedding.* New York: Anchor, 1995.

Williams, Blanche Colton. *Our Short Story Writers.* 1920. Freeport, N.Y.: Books for Libraries Press, 1969.

Wright, Richard. "Between Laughter and Tears." *New Masses,* October 5, 1937, 22–23.

——. "Blueprint for Negro Writing." *New Challenge* 2.2 (Fall 1937): 53–64.

## CAROLINA

HER EYES flew open. The birds were waking in the Carolina woods. Cleo always got up with them. There were never enough hours in a summer day to extract the full joy of being alive. She tumbled out of the big old-fashioned bed. Small Serena stirred, then lay still again on her share of the pillow. At the foot of the bed, Lily and Charity nestled together.

She stared at her three younger sisters, seeing the defenselessness of their innocent sleep. The bubbling mischief in her made her take one of Lily's long braids and double knot it with one of Charity's. She looked back at Serena, who tried so hard to be a big girl and never let anyone help her dress. She picked up Serena's little drawers and turned one leg inside out.

She was almost sorry she would be far away when the fun began. She could picture Lily and Charity leaping to the floor from opposite sides of the bed, and their heads snapping back, and banging together. As for Serena, surprise would spread all over her solemn face when she stepped into one leg of her drawers and found the other leg closed to her. She would start all over again, trying her other foot this time, only to find she had stepped into the same kettle of hot water. She would wrassle for fifteen minutes, getting madder and madder. Cleo had to clap her hand to her mouth to hush her giggles.

She would get a whipping for it. Mama would never see the joke. Mama would say it was mean to tease your sisters. You had to walk a chalkline to please her.

Sometimes Cleo tried to walk a chalkline, but after a little while, keeping to the strait and narrow made her too nervous. At home, there was nothing to do except stay around. Away from home, there were trees to climb and boys to fight, and hell to raise with Josie Beauchamp.

She climbed out of the open window and dropped to the ground at the moment that Josie Beauchamp was quietly creeping down the stairs of her magnificent house. Some day Cleo was going to live in a fine house, too. And maybe some day Josie was going to be as poor as church mice.

They met by their tree, at the foot of which they had buried their symbols of friendship. Josie had buried her gold ring because she loved it best of everything, and Cleo best of everybody. Cleo had buried Lily's doll, mostly because it tickled her to tell her timid sister that she had seen a big rat dragging it under the house. Lily had taken a long stick and poked around. But every time it touched something, Lily had jumped a mile.

Cleo and Josie wandered over the Beauchamp place, their bare feet drinking in the dew, their faces lifted to feel the morning. Only the birds were abroad, their vivid splashes of color, the brilliant outpouring of their waking songs filling the eye and ear with summer's intoxication.

They did not talk. They had no words to express their aliveness. They wanted none. Their bodies were their eloquence. Clasping hands, they began to skip, too impatient of meeting the morning to walk toward it any longer. Suddenly Cleo pulled her hand away and tapped Josie on the shoulder. They should have chosen who was to be "It." But Cleo had no time for counting out. The wildness was in her, the unrestrained joy, the desire to run to the edge of the world and fling her arms around the sun, and rise with it, through time and space, to the center of everywhere.

She was swift as a deer, as Mercury, with Josie running after her, falling back, and back, until Josie broke the magic of the morning with her exhausted cry, "Cleo, I can't catch you."

"Nobody can't never catch me," Cleo exulted. But she spun around to wait for Josie. The little sob in Josie's throat touched the tenderness she always felt toward those who had let her show herself the stronger.

They wandered back toward Josie's house, for now the busyness of the birds had quieted to let the human toilers take over the morning. Muted against the white folks' sleeping, the Negro voices made velvet sounds. The field hands and the house servants diverged toward their separate spheres, the house servants settling their masks in place, the field hands waiting for the overseer's eye before they stooped to servility.

Cleo and Josie dawdled before the stables. The riding horses whinnied softly, thrusting their noses to the day. Josie's pony nuzzled her hand, wanting to hear his name dripping in honey. And Cleo moved away. Anybody could ride an old pony. She wanted to ride General Beauchamp's roan stallion, who shied at any touch but his master's.

She marched back to Josie. "Dare me to ride the red horse," she challenged. Her eyes were green as they bored into Josie's, the gray gone under in her passion.

"No," said Josie, desperately trying not to flounder in the green sea. "He'd throw you and trample you. He'd kill you dead."

"He can't tromp me! I ain't ascairt of nothing alive. I dare you to dare me. I double dare you!"

"I won't, I won't! I'm bad, but I'm not wicked."

"I'm not wicked neither! I just ain't a coward."

She streaked to the stall and flung open the barrier. The wild horse smelled her wildness. Her green eyes locked with his red-flecked glare. Their wills met, clashed, and would not yield. The roan made a savage sound in his throat, his nostrils flared, his great sides rippled. He lowered his head to lunge. But Cleo was quicker than he was. She grasped his mane, leaped on his broad neck, slid down his back, and dug her heels in his flanks.

"Giddap, red horse!" she cried.

He flung back his head, reared, and crashed out of the stall, with Josie screeching and sobbing and sidestepping just in time.

Cleo hung on for ten minutes, ten minutes of dazzling flight to the sun. She felt no fear, feeling only the power beneath her and the power inside her, and the rush of wind on which she and the roan were riding. When she was finally thrown, she landed unhurt in a clover field. It never occurred to her to feel for broken bones. She never doubted that she had a charmed life. Her sole mishap was a minor one. She had split the seat of her drawers.

She got up and brushed off her pinafore, in a fever now to get home and brag to her sisters. She knew that she ought to let Josie see that she was still alive. The riderless horse would return, and Josie would never tell who had ridden him off. But she would be tormented by fear for as long as Cleo stayed away.

Josie would not want to eat, no matter what fancy things the white folks had for breakfast. She would not want to ride in her pony cart, no matter how pretty a picture she made. She would not want to go calling with her stylish mother, not even if she was let to wear the dress that came all the way from Paris. On this bright day the sun had darkened for Josie, and nobody but Cleo could make it shine again.

The four sisters sat around the kitchen table, eating their salt pork and biscuit and hominy, slupping down their buttermilk. Charity was nine, two years younger than Cleo, Lily was eight, Serena four. Their faces were tear-streaked. Cleo's was not, though she was the one who had got the whipping. Mama couldn't keep track of the times she had tanned Cleo's hide, trying to bring her up a Christian. But the Devil was trying just as hard in the other direction.

There Cleo was this morning, looking square in Mama's eye, telling her she must have been sleepwalking again. Couldn't remember getting dressed or tying her sisters' braids together. Just remembered coming awake in a clover field. Mama had tried to beat the truth out of her, but Cleo wouldn't budge from her lie. Worst of all, she wouldn't cry and show remorse. Finally Mama had to put away the strap because her other children looked as if they would die if she didn't.

They couldn't bear to see Cleo beaten. She was their oldest sister, their protector. She wasn't afraid of the biggest boy or the fiercest dog, or the meanest teacher. She could sass back. She could do anything. They accepted her teasing and tormenting as they accepted the terrors of the night. Night was always followed by day, and made day seem more wonderful.

Mama stood by the hearth, feeling helpless in her mind. Cleo was getting too big to beat, but she wasn't a child that would listen to reason. Whatever she didn't want to hear went in one ear and out the other. She was old enough to be setting an example for her sisters. And all they saw her do was devilment.

With a long blackened fireplace stick Mama carefully tilted the lid of the three-legged skillet to see if her corn bread was done. The rest of Pa's noon dinner—the greens, the rice, the hunk of fresh pork—was waiting in his bucket. Gently she let the lid drop, and began to work the skillet out of its covering of coals that had been charred down from the oak wood. As the skillet moved forward, the top coals dislodged. Their little plunking sounds were like the tears plopping in Mama's heart.

Sulkily Cleo spooned the hominy she hated because she mustn't make Mama madder by leaving it. Mama bleached her corn in lye water made from fireplace ashes. Pa spit tobacco juice in those ashes. He spit to the side, and Mama took her ashes from the center, but that didn't make them seem any cleaner. Mama thought everything about Pa was wonderful, even his spit.

Cleo made a face at Mama's back, and then her face had to smile a little bit as she watched the dimples going in and out of Mama's round arms. You could almost touch their softness with your eyes. A flush lay just under the surface, giving them a look of tender warmth. For all the loving in Mama's arms, she had no time for it all day. Only at night, when her work was done, and her children in bed, you knew by Mama's silver laughter that she was finding time for Pa.

Mama loved Pa better than anyone. And what was left over from loving him was divided among her daughters. Divided even, Mama said whenever Cleo asked her. Never once would Mama say she loved one child most.

On their straggling way to the mill with Pa's dinner, Cleo told her sisters about her wild ride. They were bewitched by her fanciful telling. Timid Lily forgot to watch where she was walking. Her toes uncurled. She snatched up a stick and got astride it.

Serena clung to Charity's hand to keep herself from flying. Cleo was carrying her away, and she wanted to feel the ground again. She wanted to take Pa his dinner, and go back home and play house.

Charity saw a shining prince on a snow-white charger. The prince rode toward her, dazzling her eyes with light coming nearer and nearer, leaning to swoop her up in his arms. And Cleo, looking at Charity's parted lips and the glowing eyes, thought that Charity was seeing her riding the red horse into the sun.

Her triumphant tale, in which she did not fall, grandly dismounted to General Beauchamp's applause, came to its thrilling conclusion. She turned and looked at Lily scornfully, because a stick was not a horse. Lily felt foolish, and let the stick fall, and stepped squish on an old fat worm. Serena freed her hand. Released from Cleo's spell, she felt independent again. Charity's shining prince vanished, and there was only Cleo, walking ahead as usual, forgetting to take back the bucket she had passed to Charity.

Pa was waiting in the shade, letting the toil pour off him in perspiration. His tired face lightened with love when they reached him. He opened his dinner bucket and gave them each a taste. Nothing ever melted so good in their mouths as a bite of Pa's victuals.

He gave them each a copper, too, though he could hardly spare it, what with four of them to feed and Mama wanting yard goods and buttons and ribbons to keep herself feeling proud of the way she kept her children. Time was, he gave them kisses for toting his bucket. But the day Cleo brazenly said, I don't want a kiss, I want a copper, the rest of them shamefacedly said it after her. Most times Pa had a struggle to dig down so deep. Four coppers a day, six days a week, was half a day's pay gone up in smoke for candy.

Pa couldn't bring himself to tell Mama. She would have wrung out of him that Cleo had been the one started it. And Cleo was his eldest. A man who loved his wife couldn't help loving his first-born best, the child of his fiercest passion. When that first-born was a girl, she could trample on his heart, and he would swear on a stack of Bibles that it didn't hurt.

The sisters put their coppers in their pinafore pockets and skipped back through the woods.

Midway Cleo stopped and pointed to a towering oak. "You all want to bet me a copper I can't swing by my feet from up in that tree?"

Lily clapped her hands to her eyes. "I doesn't want to bet you," she implored. "I ain't fixing to see you fall."

Serena said severely, "You bust your neck, you see if Mama don't bust it again."

Charity said tremulously, "Cleo, what would us do if our sister was dead?"

Cleo saw herself dressed up fine as Josie Beauchamp, stretched out in a coffin with her sisters sobbing beside it, and Pa with his Sunday handkerchief holding his tears, and Mama crying, I loved you best, Cleo. I never said it when you were alive. And I'm sorry, sorry, I waited to say it after you were gone.

"You hold my copper, Charity. And if I die, you can have it."

Lily opened two of her fingers and peeped through the crack. "Cleo, I'll give you mine if you don't make me see you hanging upside down." It was one thing to hear Cleo tell about herself. It was another thing to see her fixing to kill herself.

"Me, too," said Serena, with a little sob, more for the copper than for Cleo, whom she briefly hated for compelling unnecessary sacrifice.

"You can have mine," said Charity harshly. Her sweet tooth ached for a peppermint stick, and she almost wished that Cleo was dead.

Cleo flashed them all an exultant smile. She had won their money without trying. She had been willing to risk her neck to buy rich Josie Beauchamp some penny candy. Now that it was too late to retrieve Josie Beauchamp's lost hours of anxiety, Cleo wanted to carry her a bag of candy, so that when Josie got through with being glad, and got mad, she wouldn't stay mad too long.

She held out her hand. Each tight fist poised over her palm, desperately clung aloft, then slowly opened to release the bright coin that was to have added a special sweetness to the summer day.

Cleo couldn't bear to see their woe-begone faces. She felt frightened, trapped by their wounded eyes. She had to do something to change their expressions.

"I'll do a stunt for you," she said feverishly. "I'll swing by my hands. It ain't nothing to be ascairt to see. You watch."

Quickly, agilely she climbed the tree and hung by her hands. Wildly, wildly she swung, to make them forget she had taken their money, to let them see how wonderful she was.

Then a boy came by, just an ordinary knotted-headed, knobby-kneed boy. He looked at her and laughed, because to him a girl carrying on so crazy cut a funny figure. She wanted to kill him. He made her feel silly. She climbed down, and she knew he was watching her, watching the split in her drawers.

When she reached the ground, she whirled to face him, and found his feet waving in front of her. He was walking on his hands. And her sisters were squealing with delight. They had seen her walk on her hands a thousand times. What was there so wonderful about watching a boy?

She flung herself upon him, and they fought like dogs, the coppers lost irrecoverably. Her sisters circled them, crying and wringing their hands. She had to win, no matter how. She bent her head and butted him in the groin, where the weakness of boys was—the contradictory delicacy.

The fight was knocked out of him. He lay very still, his hands shielding his innocent maleness from further assault, and the blood on his lips where his anguished teeth had sunk in.

Her sisters fluttered around him. They felt no pride for her victory. Instead they pitied him. She watched them with wonder. What was there to being a boy? What was there to being a man? Men just worked. That was easier than what women did. It was women who did the lying awake, the planning, the sorrowing, the scheming to stretch a dollar. That was the hard part, the head part. A woman had to think all the time. A woman had to be smart.

Her sisters weren't smart. They thought Pa was the head of the house. They didn't know the house was run by the beat of Mama's heart. There was an awful lonesomeness in Cleo when Mama went across the river to Grandma's. She did not want to be bad then. She wanted to be good so God would send Mama back safe. But she was wildly bad again the moment Mama returned. She could not bear the way she felt inside, like laughing and crying and kissing Mama's face.

She never kissed Mama. Kisses were silly. Pa kissed Mama when he came home from work. There was sweat on him from his labor, but Mama lifted her mouth to his. His mustache prickled against her lips, but Mama did not pull away.

Looking at her sisters, standing above the suffering boy, she saw in each some likeness of Mama—in Charity the softness and roundness, the flush just under the thin skin, the silver laughter; in Lily the doe eyes, liquid and vulnerable, the plaited hair that kept escaping in curls; in small Serena the cherry-red mouth, the dimpled cheeks. She knew that she looked like Pa. Everyone said so. Everyone said she was a beauty. What was wrong with their seeing? How could looking like Pa, with his sweat and his stained mustache, make anybody a beauty? Sometimes she would stare at herself in Mama's mirror and stick out her tongue.

Now, seeing her sisters, with their tender faces turned toward the boy, a terrible sorrow assailed her. Some day they would all grow up. They would all get married and go away. They would never live together again, nor share the long bright busy days. Mama, too, would go. Mama would die. Didn't she always say that her side of the family were not long livers? They were dead before they were fifty. Dead with their loveliness alive in their still, smooth faces. When Mama was gone in a last luminous moment, there would be the look of her and the silver laughter in the children she had blessed with her resemblance.

So long as her sisters were within sight and sound, they were the mirrors in which she would see Mama. They would be her remembering of her happy, happy childhood.

She flung herself down on the ground, and her torture was worse than the boy's. For hers was spiritual suffering and immeasurable frustration. All her terror of the future, all her despair at knowing that nothing lasts—that sisters turn into wives, that men take their women and ride away, that childhood is no longer than a summer day—were in her great dry sobs.

The boy staggered to his feet in complete alarm. He thought he had hurt her in some dreadful way mysterious to girls, her breast, her belly where the babies grew. Her father would skin him alive. He made a limping dash across the road and the trees closed in.

Then her sisters knelt beside her, letting their soothing fingers caress her face. Her sobbing quieted. She jumped up and began to turn cartwheels. A wildness was in her. She was going to turn cartwheels all the way home, heretofore an impossible feat.

Mama was in the doorway, watching her hurtle down a dusty road, seeing a girl eleven years old turning upside down, showing her drawers. Mama got the strap again and laid it on hard and heavy. Cleo just grinned, and wouldn't wipe the grin off, even with the whole of her on fire and hurting. Mama couldn't bear such impudence from her own flesh and blood. She let the strap fall and sat down and cried.

Mama didn't know what made Cleo so wild. Cleo got more of her attention than all of her other children put together. God help her when she grew up. God help the man who married her. God help her sisters not to follow in her footsteps. Better for her sisters if Cleo had never been born.

Somewhere in Springfield, Massachusetts, at that moment, Bart Judson, a grown man, a businessman, too interested in the Almighty Dollar to give any thought to a wife, was certainly giving no thought to an eleven-year-old hell-raiser way down South. But for Bart, whose inescapable destiny this unknown hoyden was to be, it might have been better if her sisters had never been born.

From *The Living Is Easy*, 1948

## AT THE SWAN BOATS

JUDE REACHED the swan boats at three exactly. He had walked up to Boylston Street from his store, hurried across the Common, and crossed Charles Street to the Public Garden, where he slowed to a less anxious pace, approaching the pond with a lover's diffidence. But his heart continued to race. There were only Beacon Hill children and nurses on the walks. He looked around at the occupied benches on the green. Lila was not anywhere. He was panicky, forgetting it was just on three, and sick with the thought that her father might have exacted a promise that she would not see him again.

One of the swan boats glided to a landing. A crowd of chattering children and nurses disembarked. A tall, cream-colored child came down alone. It was Lila, her brown braid swinging behind her, wearing again those outrageous bloomers and middy blouse. She saw him and smiled delightedly.

Jude started toward her, feeling silly and ashamed of both of them. When he reached her, he could not hold back his chagrin. He scowled and said without greeting her, "I feel like I'm robbin' the cradle."

She laughed loudly and he felt even more conspicuous, aware of the watching children and nurses.

"I had to come this way or not at all."

He started to take her arm, but to these onlookers the gesture would appear to be restraint, and he could not take her hand without feeling like a father. He plunged his hands into his pockets.

"Come on. Let's walk," he said.

Her eyes twinkled into his. "I want another ride. I came, and I didn't see you, and I went on the swan boat. It's fun."

"It's foolishness," he said severely, though he had not thought so until then. It had seemed to him idyllic, and he had imagined himself proud as punch beside her, on the swan boat with the passers-by admiring his taste in women.

"Let's walk then," she said demurely. "I'll go and get my bicycle."

It was leaning against a nearby tree, and in a moment she was trundling it toward him. She looked even more like a schoolgirl, and he wondered wrathfully if he should offer to wheel it.

"Looka here," he said in sullen dismay, "you're not goin' to ride that thing, are you?" He had a picture of himself dog-trotting behind it.

She burst out laughing. "My goodness, no! It's forbidden in the park. But I had to get away somehow. So I told papa I was going to peddle over to Cousin Jessica's. Goodness, would you rather I'd come on King Cambridge? I'd have looked even sillier on a swan boat in papa's pants."

He did not think that was possible and offered grumpily, "You want me to wheel that thing?"

She looked hurt and a little stubborn. "No, thank you," she said politely. She began to push the bicycle along. "It might spoil your trousers."

He gave her a sidelong glance, wondering if she were teasing him. But her eyes were no longer laughing, and her mouth trembled slightly.

"Looka here," he said contritely, "I'm just disappointed. I wanted to show you a big time, take you to dinner and the theayter. Then you come off the boat looking like that, and it just sorta took all the wind out my sails."

"I know," she said unhappily. "I—I wanted to wear my cream silk. I even tried my hair two ways. Then papa wouldn't leave the house. He just sat around, holding his head. I thought I wouldn't get here at all. He didn't want me to leave him."

"He drank too much," Jude said unfeelingly.

She flushed. "He drinks because he's worried." She took a deep breath as if she were preparing for a plunge. "He—gambles." The flush spread to the roots of her hair.

"Oh, that ain't nothin'," Jude said heartily. "He's a man." But he was just as shocked as she was.

She looked at him gratefully, and the flush receded a little.

"But he gambles the way he drinks. Poor papa. And when he doesn't have money to gamble with, he gambles with anything. That's how he lost his stable."

"And maybe he'll win it back that same way," Jude said in an effort to cheer her.

She smiled. "Anyway, that's how I had my party." She was carefree again. Her eyes were laughing at him. "And if it hadn't been for my party, we wouldn't be here now. And you're not too sorry, are you?"

He was aware of her charm all over again, and he felt a fool to have been annoyed by a pair of bloomers and a middy blouse.

"We got years and years to go to the theayters, Miss Lila. And a day like this, with us walking 'longside a bicycle, maybe it's a day to remember. There's just me and you, and all these trees and flowers. I guess I'm happy. I guess I'm real happy. I wish I'd bought some peanuts. I'd just like to sit on the grass and crack peanuts like a boy."

For a moment her face had that still remoteness, then she said gently, "Let's sit over there. I'm sorry about the peanuts. I started to bring some candy, hard ones, but I thought you'd think it was silly."

They left the walk and went across the short springing grass to a big-boled tree. Lila sat down, with her back against the tree, and her hands clasped round her hunched up knees. Jude flung off his hat and sat down beside her, wanting to take off his shoes and wiggle his toes.

"Man alive, this is nice," he said. "I ain't really sat in this park since the first night I came to Boston."

She said softly, "I come here lots."

"Who you come with?" he asked jealously.

"Just me," she said in surprise. "I like to be by myself."

"You ain't met the right sort of man." He looked at her long braid of hair. "You ain't met any real men at all." He beamed happily. "'Cept me."

"And papa," she said proudly. "He's the best man alive. I'll never leave him."

"Last night," he reminded her, "you was goin' to run off and go on the stage."

"I've changed my mind," she said firmly.

"Oh, you," he scoffed. "You'll change your mind again."

"It's because I'm a girl. I should have been a boy. Then I'd have gone to college and been a doctor."

"You got hands for healin'?" he asked doubtfully.

"Then a lawyer," she insisted stubbornly. "Something in a man's world anyway."

"You're kinda like me," he said admiringly. You got get-up and go. You'd be the kind of wife that'd get behind a man and make him climb."

She regarded him seriously. "You ought to get married, Mr. Crumb. You talk a lot about it."

He pulled down his mouth and tried to sound modest. "I been thinkin' a lot about it. I can afford to think about it. I'm pretty well fixed."

She looked surprised. "Would you marry a girl who'd marry you for your money? I'd never marry anybody unless it was for love." The word, so boldly stated, startled her. She blushed and stared at her sleeves and frowned like an embarrassed schoolboy.

"That's what I like about you," said Jude. "You're a square-shooter. Miss Jessie, now. You'd never know where you stood with her."

She smiled at him and that look of remoteness and self-completion came into her eyes. "Cousin Jessie's not hard to understand. She's more your kind than I am, Mr. Crumb. She wants all the things you want for a woman. She'd be the kind that'd make a man climb. If you married her, I'd sort of be your cousin. And then papa would have to let you call on me."

The absurd naiveté of her last words destroyed whatever anxiety Jude was beginning to feel. He burst out laughing, and could not resist tweaking her braid and tickling the nape of her neck with the curl of its end.

"Miss Lila, you're a caution, and no mistake!"

She jerked her hair free and jumped up. She was hurt, and she did not want him to see it. He was treating her like a child, and a moment ago she had thought he was almost proposing. She was ashamed of that thought and prayed that he had not guessed it was in her mind.

"You know how to ride a bicycle?" she asked roughly.

He grinned. "You fixin' to teach me?"

"I don't care," she said, and jerked her shoulders impatiently. "I get tired just sitting still. Sitting in the park is for—is for sweethearts. I like to keep doing things."

She righted the bicycle and propelled it to the path. She looked back over her shoulder. He was still sitting there watching her, with that hateful smirk on his lips.

"Get a move on," she said wrathfully.

He got up with alacrity and came to her. He saw that she was ready to cry, and he wanted to blurt out his love for her.

His face filled with strain. "Miss Lila, listen, I'm a man of plain words—"

She could not bear to look at him. Every instinct told her he was going to propose, and she did not want to hear him out and find that she had guessed wrong again.

She banged the bicycle on the path. "Get on," she said sharply. "Get on and peddle. I'll help you balance. I'm strong as anything. I'm just like a boy."

They teetered off down the road, and Jude felt silly, and his trouser legs caught in the pedals. Lila struggled along at his side, shouting instructions in a cross and tiring voice, and grunting intermittently. Suddenly Jude could balance by himself, and presently he was rattling off alone, with Lila sitting by the roadside, with her knees hunched up, beginning to enjoy herself. Then they took turns, and Lila showed off, doing tricks and laughing uproariously. Jude tried the simpler tricks, and fell and skinned his knees, and laughed as hard as Lila.

It was six before they were thoroughly spent and ravenous. The setting sun bathed them both in soft light. Lila was luminous, and Jude's blue-flecked eyes and sweat-streaked face were glowing with simple happiness.

They stood on either side of the bicycle smiling at each other. Their look was frank and filled with comradeship. In this moment each thought the other the nicest person on earth. Lila saw the days ahead and the active things they would do together. Jude was not really old. She would teach him to play, and that would prolong her play period, too. The dreary prospect of adult behavior was no longer imminent and awesome. This man was her own kind. With him she could stay out of stuffy parlors and roam the limits of her world without the impediments of stays and sweeping dresses.

Jude looked at the little tendrils of hair curling on Lila's damp forehead. Tiredness had put two dark smudges under her shining eyes, but because of the healthy pink that suffused her cheeks and the tiny beads of sweat on her upper lip, she simply looked like a child who had played too hard. Jude had a sudden selfless wish that she could stay that way forever. That way was such a happy way. He knew with a pang that he could not be certain that an older Lila would be another Christine, for he could not imagine a young Christine as a carefree Lila. If only he had brought some food! He did not want to leave the park. He was afraid they would leave forever the enchanted gardens.

"Let's go," said Lila. "I'm starving. Aren't you?"

"I guess I am," Jude said heavily. "You think we look too bad to go to a restaurant?" He could not bear to leave her. Perhaps they could come back afterwards and find the same magic under the moon.

"You smell," said Lila solemnly.

He was terribly humiliated. "I reckon I do," he replied in confusion, "but I had a bath yesterday just a little bit before your party."

Her eyes began smiling. "I was teasing. I sort of like the way you smell, like ripening fruit and black earth. I could smell it last night, only the soap smell was stronger. You use scented soap," she added accusingly.

"I bought it for your party," he admitted. "Matter o' fact, I scrubbed first with laundry soap, then I washed all over again with that sweet soap, and then I sprinkled with cologny water. It's hard to keep clean in my kind of work."

For a moment her eyes were wistful and faraway. "It doesn't matter. It's a man's work. Merchant ships and windburned sailors, and the bog dray horses on the docks. Oh, if I were you, I'd have gone to sea on one of those ships a long time ago."

"You want to come see me unload someday," he asked eagerly. "Tomorrow the Jamaica boat's due in. It's bringing bananas, and mangoes, and guavas. I'll be down with my men helping unload."

She shut her eyes tightly, then opened them, and they were full of tears. "Mr. Crumb, this is one of the happiest days of my life. You make me glad I'm grown-up. If I'd been younger, you wouldn't have noticed me, and I'd have missed so much that's going to be fun. Oh, Jude, I - I almost love you."

The moment was so perfect that he dared not speak. She, of her own volition, had spoken the words that were needed to bind them. Now she was his, and the consummation of the long years of search was only a matter of months or even weeks. She was seventeen, but Christine had been as young a bride, and as inexperienced. He would be gentle with Lila. He would wait until she wanted him. If her family had let them alone, he could have marked time until she was twenty. With his mind and his heart he knew that she would never marry any other man. He had seen her men. They were not her kind. His smell of fruit and damp black earth, the tales on his tongue of ships and cargoes, the rippling muscles in his strong black arms, his bold ambition, these were the things she wanted. He thought this with exultant egoism and without irony.

When the moment passed, Jude said gently, "Thank you, Miss Lila." He was a man, and he could not state his love like a timid boy as she had done. He would not frighten her with a forthright proposal. There would be a better time, though there could never be a better place.

Lila's held in breath escaped on a sigh of gratitude that Jude had not misunderstood nor thought her forward. She sent him a quick smile, and they trudged to the park gates in a blissful companionable silence.

Outside the gates they paused, and Lila straddled her bicycle.

"You got a long ride ahead," Jude said solicitously, "and you must be tired."

"I'm too happy to care," said Lila. "I'll feel like I'm flying. What time shall I come tomorrow, and where?"

He gave her the address of his store and named an early hour, and thought with satisfaction of how Miss McGinty would gape with envy at the beautiful girl who was going to be his bride, and then wondered worriedly if Miss McGinty would think he was a cradle robber.

"What you going to wear," he asked anxiously.

"Oh, I'll look grown-up," she protested in distress. "I'll wear a shirtwaist, and my sailor hat, and my pointed shoes, and maybe a corset." Her voice trailed off unhappily.

He looked at her, and knew that she wanted to come the way she was, and that, in an incurious world, he would have let her.

"That will be fine," he said without heartiness.

She touched his hand lightly. "Good-by, Mr. Crumb." Abruptly she rode away, pedaling very fast. She did not look back, and her long braid swung like a pendulum. Jude stared after her and thought of the soft-haired son she would bear him, and wondered with bleak amusement if she would ride him on her handlebars. He turned and walked to the trolley.

Circa 1940

# BLACKBERRYING

MRS. AYER is a middle-aged Negro woman of average height, rather heavy, with straight features, ruddy brown complexion and wavy dark hair. She was born in Camden, S.C., where she received a grammar school education, and moved to Charleston, S.C. when she was married. For the last six years she has been living in New York, where her four daughters, two married, two single, live. One of her daughters is the proprietor of a beauty parlor where Mrs. Ayer likes to spend the day, when she isn't too busy.

Her principal interests are her children and church work (she is a Methodist), but she finds that she is too busy with domestic work to get much time for church activities. Although her children all live in New York, she is beginning to be anxious to return to her home in the South, and hopes to leave as soon as her youngest daughter is married. In spite of her years in the North, her "Geechee" accent is still perceptible.

Once or twice a year, around where I lived, most women with families would pack up for three or four days and go blackberry picking. My mother had some distant relatives in a little place called Ninety-Six, not very far on the train from Camden. I remember the first time she took me to Ninety-Six when she went to pick berries.

We—she did—started getting ready about a week before we left. She boiled her Mason jars (heavy, glass quart jars for canning) and boiled the rubber collars (heavy rubber bands which were put on before the cap was screwed on the jar to make the canned goods airtight), and she boiled the caps to fit on the jars. Then she packed about fifteen jars and collars and caps in a big basket and in suitcases so she could carry them without much trouble. Clothes didn't matter much. You had two or three gingham dresses and a pair of shoes and two pair of socks and that was about all.

The first time I went, my mother just took me. She left my brother and sister at home. I was the youngest and she thought she had to take me, and she didn't want to take the others because she didn't know how much room the lady where we were going to stay had. I was about seven then.

We got on the train and I guess we rode two-three-hours—trains went slower then than they do now. Ninety-Six is a little flag station and when we got there, the woman's husband where we were going to stay met us at the station (it was just a little shed, really) with a horse and buggy. He lived about three miles from the place where the train stopped.

When we got there, there were two other women with their children. It was always like that. More than one woman came to stay at a house during picking time. This time you went to this place, the next time, you went somewhere else. And your relatives and maybe one or two of your best friends were the ones who came to pick berries together. This time I'm telling you about, there were two other women and their children. I believe (she stopped to count) there were twelve or thirteen children in that house at one time. Miss (Mrs.) Mary (her hostess) herself had seven children, I made eight, and one woman had two children, and the other one had two or three. I can't remember exactly.

We didn't do anything but play that first day. The grown folks got their jars together in the kitchen, and collected big pots and pans to put the berries in when they picked 'em. I guess they talked the rest of that day since maybe they didn't see each other more than once or twice a year. When we got ready to go to bed, the girls were put together in the parlor on pallets to sleep, and the boys were put in the dining room. I know there were five of us girls sleeping on a pallet on the floor once. I don't know where the grown folks slept. I don't remember whether they slept on pallets or not. I guess not since the children gave up their beds and slept on pallets. I do know that sometimes as many as four women slept together in one room.

We got up early in the morning and had breakfast as soon as it was light. We had salt pork and hominy grits and hot biscuits and maybe one or two other things. Then the boys helped the women take the pans out and pile 'em in the wagon. One of the boys drove the mules, and two women sat on the seat of the wagon and the other two sat in the back with as many of the children as could go. Sometimes the other children would want to go, and they'd hang on to the side of the wagon or behind it. If you didn't have room to go, you'd just walk along behind the wagon.

You'd take food along to eat in the middle of the day because you stayed all day. Everybody would pick, the women and the children. You didn't put the berries in any special basket. You figured out how much everybody would get after you got back to the house. And everybody always got the same share. When you filled one big pan, you'd start filling another one, and you kept on 'till you'd picked as many as you could. 'Course the children ate more than they picked, and sometimes they'd run off and play.

I remember once I had on shoes and everybody else was barefooted. They called me a city chap, and they played tricks on me. Once they ran off from the grown folks and I followed 'em. We came to a little crick and they ran right on through it to the other side. I wanted to follow 'em but I had on a nice little gingham dress and shoes. They had on overhalls (overalls) and no shoes so it was easy for them to get wet. I stood on the side for a minute just looking at 'em and trying to make up my mind about getting over to the other side. They got tired of waiting on me, and one of the big girls came back over and threw me in the crick. Then she ran on across and they all ran and hid. When I finally got out of the water, I couldn't find 'em anywhere. I stood there cryin' and yellin' and finally, it seemed like hours to me—they came back and got me.

When the grown folks got through picking—they always carried enough utensils to hold enough berries to keep 'em picking 'till sundown—if the children had strayed off playing, they'd holler for the children. Then going back, more had to walk or hang on because the pans would almost fill the wagon.

That night we wouldn't do much. Everybody was tired, and we'd have a big, hot supper, and then go to bed. Sometimes the children would make a lot of noise since so many of them were together and the grown folks would have to come in and stop the fuss, but most of the time the whole house was quiet by nine o'clock and everybody was asleep.

Then, the next morning the canning would start. They would put the wash pots out in the yard and start a fire under going. Most women had at least two wash pots, and some had three and four. They were heavy old iron, black pots about two feet deep, and they stood on three squatty legs about six inches tall. Tall enough to make a hot fire under. The women used them to boil their clothes in to make 'em white on wash-day. They'd fill these wash-pots with water and put the Mason jars in again to boil. Sometimes they'd let the big children take the jars out on long sticks. You see, when they boiled their clothes, they had a wooden stick—most often a broom handle—that they stirred the clothes with. They'd use this stick to put in the mouth of the jar and lift it out. When they got through sterilizing the jars, they'd pour the water out and put some more in, and then put in the berries. They used the pots for different things. I think they made jam in them and started the wine in them, but I think they made the jelly in the house in the kitchen. I don't remember that very well. They worked almost all day. Then when they were ready to divide it up, one woman would fill a jar, then another one, and so on 'till everybody had one jar full. You kept that up 'till everybody had as much as everybody else. 'Course if there was a little left over, you'd eat as much of it as you could that night for supper and the rest you left to the woman whose house you were in. You didn't give her anything for lettin' you stay there except that everybody would give her three or four quarts of jelly or jam or whatever you made.

Nobody ever went home the night they finished canning. They'd sit around and talk, and maybe decide where they'd go to can the next time. It was only berries or maybe watermelons if you were going to make watermelon rind preserves that you went out like that to pick and can. Peaches and apples and plums and things like that, you canned at home by yourself because you just bought whatever you wanted to put up.

The next day you went back home. I remember when we went, we were the only folks who came on the train. The others came in horse and wagons. They would leave early in the morning, and most of the time we were the last to leave because we had to wait for the train.

2524 Seventh Avenue, New York City
WPA Federal Writers' Project
November 2, 1938

# QUILTING

MRS. MAYME REESE, the informant, was born in April 1879, in Charleston, South Carolina. Prior to moving to New York City, she lived in Newberry, South Carolina, with her husband, three sons, and a daughter. She especially enjoys weekly out-of-town visits to her grandchildren.

Mrs. Reese was very friendly to the interviewer and readily agreed to a second interview sometime in the future. She apparently has a very excellent memory and seems willing to reminisce. Although she spoke with a vestige of the Gullah dialect, the interviewer could not take it down because it was not phonetically distinct enough to note the variations. There was no trace of the "Geechie" manner of speaking so far as transposition of word order was concerned.

I can't remember what games I played when I was a girl off-hand like this. Games and songs—I'll have to think about it and tell you the next time you come. We played almost the same games the children play today—some of them about the same, some of them different.

Did you ever hear about quilting parties? We used to have quilting parties at least twice a year. One time we would meet at one house and one time at another; you'd keep on that way until the quilt was finished. Well, say there'd be three or four ladies who were good friends. If I was making the quilt, I'd set up the frame (quilting frame) in my house and the other two or three ladies would come to my house and spend the day quilting. I'd have it all ready for the quilting to start. Maybe I'd have been sewing scraps together for a year until I got the cover all made.

Then when my friends would come, the cover would be all ready and there wouldn't be anything to do but start working on the padding. If there were four ladies, each would take an end. (Gestures) I'd take this end, the other two would take the ends over there. You'd decide before how you were going to make the stitches. If you were going to have a curving stitch, you'd sew one way. If you were going to quilt block fashion, you'd sew that way. (Make the stitches in the pattern of a square of a size decided upon.)

The ladies who would come to help you would come as early in the morning as they could. Sometimes you all had breakfast together. If you didn't, you had dinner together and a little snack off and on during the day. If it was at my house and nobody was coming early enough for breakfast, I'd put something on the sideboard—the buffet—that everybody could reach if they got hungry before time to sit at the table. Sometimes there'd be sweet potatoes, some smoked pork, bread, maybe some syrup, and things like that. Then when you had dinner, there'd be the regular things everybody had at home. If somebody came way in (from the country or a town 8 or 9 miles away), they'd have supper and stay all night.

Depending upon how many quilts you needed a year or just wanted to make, there'd be that many quilting parties for ladies who were intimates. If none of my friends were going to make quilts in a year, then they'd keep coming to my house maybe twice a week until we got it finished. If you worked right along and didn't stop to talk—'course most of the time we stopped to gossip a little—you could finish a quilt in a day or two. All that depended on the pattern, too. If somebody else was making a quilt, we'd go to their house and exchange labor 'till they got their quilt done.

Whenever we had a quilting party, the men-folks had to look out for themselves. They ate cold food if they came in hungry in the day and if we finished working soon enough, they'd get their supper on time. If we didn't, they just had to wait. They didn't mind. If they fussed, we'd remind 'em 'bout keeping warm in the winter.

In the fall when they had the county fairs, sometimes we'd take our quilts out to fair-grounds for exhibition. Each lady picked out her best quilt—the prettiest color, the prettiest pattern and the best stitches—and took it to the fair to try to win the prize . . . No, it didn't make any difference if your prettiest quilt had been quilted by three or four other people. You see you already had the pattern and you'd already put the pieces together so that much was your own idea. And that counted more than the help you got—and the results you got—when you were putting it on the frame. Sometimes a church club would make a quilt and enter it in the name of the church. Even if they put it in the club's name, the club would give the money to the church if they won. Once I won the prize for my own quilt and once I was one of a group that won. The prize most often was five dollars. Sometimes it was ten. One year they couldn't get the money together and they gave the winner some prize preserves, some pieces of fancy-work and something else that had won first prize in other contests instead of the money. I don't remember if that was one woman or whether it was a club. 'Course you'd rather have the money than that stuff 'cause everybody could can fruit and do tatting and crocheting and things like that and they could make their own things. But you couldn't act nasty about it. Anyhow, it didn't happen but once as I remember it.

Sometimes rich white women would hear that such and such a person had won the prize for pretty quilts and they'd come and ask that person to make them a quilt. Sometimes they'd make it and sometimes they wouldn't. If they did make it, they'd get around five dollars. Sometimes they'd furnish the scraps and sometimes they wouldn't. Most of the time, though, they'd buy pieces of goods and give it to the person who was making the quilt to cut up. They'd get different colors and they'd say what pattern they wanted.

Sometimes they'd have quilting parties in some of the churches. Of course not every church did that. But those that did had quite a few women members who went to quilt. They'd get some little boys to take the quilting frame to the church in the morning and then they'd go in the afternoon. I guess they'd quilt for two-three hours. Most of the time when they did that, they'd be making the quilt to sell to raise money for the church.

Things like that were nice. Sometimes I wish I could go back to that kind of life for a while but times have changed so. They won't ever be like that again. But I guess it's just as well. Nowadays, there are other things to occupy people's minds.

1 St. Nicholas Terrace, New York City
WPA Federal Writers' Project
September 21, 1938

## PROLOGUE TO A LIFE

IN 1896 LUKE KANE had met and married Lily Bemis. He had been very much in love with her. And she had literally fallen at his feet, stumbling over his bicycle, lying flat before the back door, and sprawling before him, her full skirts billowing about her, and quite all of the calves of her legs showing.

Luke, in an instant, was out of the kitchen, and had gathered the hired girl in his arms, and was cursing his bicycle and soothing her in the same breath.

She was small and soft. Though her face was hidden against his breast, he saw that her arms were golden, and her dark hair wavy and long.

"Is that your old bicycle?" Lily asked tearfully. "You're fixin' to kill somebody."

"Ain't I the biggest fool!" he agreed.

She got herself out of his arms and, sitting down on the steps, she tried to do things with her clothes and hair.

"What anybody'd put an old bicycle right in the doorway for—"

But he was staring into her eyes.

"How long you been working for Miz Trainor?"

"I've seen you before," she told him. "Lots."

"Yeh? Don't you speak to nobody?"

"Gentlemen to whom I been introduced. Oh, yes."

"I'm somebody round these parts," he boasted. "Ever heard of Manda Kane?"

"Sure. We get our fancy cakes from her when we're having parties and things."

"I'm her son," he informed her, proudly. "I been up here delivering. "My name's Luke."

"Yeh?" Her eyes were bright with interest. "Mine's Lily Bemis."

"Come from the South?"

"Born there. Yes. But I came up with the Mitchells when they came. That's been five years. But then old Miz Mitchell died, and the two girls got married. I never cared much for old Mister Mitchell, so I came on to Springfield. 'Cause Mamie Cole went on to Boston and said I could take her place here. I knew Miz

Trainor was good and all, and didn't have no small children. So I sorta thought I'd try it. Gee, I'm young and everything. If I don't like it here, I can travel on."

He plumped down beside her.

"Listen," he said softly, "I hope you'll like it here."

Her eyes were two slits and dangerous.

"Why—Luke?"

"'Cause, then," he said huskily, "you'll stay. And I can be likin' you."

She bent to him suddenly. "You're the funniest coon. Your eyes are blue as blue."

"Yeh. It's funny, black as I am," he said modestly.

She put two slim yellow fingers against his cheek. "You're not black at all. You're just dark brown. I think you're a beautiful color."

His eyes that were like a deep sea glowed with gratitude. "I sorta like yours the best."

"Oh, me, I'm not much!" she said carelessly. "What makes you think I'm pretty?"

"I dunno. You're so little and soft and sweet. And you ain't so shy."

She was instantly on her feet. "If you think I'm bold, sitting out here with you, when we never been introduced—"

"Looka here!" He was on his feet, too. "Women's the funniest things. I'm liking you 'cause you're not like everyone else, and you're bristling! I can have any girl in this little old town of Springfield I want. But I'm not making up to any 'cause I ain't found none that suited me. My mother's orful particular. We got a name in this town. You're the first girl I'm liking, and you're cutting up!"

But she was inside of the screen door now, and he saw her hook it. She came very close to it, but she was careful not to press her nose against it.

"Listen, Mr. Kane, I like you, too. I want to meet you proper. What would folks say if they knew we met like this? Me with two buttons off my shirtwaist and my hair net torn? But tomorrow's prayer meeting night, and I'm going. I'm an A.M.E. If that's your church, too, you come on over. I'll get Miz Hill to get Reverend Hill to introduce us proper."

He gulped. "Can I bring you home after?"

She considered it. "Maybe I'll let you be keeping my company," she promised.

There followed a whirlwind month of courtship. Lily had a hundred moods. They were a hundred magnets drawing Luke. She did not love him. Deep within her was an abiding ambition to see her race perpetuated. Though she felt that her talents were of a high order, she knew she would escape greatness through her lack of early training. And she had the mother instinct. Thus she would rather bear a clever child. In her supreme egoism she believed the male seed would only generate it. She would not conceive of its becoming blood of her child's blood, and flesh of her child's flesh. Men were chiefly important as providers. She would have married any healthy man with prospects. . . .

Late in the summer Lily and Luke were married. Lily didn't want a church wedding. They were married in Reverend Hill's front parlor. Miz Hill and Manda Kane stood up with them. Ma Manda was tearful. She was losing her only son to a low-voiced yellow woman. She knew the inescapable bond of soft skin and hair.

Lily, standing quietly by Luke's side, felt a vast contentment. She respected the man she was marrying. She faced the future calmly. She only wanted their passion to be strong enough to yield a smart and sturdy son.

Later that day they were on a train that was bound, by the back door route, for Boston. They sat in the coach with their little belongings piled all about them. Luke made sheep's eyes at Lily and felt very proud. He was wondering whether it was obvious that they had just been married. He rather wanted the phlegmatic passengers to admire his golden bride.

He drew her round dark head on to his shoulder, and caught his hand in the tendrils of her hair.

"Guess I'm the happiest man in the world, and the proudest."

"Ho, you're not proud of me!"

"You are the moon and the stars, Lily, and the bright sun."

She twisted her head and looked deep into his kind eyes.

"Luke, do you love me as much as that?"

"You watch me," he told her. "I'll bring you the world on a silver platter. Lily, I'll make you a queen."

She rubbed her little hand up and down his arm.

"How much money we got now, Luke?"

"Enough," he boasted, "to live like millionaires for maybe a week in Boston."

"Luke," she said earnestly, "we're not going back. Ever."

He was pleased. "Our honeymoon will last wherever we are."

She was almost impatient. "It ain't that!"

He drew away from her and stared down at her hard.

"What in the name of God—"

"Let's eat," she said, and dug about for Ma Manda's hamper.

She put the linen napkin on her lap and laid out the sandwiches, licking her fingers when the mayonnaise or jam or butter had oozed through.

"Chicken," she announced, "and ham, and I reckon this is po'k, Luke!"

He balanced the coffee on his knee. "There's cups somewheres, Lily."

Presently they were hungrily eating, Luke almost wolfishly.

"We've caught our train," said Lily, with a little nervous laugh. He was making her rather ill.

He took a great gulp of coffee.

"Always was a fast eater. Father before me was."

Her hand tightened over his. "You could die," she said with real concern, "of indigestion."

He ducked his head suddenly and kissed her wrist. "But I'll make you your million before I do."

Thus she let him go back to his eating, and she gave him an almost indulgent smile.

Once in the vast South Station they stood for a moment, bewildered. They both felt newly married and foolishly young. Lily had a sudden sense of panic. Suppose Ma Manda never forgave them. Suppose Luke died or deserted her. Suppose she was never able to bear a child.

And then she saw Mamie Cole coming toward them. She flew into her arms.

"The blushing bride and groom!" cried Mamie, and offered her cheek to Luke.

"Well, it's nice to see you," said Luke, rather shyly after kissing her.

"I'm only off for an hour," she explained, "so we better get up to the flat. I got you three real nice rooms, Lily, in front."

"Three—?" echoed Luke. His voice fell in disappointment. "I kinda thought—a hotel—"

"Luke!" Lily caught his arm fast. Her brown eyes were dark with pleading. "Luke, it's not a hotel room I want. It's a home."

He asked in bewilderment: "Here—in Boston?"

"Listen, we're not going back. We're laying our corner-stone here. There's far and away more business in Boston than in Springfield. Just you see. I want my husband. Luke, I want my home. I want my—son. Back home we'd have to live with your mother. She's got that big house. And, Luke, I can't get along with no women. I almost hate women. They're not honest. They're weaklings. They care about cheap things. God knows you're going to find it hard to live with me—and you love me. I don't want nothing but my man and my son. That's me, Luke."

He had the most terrible longing to take her in his arms. "Your man and your son? Lily, my girl, you've got your man. By God, you'll have your son. . . ."

In 1898 Lily gave birth to twins.

They were boys, with Lily's soft yellow skin and fine brown eyes, and all about them the look of her, somehow. Jamie and John. They were completely sons of Lily. To her they were gods.

Luke had been getting on in a fair sort of way before the twins were born. He had opened a tiny lunch stand in the South End. Lily had been helping with the cooking. After a barely perceptible start, business had picked up nicely. Luke could cook almost as well as his mother. And Lily, growing prettier and plumper every day, and rapidly learning badinage, was an obvious attraction.

She worked until the week before the twins were born. Then Ma Manda, in panicky self-reproach, hurried on to Boston, saw to it that a proper girl was hired, packed Lily off to the New England Hospital, and looked about at houses. She decided on a red-brick one on a quiet street in Brookline, and bought it through a profiteering agent. She ordered atrocious furniture on the credit plan (Lily returned it piece by piece later), and awaited the birth of her grandchild in grim satisfaction.

To the triumphant Lily the world existed for two golden babies. These were her lives to shape and guide. These were her souls to expand. She, with her constant faith, must quicken their geniuses.

So the years passed. Jamie and John were three and able to read. Then John at four could bang out a harmony on the new upright piano. Jamie at six was doing third grade lessons. . . .

They were nine. And Lily's pride, and joy, and love, and life. They had not cried in their cradle. They had never been jealous of each other. They had given her and Luke wholeheartedly their love. They wrote regularly and beautifully to their grandmother. Their teachers adored them. Despite their talents, they were manly, and popular with children. They had never been ill. They were growing like weeds. John, at the Boston Conservatory, had been singled out as an extraordinary pupil. His little sensitive face had stared out of many daily papers. Jamie, in the seventh grade, leading his class, was the marvel of his school. He could solve the mathematical problems of high school students. He could also discuss his future with calm assurance. . . .

Lily was thirty-two now. And a housewife. Occasionally she swept into the shop which had been yearly enlarged until it comprised three wide windows and twenty-two tables. The doctors and lawyers who frequented the place would rise and eagerly greet her. She was completely complacent. She was fat, but her skin was firm and soft to Luke's touch. Her eyes were clear and content. There were always tender anecdotes about her boys. Jamie and John. The realization of her dreams, the growing fulfillment of her hopes, the latent genius quickening.

She walked in peace. She knew ten years of utter harmony. She was therefore totally unprepared for any swift disruption.

In 1908 the twins were ten. Though they were young men now with certain futures, they were still very charming, and went swimming or skating with the boys on their block whenever they were called for. . . .

It was on the last day of March, going all too meekly like a lamb, that Lily, in her kitchen, making the raisin-stuffed bread pudding the twins adored, sat down suddenly with her hand to her throat, and her heart in a lump against it. She was alone, but she knew she was not ill. She made no attempt to cry out to a neighbor. She could see, as clearly as though she stood at the pond's edge, the twins, their arms tight about each other, crashing through the treacherous ice, making no outcry, their eyes wide with despair, dragged swiftly down, brought up again to break her heart forever, and Jamie's red scarf, that Ma Manda had knitted for him, floating. . . .

Within twenty minutes three frightened children brought her the news. Two days later their bodies were found. Lily identified them in a dim dank morgue.

The twins lay together in a satin-lined casket in the flower-filled parlor. They were very lovely in their last sleep. The undertaker's art had restored them and enhanced them. There was about their mouths that too exquisite beauty that death brings to the mouths of children who die in pain. Dead, they were more similar than living. And it was James who looked like John. . . .

James and John were Lily. James and John were dead. Only the fact that she had watched her heart and soul flung into the earth with her sons kept Lily's body alive. She was spiritually a dead woman walking in the patient hope of physical release. There was no youth in her any more. Her body was no longer firm, but flabby. Her eyes were lusterless. Her lips that had always been a little too thin were a line now that went sharply down at each corner. And the voice that had bantered richly with her boys, that had thrilled like a girl's at the intimate bass of a man, was quavering, and querulous, and, all too often, still. . . .

Ma Manda stayed on. Lily wanted it. They were held by their mutual bereavement. The twins, dead, were more potent than ever they could have been, living. Now Lily and Ma Manda knew there was nothing these boys could not have done, no world they would not have conquered, had they lived.

Ma Manda one weekend returned to Springfield, sold her house and the two fine mares, and her business and her lease to a prosperous German. Her only sentimentalities were two ribboned packets of letters.

Luke was sorry that the twins were dead, but his heart was not broken. Lily was his world. While she lived there was hope, and love, and life. He had no real conception of the genius of the twins. He had always thought of them as smart little boys. Now death had shattered their spell for him. He even wondered vaguely why it did not occur to Lily she might have another child.

One night, after a silent meal that Luke had cooked himself to tempt the too light appetite of his women, Lily rose abruptly from the supper table, and with the knuckles of her clenched fists showing white, said in a voice that she tried to keep steady: "Luke, I'm sleeping in the twins' room tonight. I—I guess I'll go on up now. G'night, Ma Manda. 'Night, Luke."

An hour later, when he softly tried the door, it was locked.

A year passed. Lily, a little mad in her constant communion with her dead, had grown somehow hauntingly lovely, with her loosened hair always tangled, her face thin and pale and exquisite, and her eyes large and brightly knowing. Now she was voluble with Ma Manda, though there were no notes in her voice. She kept up a continual stream of pathetic reminiscences. And she went about her house with her hands outstretched briefly to caress some memorial to her boys.

Ma Manda indulged her. To her there was only beauty in Lily's crazy devotion. She had loved Luke's golden sons more than she had ever loved Luke. As with Lily, throughout their growing, they had become her sole reality. With the ancients' idea of duty, she kept their memory fresh, her sorrow keen. She went regularly to a Baptist church and wailed when the preacher harangued the dead.

And always for Luke, in his starved normal passion, surprisingly not the brute, Lily's light body was a golden mesh.

Lily had sat by an open window, staring up at the stars, her bare feet on a chilled floor, her nightgown fluting in the wind. Presently she had begun to sneeze. Soon her eyes and her nose were running. When she got into Jamie's white bed, she felt a great wave engulf her. In the morning she was very ill.

Lily felt that she was dying. And she was afraid to die. She hated pain. She had given no thought to death before the death of her twins. After that she had thought of her going as only a dreamless sleeping and a waking with her sons. Now there was something in her chest that was making her last hours torture. And a cough that tore her from the hot pillows and started that jerk and pull in her heart. Sometimes her breath was a shudder that shook her body.

In the first hours of the third night, she clutched at Ma Manda and stared up at her with eyes so full of piteous appeal that Ma Manda said sharply and involuntarily: "Lily, my child, you best let Luke in. He's a great one for healing. There's the power of the Almighty in his hands."

Lily made a little gesture of acquiescence. Ma Manda went softly, fumbling in her tears.

Luke bent over Lily. His blue eyes burned. They were dark and deep and glowing. She felt her own eyes caught in them. Felt her senses drowning. He flung one hand up to the sky, the fingers apart and unbending. The other he pressed against her chest till his flesh and her flesh were one.

He was exalted and inspired. The muscles leaped in his arm. He was trembling and black and mysterious.

"Lily, my girl, God's going to help you. God in His heaven's got to hear my prayer! Just put your faith in me, my darling. I got my faith in Him. I got a gift from the heavenly Father. Praise His name! Lily, my Lily, I got the power to heal!"

Strength surged out of him—went swinging down through the arm upraised, flashed through his straining body, then shot down and tingled in his fingers which had melted into her breast. They were like rays, destroying. Five streams of life, pouring into her sick veins, fierce, tumultuous, until the poison and the pain burst into rivulets of sweat that ran swift and long down her quivering body, and presently left her washed clean and quiet and very, very tired.

Then Luke's words came in a rush, in the voice of one who had fought a hard fight, or run a long race, yet deep and tremblingly beautiful.

"God, be praised! God, the Maker, we humbly thank Thee! Thou heard! Thou heard!! Thou gave me strength to heal! O God, this poor child—my Lily—she's well! She can rise and take up her bed and walk! O God, Thou art the Father of all living! Thou art life! Thou art love! Thou art love!! Thou art love!!!"

He slumped down on his knees and burst into wild tears. His head went bumping against Lily's breast.

In her relief and gratitude and wonderment, she felt her first compassion for her husband. In his weakness she was strong. She was a mother.

He clung to her. He was a man sick with passion. Presently she said: "Lie with me, Luke," and drew him up into her arms.

For Lily, and for Luke, and for Ma Manda, after a week or two, that night, crowded out of their consciousness, might have never been. Lily went back to her inner life; Ma Manda to the spiritual needs of her daughter-in-law and the physical needs of her son; Luke to the old apathetic content in Lily's apparent contentment.

But one Sunday morning as he lay staring at a bright patch of sunlight on the wall and hearing faintly the bells of the Mission Church without emotion, the door creaked sharply.

Lily came in and stood at the foot of his bed. He sat up in real surprise and made a vague gesture toward his bathrobe.

Her eyes were level into his and full of scorn. Her face was pale and proud. Her lips were a thin twist of contempt.

She was so lovely and so terrible in her fury that he caught his breath. He scuttled down to the foot of the bed and gripped her wrist tight. "Lily, you sick? For God's sake, what ails you?"

She flung her arm free. "I'm going to have a child. Another child! Well, it's yours. I've borne my babies. And I've buried them. This is your little black brat, d'you hear? You can keep it or kill it. If it wasn't for my babies in heaven, I'd get rid of it with the deadliest poison. But I can't damn my soul to hell for a wretched child that may be born dead. And if it lives"—her voice was a wail— "I curse it to my despair!"

For the first time since his childhood, Luke flung himself down full length on the bed and cried. . . .

In the months that followed, Ma Manda and Luke, in their terrific watchfulness, had a nine months' travail, too.

Lily's child was born on a spring morning in a labor so fierce that both of them, after hours of struggle, lay utterly spent; the child in the big white crib that had been the twins', the mother, for the last time, on her own great mahogany bed.

Lily was conscious, and calm. She was dying as she had wanted to die, painlessly. She felt no curiosity about her baby. She had heard a sharp whisper, "It's a girl," which she had half expected, and had turned her face from the sound of it to summon all of her strength for a bitter chuckle.

Presently Luke came to stare down at her. His eyes were filled with great desperation. He, too, had forgotten the new baby. Lily was dying.

"Lily"—his voice was deep and tender—"just put your faith in God. My Father has never failed me. He'll pull you through."

She was quietly exalted. "I have come through."

"Lily, I love you. Don't act that way. Put your hand in mine. Let me help you, my darling."

His hand went out to her. She saw the fingers stiffen, straighten, and the muscles pulling in his arm.

But she made no move.

"Are you too weak? Let me raise your hand. The power of God is in me. It leaps like a young ram. Only touch me, Lily!"

Ma Manda, kneeling at the foot of the bed, wrung her hands and wailed, "Only touch him, Lily!"

Her eyes were wide and seeking. Her mouth was tremulous and beautiful. With a tremendous effort she raised herself up from her pillow. Her braids went lopping over her breasts.

Her hands went out, slowly, gropingly. Luke waited, quivering, his heart in his mouth.

But then she sighed sharply. Her hands clasped tightly. Her eyes were passionate. Her face was glorious.

It was Ma Manda who scrambled to her feet and laid her back on the pillow and knew that she was dead, and gently brushed the lids over her eyes. In the instant when her soul leaped to the sun, the new baby whimpered, once, then again, and was still. Luke turned toward it with a furious oath. He bent over the crib and looked down at the tiny dark bundle that was scarcely anything at all, with its quiet hands and shut eyes.

In the sudden hope that it had died, he put his hand over its heart. The baby opened its eyes. They were blue—as deeply blue as his own, but enormous and infinitely sad. It was their utter despairing that moved him. He felt for this child a possessive tenderness such as the twins had never inspired. It was a woman-child. He understood her frailty.

So he knelt and slapped her face hard, and breathed into her mouth, and cried out Lily! Lily! naming her. He urged the strength in his spatulate fingers to quicken the beat of her heart. He prayed, "God, be merciful!" again and again.

She broke into a lusty wail and fell into a normal sleep, with the tears still wet on her cheeks.

Lily was dead, and Lily was not dead. A mother is the creator of life. And God cannot die.

From *The Saturday Evening Quill*, April 1929

# HANNAH BYDE

ONE COMES upon Hannah in her usual attitude of bitter resignation, gazing listlessly out of the window of her small, conventionally, cheaply furnished parlor. Hannah, a gentle woman crushed by environment, looking dully down the stretch of drab tomorrows littered with the ruins of shattered dreams.

She had got to the point, in these last few weeks, when the touch of her husband's hand on hers, the inevitable proximity in a four-room flat, the very sound of his breathing swept a sudden wave of nausea through her body, sickened her, soul and body and mind.

There were moments—frightful even to her—when she pictured her husband's dead body, and herself, in hypocritical black, weeping by his bier; or she saw her own repellent corpse swirling in a turgid pool and laughed a little madly at the image.

But there were times, too—when she took up her unfinished sack for the Joneses new baby—when a fierce, strange pain would rack her, and she, breath coming in little gasps, would sink to the floor, clutching at the tiny garment, and, somehow, soothed, would be a little girl again with plaited hair, a little eager, visioning girl—"Mama don't cry! Some day I'll be rich an' ev'rything. You'll se, mama!"—instead of a spiritless woman of thirty who, having neither the courage nor strength to struggle out of the mire of mediocrity, had married, at twenty, George Byde, simply because the enticing honeymoon to Niagara would mark the first break in the uneventful circle of her life.

Holiday crowds hurrying in the street . . . . bits of gay banter floating up to her . . . . George noisily rustling his paper . . . . Wreaths in the shop window across the street . . . . a proud black family in a new red car . . . . George uttering intermittent, expressive little grunts . . . . A blind beggar finding a lost dollar bill . . . . a bullying policeman running in a drunk . . . . George, in a reflective mood, beating a pencil against his teeth—

With a sharp intake of breath she turned on him fiercely, her voice trembling with stifled rage, angry tears filming her eyes.

"For God's sake, stop! You'll drive me mad!"

He dropped his paper. His mouth fell open. He got to his feet, a great, coarse, not unkindly, startled giant. "Hannah, I ain't—What under the sun's the matter with you?"

She struggled for composure. "It's nothing. I'm sorry. Sorry, George." But her eyes filled with pain.

He started toward her and stopped as he saw her stiffen. He said quietly, "Hannah, you ain't well. You ain't never bin like this."

She was suddenly forced into the open. "No," she said clearly, "I'm not well. I'm sick—sick to death of you, and your flat, and your cheap little friends. Oh," she said, her voice choked with passion, "I'd like to throw myself out of this window. Anything—anything to get away! I hate you!"

She swayed like some yellow flower in the wind, and for a moment there was the dreadful silence of partial revelation.

He fumbled, "No, no, hon. You're jes' nervous. I know you women. Jes' you set down. I'll go see if Doc's home."

She gave a deep sigh. Habitual apathy dulled her tone. "Please don't bother. I'm all right. It's nerves, I guess. Sometimes the emptiness of my life frightens me."

A slow anger crept over him. His lips seemed to thicken. "Look here, Hannah, I'm tiahed of your foolishness. There's limits to what a man will stand. Guess I give you ev'rything anybody else's got. You never have nothing much to do here. Y' got a phonygraph—and all them new records. Y' got a piano. I give you money las' week to buy a new dress. And yesterday y' got new shoes. I ain't no millionaire, Hannah. Ain't no man livin' c'n do better'n his best."

She made a restless, weary little gesture. She began to loathe him. She felt an almost insane desire to hurt him deeply, cruelly. She was like a taunting mother goading her child to tears.

"Of course I appreciate your sacrifice." Her voice shook a little with rising hysteria. "You're being perfectly splendid. You feed me. You clothe me. You've bought me a player piano which I loathe—flaunting emblem of middle-class existence—Oh, don't go to the trouble of trying to understand that—And a stupid victrola stocked with dreadful noises of your incomparable Mamie Waters. Oh, I'm a happy, contented woman! 'There never is anything to do here.'" She mocked in a shrill, choked voice. "Why, what in God's name is there to do in a dark, badly furnished four-room flat? Oh, if I weren't such a cowardly fool, I'd find a way out of all this!"

The look of a dangerous, savage beast dominated his face. He stood, in this moment, revealed. Every vestige of civilization had fled. One saw then the flatness of his close-cropped head, the thick, bull-like shortness of his neck, the heavy nose spreading now in a fierce gust of uncontrollable anger, the beads of perspiration that had sprung out on his upper lip, one wondered then how this gentle woman Hannah could have married him. Shut her eyes against his brutal coarseness, his unredeemed ignorance—here no occasional, illiterate appreciation of the beautiful—his lack of spiritual needs, his bodily wants.

And yet one sees them daily, these sensitive, spiritless Negro women caught fast in the tentacles of awful despair. Almost, it seems, they shut their eyes and make a blind plunge, inevitably to be sucked down, down into the depths of dreadful existence.

He started toward her, and she watched his approach with contemptuous interest. She had long ceased to fear him. She had learned to whip him out of a mood with the lash of her scathing tongue. And now she waited, almost hoping for the miracle of his heavy hand blotting out her weary life.

He was trembling. His eyes were black with rage. His speech was thick. "By God, you drive me mad! If I was any kind of man I'd beat you till you ran blood. I must have been crazy to marry you. You—you—!"

There was a sharp rapping at the door, drowning his crazy words. Hannah smiled faintly, almost compassionately.

"The psychological moment. What a pity, George."

She crossed the floor, staggering for an instant with a sudden, sharp pain. She opened the door and unconsciously caught her lip in vexation as she admitted her visitor.

"Do come in," she said, almost dryly.

Tillie entered. Tillie, the very reticent, very pretty, very silly wife of Doctor Hill: a newly wed popular girl finding matrimony just a bit cramping.

She entered boldly, anticipating and ignoring the palpable annoyance in the stern set of Hannah's face. She even shrugged a little, a kind of wriggling that her friends undoubtedly called "cute." She spoke in the unmistakable tone of the middle-class Negro.

"Hello, you! And big boy George! I heard you all walking about downstairs, so I came on up. I bin sittin' by myself all evenin'. Even the gas went out. Here it's New Year's eve, I'm all dolled up, got an invite to a swell shebang sittin' pretty on my dresser—and my sweet daddy walks out on a case! Say, wouldn't that make you leave your happy home?"

George enjoyed it. He grinned sympathetically. Here was a congenial, jazz-loving soul, and, child-like, he promptly shelved his present grievance. He wanted to show off. He wanted, a little pathetically, to blot out the hovering bitterness of Hannah in the gay comraderie of Tillie.

He said eagerly, "Got some new records, Tillie."

She was instantly delighted. "Yeh? Run 'em round the green."

She settled herself in a comfortable chair and crossed her slim legs. Hannah went to the window in customary isolation.

George made a vain search of the cabinet. "Where're them records, Hannah?" he asked.

"On the table ledge," she murmured fretfully.

He struggled to his feet and shuffled over to the table. "Lord," he grumbled, "you ain't undone 'em yet?"

"I've been too tired," she answered wearily.

He and Tillie exchanged mocking glances. He sighed expressively, and Tillie snickered audibly. But their malicious little shafts fell short of the unheeding woman who was beating a sharp, impatient tattoo on the windowpane.

George swore softly.

"Whassa matter?" asked Tillie. "Knot?"

He jerked at it furiously. "This devilish string."

"Will do," she asserted companionably. "Got a knife."

"Yep." He fished in his pocket, produced it. "Here we go." The razor-sharp knife split the twine. "All set." He flung the knife, still open, on the table.

The raucous notes of a jazz singer filled the room. The awful blare of a frenzied colored orchestra, the woman's strident voice swelling, a great deal of "high brown baby" and "low down papa" to offend sensitive ears, and Tillie saying admiringly, "Ain't that the monkey's itch?"

From below came the faint sound of someone clumping, a heavy man stamping snow from his boots. Tillie sprang up, fluttered toward George.

"Jim, I'll bet. Back. You come down with me. G. B., and maybe you c'n coax him to come up. I got a bottle of somethin' good. We'll watch the new year in and drink its health."

George obediently followed after. "Not so worse. And there oughta be plenty o' stuff in our ice-box. Scare up a little somethin' Hannah. We'll be right back."

As the door banged noisily, Hannah, with a dreadful rush of suppressed sobs, swiftly crossed the carpeted floor, cut short the fearful din of the record, and stood, for a trembling moment, with her hands pressed against her eyes.

Presently her sobs quieted, and she moaned a little, whimpering, too, like a fretful child. She began to walk restlessly up and down, whispering crazily to herself. Sometimes she beat her doubled fists against her head, and ugly words befouled her twisted lips. Sometimes she fell upon her knees, face buried in her outflung arms, and cried aloud to God.

Once, in her mad, sick circle of the room, she staggered against the table, and the hand that went out to steady her closed on a bit of sharp steel. For a moment she stood quite still. Then she opened her eyes, blinking them free of tears. She stared fixedly at the knife in her hand. She noted it for the first time: initialed, heavy black, four blades, the open one broken off at the point. She ran her fingers along its edge. A drop of blood spurted and dripped from the tip of her finger. It fascinated her. She began to think: this is the tide of my life ebbing out. And suddenly she wanted to see it run swiftly. She wanted terribly to be drained dry of life. She wanted to feel the outgoing tide of existence.

She flung back her head. Her voice rang out in a strange, wild cry of freedom.

But in the instant when she would have freed her soul, darkness swirled down upon her. Wave upon wave of impenetrable blackness in a mad surge. The knife fell away. Her groping hands were like bits of aimless driftwood. She could not fight her way through to consciousness. She plunged deeply into the terrible vastness that roared about her ears.

And almost in awful mockery the bells burst into sound, ushering out the old, heralding the new: for Hannah, only a long, grey twelve month of pain-filled, soul-starved days.

As the last, loud note died away, Tillie burst into the room, followed by George and her husband, voluble in noisy badinage. Instantly she saw the prostrate figure of Hannah and uttered a piercing shriek of terror.

"Oh, my God! Jim!" she cried, and cowered fearfully against the wall, peering through the lattice of her fingers.

George, too, stood quite still, an half empty bottle clutched in his hand, his eyes bulging grotesquely, his mouth falling open, his lips ashen. Instinctively although the knife lay hidden in the folds of her dress, he felt that she was dead. Her every prophetic, fevered word leaped to his suddenly sharpened brain. He wanted to run away and hide. It wasn't fair of Hannah to be lying there mockingly dead. His mind raced ahead to the dreadful details of inquest and burial, and a great resentment welled in his heart. He began to hate the woman he thought lay dead.

Doctor Hill, puffing a little, bent expertly over Hannah. His eye caught the gleam of steel. Surreptitiously he pocketed the knife and sighed. He was a kindly, fat, little bald man with an exhaustless fund of sympathy. Immediately he had understood. That was the way with morbid, self-centered women like Hannah.

He raised himself. "Poor girl, she's fainted. Help me with her, you all."

When they had laid her on the couch, the gay, frayed, red couch with the ugly rent in the center Hannah's nerve-tipped fingers had torn, Jim sent them into the kitchen.

"I want to talk to her alone. She'll come around in a minute."

He stood above her, looking down at her with incurious pity. The great black circles under her eyes enhanced the sad dark beauty of her face. He knew suddenly, with a tinge of pain, how different would have been her life, how wide the avenues of achievement, how eager the acclaiming crowd, how soft her bed of ease, had this glorious golden woman been born white. But there was little bitterness in his thoughts. He did not resignedly accept the black man's unequal struggle, but he philosophically foresaw the eventual crashing down of all unjust barriers.

Hannah stirred, moaned a little, opened her eyes. In a quick flash of realization stifled a cry with her hand fiercely pressed to her lips. Doctor Hill bent over her, and suddenly she began to laugh, ending it dreadfully in a sob.

"Hello, Jim," she said, "I'm not dead, am I? I wanted so badly to die."

Weakly she tried to rise, but he forced her down with a gentle hand. "Lie quiet, Hannah," he said.

Obediently she lay back on the cushion, and he sat beside her, letting her hot hand grip his own. She smiled, a wistful, tragic, little smile.

"I had planned it all so nicely, Jim. George was to stumble upon my dead body—his own knife buried in my throat—and grovel beside me in fear and self-reproach. And Tillie, of course, would begin extolling my virtues, while you—Now it's all spoilt!"

He released her hand and patted it gently. He got to his feet. "You must never do this again, Hannah."

She shook her head like a wilful child. "I shan't promise."

His near-sighted, kindly eyes bored into hers. "There is a reason why you must, my dear."

For a long moment she stared questioningly at him, and the words of refutation that leaped to her lips died of despairing certainty at the answer in his eyes.

She rose, swaying, and steadied herself by the feverish grip on his arms. "No," she wailed, "no! no! no!!"

He put an arm about her. "Steady, dear."

She jerked herself free, and flung herself on the couch, burying her stricken face in her hands.

"Jim, I can't! I can't! Don't you see how it is with me?"

He told her seriously, "You must be very careful, Hannah."

Her eyes were tearless, wild. "But, Jim, you know—You've watched me. Jim! I hate my husband. I can't breathe when he's near. He—stifles me. I can't go with it. I can't! Oh, why couldn't I have died?"

He took both her hands in his and sat beside her, waiting, until his quiet presence should soothe her. Finally she gave a great, quivering cry and was still.

"Listen, Hannah," he began, "you are nervous and distraught. After all, a natural state for a woman of your temperament. But you do not want to die. You want to live. Because you must, my dear. There is a life within you demanding birth. If you seek your life again, your child dies, too. I am quite sure you could not be a murderer.

"You must listen very closely and remember all I say. For with this new year—a new beginning, Hannah—you must see things clearly and rationally, and build your strength against your hour of delivery."

Slowly she raised her eyes to his. She shook her head dumbly. "There's no way out. My hands are tied. Life itself has beaten me."

"Hannah?"

"No. I understand Jim. I see."

"Right," he said, rising cheerfully. "Just you think it all over." He crossed to the door and called, "George! Tillie! You all can come in now."

They entered timorously, and Doctor Hill smiled reassuringly at them. He took his wife's hand and led her to the outer door.

"Out with you and me, my dear. We'll drink the health of the new year downstairs. Mrs. Byde has something very important to say to Mr. Byde. Night, G. B. Be very gentle with Hannah."

George shut the door behind them and went to Hannah. He stood before her, embarrassed, mumbling inaudibly.

"There's going to be a child," she said dully.

She paled before the instant gleam in his eyes.

"You're—glad?"

There was a swell of passion in his voice, "Hannah!" He caught her up in his arms.

"Don't," she cried, her hands a shield against him, "you're—stifling me."

He pressed his mouth to hers and awkwardly released her.

She brushed her hands across her lips, "You've been drinking. I can't bear it."

He was humble. "Just to steady myself. In the kitchen. Me and Tillie."

She was suddenly almost sorry for him. "It's all right, George. It doesn't matter. It's nothing."

Timidly he put his hand on her shoulder. "You're shivering. Lemme get you a shawl."

"No." She fought against hysteria. "I'm all right, George. It's only that I'm tired." She went unsteadily to her bedroom door, and her groping hand closed on the knob. "You—you'll sleep on the couch tonight? I—I just want to be alone. Good night, George. I shall be all right. Good night."

He stood alone, at a loss, his hands going out to the closed door in clumsy sympathy. He thought: I'll play a piece while she's gettin' undressed. A little jazz'll do her good.

He crossed to the phonograph, his shoes squeaking fearfully. There was something pathetic in his awkward attempt to walk lightly. He started the record where Hannah had cut it short, grinning delightedly as it began to whir.

The jazz notes burst on the air, filled the narrow room, crowded out.

And the woman behind the closed door flung herself across the bed and laughed and laughed and laughed.

From *The Messenger*, July 1926

## THE BLACK DRESS

THEY SENT me word that morning that old Mr. Johnson had died in the night. It was not really a surprise to me. I knew he had been lingering for weeks.

That was my chiefest reason for writing to Margaret. Deep in his heart old Johnson, her father, loved her very much. It would not be so hard for him to go with her hand in his. Margaret I knew had forgiven him his early injustice. I felt she would be glad to brighten his last pain-black days. They would not be many. He could not live beyond the year, and it was Christmas week when I wrote her to come.

I did not mention her father's hopeless illness. I simply asked her, for old time's sake to come and hang up her stocking with mine, as we had done when we were very young.

Her acceptance came in a day or two. She was between shows and husbands. It would be good to see me after twelve long years. Did I still have dimples? Would I find her changed? For better, for worse?

I wondered. Margaret and I had been like sisters all our growing years. I suppose she loved me more than she loved anyone else. She had only an impatient tolerance for her bigoted father. But the years had probably softened this into something nearer affection. After all, he was her only living relative.

To my knowledge she never wrote him. Nor did she write me. Occasionally I would get a telegram of extravagant endearment, and very often a generous check. My babies who had never seen her, spoke of her as Aunt Margaret.

I wrote her regularly. She had always seemed hard to the home folks, but I felt I understood her. She was not hard. She was simply unsentimental. She had one goal, the stage. She had had to fight the whole community, beginning with her father, to make them accept the theatre as a legitimate profession. The fight with her father had been long and bitter. The neighbors had taken his side. Naturally that did something to her spirit. When she left home at eighteen, it was not a girl but a bitter woman who said good-by to me, the only one to bid her good-by and God-speed.

I hoped the years had taken the edge off her bitterness. I always mentioned her father in my letters. Toward the last I would say he sent love. For old Johnson did love Margaret. And I am sure, on the lonely nights, he wished very much he could unsay the things that had sent her from him. Well, while there is life, it is not too late. At least he could say he was sorry he had said them. That was in my mind, knowing the time, his time, was so short, when I wrote to Margaret.

The hospital called me the morning of Christmas eve. They asked me the address of old Johnson's nearest of kin. I gave them Margaret's before I realized she would be in town that evening. After I hung up I hoped she had already left. For I could tell her more tenderly than a cold telegram.

Someone rang my bell. It was the boy with the tree my husband had bought on his way to work. The children were wild. And when I saw their excited faces, I suddenly and selfishly decided that I could not bring death into my house to mar the happiest day of their year.

No, Margaret must wait until tomorrow evening to be told. I would tell her after the last tired child had been tucked into bed. In the meantime I would make some arrangements with an undertaker.

I knew this was the most wicked thing I would ever do in my life. But, oh, she would understand when we stood and smiled down at the sleeping children that it would have been cruel to spoil their day with our grown-up grief.

Early that evening a taxi rolled up. A woman got out. I flew downstairs to open my door with words of gay greeting or solemn condolence ready on my lips. Margaret's dear familiar face was radiant. She did not know. I held her fast in my arms.

I shall never forget our happy evening. She was like a sprite, never still. She fell in love with small Margaret. Once she said fiercely to the shining faces, "Be happy. Let nothing stand in the way of your being happy." I thought, How hard her beautiful face is. It is only I who know she is not hard.

We were tired at last. Sentimentally we were going to sleep together. My husband was banished to a cot in the dining room, and sometime during the night he would fill our stockings.

Margaret and I were in my room together. She opened her bag to fetch out the stocking. On the top lay a black dress, looking as if it had been stuffed in hastily. I caught my breath sharply. She followed my glance.

She said indifferently, "This went in at the last moment. It'll have to be pressed before I wear it."

My throat went dry. For the first time in my life I was going to sleep with a stranger.

From *Opportunity: Journal of Negro Life*, May 1934

# MY BABY

ONE DAY during my tenth year a long time ago in Boston, I came home from school, let myself in the back yard, stopped a moment to scowl at the tall sunflowers which sprang up yearly despite my dislike of them, and to smile at the tender pansies and marigolds and morning-glories which father set out in little plots every spring, and went on into the kitchen. The back gate and back-door were always left open for us children, and the last one in was supposed to lock them. But since the last dawdler home from school had no way of know-ing she was the last until she was inside, it was always mother who locked them at first dark, and she would stand and look up at the evening stars. She seemed to like this moment of being alone, away from the noise in the house.

We were a big house. Beside the ten rooms, and the big white-walled attic, there were we three little girls and the big people, as we used to call them. Fa-ther, our mothers, grandpa, and the unmarried aunts. Presently, as I shall tell you, there were two more little ones. Grampa used to say that if we lived in the Boston Museum, which was the biggest building grampa had ever seen, we'd still need one more room. That was a standing joke in our house. For besides this permanent collection, there were always visiting relatives and friends, for we had a nice house, and we were a hospitable family.

My room was the big third-floor front bedroom. Mostly I shared it with mother. I remember everything in that room, the big brass bed that had been father's wed-ding present to mother, the wicker settee and the wicker rocker and the wicker armchair, that had once seen service in the parlor until superseded by mahogany, and now creaked dolefully on damp nights, making me think of ghosts. There was a built-in marble wash-stand in the room, and I think mother was very proud of this fixture. There were taps for running hot and cold water, and on Saturdays and Sundays and holidays the hot tap was really hot. The New England winters were cold then, and although our old-fashioned house had a furnace that sent up some semblance of heat through the registers, there were coal stoves in nearly all the rooms. In my room was a little pot-bellied stove, and I knew how to tend it my-self. At night I would sift the ashes and bank the fire, and in the mornings I would scoot out of bed onto the freezing carpet, run to the stove, bang the door shut, open the drafts, race back to bed and lie on my belly doing my algebra until the room had warmed enough for me to dress. My room, for some reason, became the hub of the house. I think it was because that little pot-bellied stove was one of the only two on the top floor. And whereas I left my window for mother to open, so I wouldn't cool off the house before it was bedded down for the night, my cousin, in whose room was an ancient, evil, ugly stove, let her fire go out, flung open her window, and shut her door against intruders.

At night everyone came into my room to warm himself before going to bed, and an aunt stopping in to toast for a moment before my banked fire and finding another aunt present would fall into conversation, and by and by all the other members of the family, except father and grampa who couldn't come in their nightshirts, would drift in and settle in the wicker furniture, and the rocking chair would sing back and forth, and someone would ask, "Is that child asleep?" And someone would answer, "If she isn't, she'd better be."

They would sit there until the banked fire gave out no more heat. Then they would sigh and heave themselves up, and their heavy bodies would pad out of the room. Mother would crack the window and let in the stars and turn out the flickering gaslight. Sometimes she slipped in beside me, sometimes not. I would lie and listen to the creaks and groans of the many bedsteads, and it seemed to me a fine and safe thing to have a big family.

That day in my tenth year when I came home from school, my mother was not in the kitchen. This seemed odd, for the children in our Irish neighborhood were often bellicose, and mother stood ready at all times to rush out and rescue us. I could not fight when I was a child. I shook too much and was too ashamed. But my mother and the cousin who was eleven months older than I were great battlers. It was wonderful to hear my mother tearing into an Irish termagant with a sailor's tongue, and to see my girl cousin triumphantly straddling a thirteen-year-old bully. My mother and my cousin were so much alike that sometimes I had the mean thought that I was not really my mother's child. And oddly enough, my mother's sister was shy and soft and dark like myself. My cousin and I used to wonder quite seriously if our mothers, for some reason, had switched us.

When I could not find my mother in the kitchen, I went softly down the hall to the parlor. I did not call her in the fear that if there were company, I would be summoned. The parlor door stood open but my cautious peeking revealed no one inside. Suddenly, I heard movement in the upstairs sitting room. I went back down the hall and up the back stairs, and sitting down on the top step, I had a clear view of the front room.

Now, looking back, I do not remember the room's furnishings. I can only recall that almost center in the room was a big table-desk that had once been in father's office, and beside this desk sat a strange white woman with a little brown girl in her arms. I could not see my mother, but I was aware of her presence in that room. Grampa was probably in the grandfather chair, chewing tobacco, spitting into a tin can when it was summer and into the stove when it was winter, not listening to the conversation of the women. My father and my widowed aunts were at work.

My mother and the woman spoke in low voices, and I did not hear anything they said. I wished I could see the baby more clearly, for I loved babies. She was good, hardly stirring, and never uttering a sound. Presently the woman rose. I scrambled down the back stairs as quietly as I could.

That night at supper my mother asked us how we would like a baby boy and girl to play with. We were wildly excited, for we were beginning to think we were too big to play with dolls and it was hard not to have something to fondle. Well, we'll see, said my mother and sent us out front to play, with grandfather at the parlor window to watch us so that the roving bands of Irish boys from Mission Hill way would not bother us. We knew that the big people were going to talk about the white lady and wanted us out of ear-shot.

The day the babies came is as clear in my mind as if it were yesterday. It was a Saturday. We had not come home from dancing school, held in the spacious home of a Negro woman who had known a better day, where we were taught parlor prancing by a young and lovely Irish girl, whose mother accompanied her to class because some of the seniors were boys of eighteen, and our teacher was only twenty-one. She was engaged and was not interested in the boys at all except as one boy danced better than another. Nor were the boys interested in her since they were all in school and there were several prettier girls in the class. Now it seems strange that we had a white dancing teacher, but in those days it was the fashion. If you went to a Negro teacher, it was an admission that you could not afford to pay a white one.

When we rang the front bell, mother came to the door. She smiled and said that the babies had come, and that they were to sleep with me because my bedroom was the biggest. My cousins raced upstairs to see the newcomers. I stayed behind to ask questions. Actually I could not bear the exquisite moment when I would hold two real babies in my arms. I asked my mother how long they would stay. She said they would stay indefinitely for their mother had gone to work to support them. She was, in fact, going to work as nursemaid for a friend of my unmarried aunt's employer. I asked my mother where their father was. She hesitated for a moment, then said that their father had not been very good to them, and that was why they were here, and I must love them a lot so they would not miss their mother too much.

With my heart bursting with love for these babies, I went slowly upstairs. Finally, I reached my room, and I heard my cousins crowing delightedly. At the foot of my bed sat a little boy in pajamas. He looked about three. His hair was very blond and curly, his skin very pink and white. He looked like a cherub as he bounced about outside the covers and chattered in utmost friendliness to my cousins. I started toward him, for I wanted nothing so much as to hug him tight. My cousins began telling me excitedly what a darling he was. I was almost upon them when suddenly I stopped. I did not do it willfully. Some force outside me jerked me to a halt. The smile left my face and involuntarily I turned and looked toward the head of the bed.

There was that baby girl, staring solemnly at me. I went slowly toward her. I had forgotten the boy was on earth. I stood above her. She was no more than two. Her hair was as curly as the boy's but softer and longer and brown. Her wide serious eyes were brown, too. She was copper-colored. In all of my life I have never seen a lovelier child. I do not know how long we stared at each other unthinkingly. As clearly as if I had spoken aloud, I heard a voice inside myself say to the inward ear of that child, I am going to love you best of all. Then I turned away without touching her and in a minute had joined my cousins who had already decided the boy would be the most fun.

The months passed, and the girl and I became inseparable. When I came home at half-past two there was her little face pressed to the window-pane, and no one had told her the time. From the moment I entered the house, I was her mother and she was my child. Their own mother came to see the children on the one day a week that she was free. But she was so young, only twenty-one and she had been caring for babies all week, and so after a few minutes with them, mother sent her out to see her young friends. My mother treated her like a child which seemed odd to me then. I learned that my mother was her aunt by marriage, and that she remembered the day she was born. I was told she had played with us when we were babies just as we played with her children now. I knew then that she was not white.

The hard winter had set in when father had to shovel a path from the house to the sidewalk before we children could leave for school. The snow was banked as high as our shoulders. There are no such winters now. We were little girls and we wore boy's storm boots that laced to our knees as did all the other little girls. We wore flannel shirts and drawers that made us itch like mad and red flannel petticoats. Some bitter mornings the bells sounded over the city which meant it was snowing too hard for school. The babies scarcely left the house that winter, for mother said they were packed with cold. I think the house was warmer than it ever had been, and sometimes father grumbled about the cost of coal. Grampa gave the babies a mixture of white vaseline, lemon juice and sugar. Mother borrowed my allowance money regularly for patent medicines. They worked on those children all winter. When it was spring, it seemed that Grampa and my mother had succeeded, for the children had gained and grown taller.

The girl was as much a part of me now as my arm. She had grown even closer to me after the long, uncertain winter. I had forgotten the years when she had not been with me. I could not imagine a life without her. As young as she was, and as young as I was, there was an understanding between us of amazing depth. The family remarked on our oneness. Her own mother knew without jealousy that the baby loved me best.

Death came on her quietly, and on what mild spring breeze it could have blown we never knew. There was a day when she whimpered and sucked on her thumb, a habit we had broken. I do not remember if the doctor came; I only remember that it seemed to me I could not bear to see her lying there, not whimpering now, but still sucking on her thumb with nobody telling her not to, and her eyes enormous and with a look of suffering.

Then one day—it may have been the next day, it may have been the next year, for the pain I suffered with her—my mother wrapped her up and took her to the hospital. When mother had gone, I slipped out of the house and trailed her like a little dog. It was a short walk from our house to the Children's Hospital. Mother went inside, and I stood on the sidewalk opposite and stared up at the hospital windows. I guess the waiting room was on the second floor, for suddenly I saw my mother in line at a second floor window. She did not see me, and I cannot say if the baby saw me or not. She lay listlessly in mother's arms pulling on her thumb. I stared at her with my hands pressed tight in prayer until they had passed out of sight. Then I ran home and crawled under the bed and lay there quivering, unable to cry, until I heard mother's weary step in the hall. We children ran to her, and when we saw she had returned without the baby, we could not bear to ask her what the doctor had said. She would not tell us. She only said the doctor would take good care of her and that she would soon be well.

It is so long now that I cannot remember how long it was. Perhaps a week passed, perhaps a month. One night in my sleep I heard the front door bell or the telephone ring. The next thing I remembered was the soft sound of my mother's sobs. I sat up and stared at her. The boy's blond head lay on the pillow, his face sweet in sleep. My mother looked at me. I did not know why she had come into my room unless to reassure herself that there was life in death. She came to me and hugged me tight, and said in a choked whisper that the baby was dead. Then she straightened almost sternly and told me to go back to sleep. I did not cry. I just felt surprised for a minute and then went to sleep almost instantly. I was ten and I was smart for my age. I had been told that the baby was dead, and I had seen the grown-ups' strained faces, but did not know what death was. The last time I had seen the baby she had been alive. It was not until I looked down at her little white coffin that I knew that she was not. Had she died without pain, she might have looked otherwise. But the sudden swift disease had ravaged her. A bandage covered her eyes, and the agony had left its mark on her mouth. She did not look like a sleeping child. Perhaps the undertaker had not yet perfected his art. This was death unbeautiful and unmistakable. The only mourners were my family.

The mother came home with us that night. I remember her white, frightened, little-girl's face, and my mother's tenderness. She did not go back to work. There was a week of family conferences, for we children practically spent the whole week outdoors.

Then one day we came home from school, and the boy and his mother had gone. My mother said they had gone far away to another city. She talked to us very seriously, and her eyes were filled with sadness and something that looked like shame. Her words came out slowly, as if reluctantly. Sometimes she could not look at us. She said the boy and his mother would never come back. They had gone away to begin a new life. If anyone asked us about them, we must say we had never known them. We knew by her face that we must not ask any questions. We went away from her, and we could not play, nor could we look at each other.

So summer came again, and an aunt from the South came to visit us, bringing her two little boys. My cousins had a child apiece and were wildly happy. Mother and the aunts were happy, too, for they had not seen their sister in years.

One day a strange dark man came to our house and talked in an angry voice to my mother. She talked back to him the same way she talked to the Irish termagants. I heard her tell that man that his baby had died because he had neglected it. She told him that his wife and son had gone away, and thrust him out of the house.

Sometime after that a letter came for my mother. I saw her hands tremble when she opened it. She did not say anything to us, but that night she read it aloud to her assembled sisters. My cousins were in the attic playing with the two little boys, and my mother thought I was with them. Actually I was lying underneath my bed, crying for that dead baby. There was not a night for a good six months that I did not cry for her. When I heard my mother and my aunts, I crammed my fist into my mouth. How could I tell them I was crying for a child I was supposed never to have heard of?

My mother and the aunts settled in the wicker furniture. Somebody carefully shut the door. Then mother read the letter. I do not remember everything it said. All that I remember is something about a marriage, and something about a new life, and something about a husband being white. Mother opened my little pot-bellied stove, thrust the letter in, and struck a match to it. Suddenly the sisters silently converged and watched the letter burn. When the letter was ashes, mother shut the stove door. I heard my unmarried aunt murmur, "God help her to be happy." Then they filed out, and one of them called upstairs sharply for the children not to make so much noise. They went back downstairs. I took my fist out of my mouth, and I cried even harder, for now there was much more to cry about.

131 West 110th Street, New York City
WPA Federal Writers' Project
December 8, 1938

# MAMMY

THE YOUNG NEGRO welfare investigator, carrying her briefcase, entered the ornate foyer of the Central Park West apartment house. She was making a collateral call. Earlier in the day she had visited an aging colored woman in a rented room in Harlem. Investigation had proved that the woman was not quite old enough for Old Age Assistance, and yet no longer young enough to be classified as employable. Nothing, therefore, stood in the way of her eligibility for relief. Hers was a clear case of need. This collateral call on her former employer was merely routine.

The investigator walked toward the elevator, close on the heels of a well-dressed woman with a dog. She felt shy. Most of her collaterals were to housewives in the Bronx or supervisors of maintenance workers in office buildings. Such calls were never embarrassing. A moment ago as she neared the doorway, the doorman had regarded her intently. The service entrance was plainly to her left, and she was walking past it. He had been on the point of approaching when a tenant emerged and dispatched him for a taxi. He had stood for a moment torn between his immediate duty and his sense of outrage. Then he had gone away dolefully, blowing his whistle.

The woman with the dog reached the elevator just as the doors slid open. The dog bounded in, and the elevator boy bent and roughhoused with him. The boy's agreeable face was black, and the investigator felt a flood of relief.

The woman entered the elevator and smilingly faced front. Instantly the smile left her face, and her eyes hardened. The boy straightened, faced front, too, and gaped in surprise. Quickly he glanced at the set face of his passenger.

"Service entrance's outside," he said sullenly.

The investigator said steadily, "I am not employed here. I am here to see Mrs. Coleman on business."

"If you're here on an errand or somethin' like that," he argued doggedly, "you still got to use the service entrance."

She stared at him with open hate, despising him for humiliating her before and because of a woman of an alien race.

"I am here as a representative of the Department of Welfare. If you refuse me the use of this elevator, my office will take it up with the management."

She did not know if this was true, but the elevator boy would not know either.

"Get in, then," he said rudely, and rolled his eyes at his white passenger as if to convey his regret at the discomfort he was causing her.

The doors shut and the three shot upward, without speaking to or looking at each other. The woman with the dog, in a far corner, very pointedly held her small harmless animal on a tight leash.

The car stopped at the fourth floor, and the doors slid open. No one moved. There was a ten-second wait.

"You getting out or not?" the boy asked savagely.

There was no need to ask whom he was addressing.

"Is this my floor?" asked the investigator.

His sarcasm rippled. "You want Mrs. Coleman, don't you?"

"Which is her apartment?" she asked thickly.

"Ten-A. You're holding up my passenger."

When the door closed, she leaned against it, feeling sick, and trying to control her trembling. She was young and vulnerable. Her contact with Negroes was confined to frightened relief folks who did everything possible to stay in her good graces, and the members of her own set, among whom she was a favorite because of her two degrees and her civil service appointment. She had almost never run into Negroes who did not treat her with respect.

In a moment or two she walked down the hall to Ten-A. She rang, and after a little wait a handsome middle-aged woman opened the door.

"How do you do?" the woman said in a soft drawl. She smiled. "You're from the relief office, aren't you? Do come in."

"Thank you," said the investigator, smiling, too, relievedly.

"Right this way," said Mrs. Coleman, leading the way into a charming living room. She indicated an upholstered chair. "Please sit down."

The investigator, who never sat in overstuffed chairs in the homes of her relief clients, plumped down and smiled again at Mrs. Coleman. Such a pleasant woman, such a pleasant room. It was going to be a quick and easy interview. She let her briefcase slide to the floor beside her.

Mrs. Coleman sat down in a straight chair and looked searchingly at the investigator. Then she said somewhat breathlessly, "You gave me to understand that Mammy has applied for relief."

The odious title sent a little flicker of dislike across the investigator's face. She answered stiffly, "I had just left Mrs. Mason when I telephoned you for this appointment."

Mrs. Coleman smiled disarmingly, though she colored a little. "She has been with us ever since I can remember. I call her Mammy, and so does my daughter."

"That's a sort of nurse, isn't it?" the investigator asked coldly. "I had thought Mrs. Mason was a general maid."

"Is that what she said?"

"Why, I understood she was discharged because she was no longer physically able to perform her duties."

"She wasn't discharged."

The investigator looked dismayed. She had not anticipated complications. She felt for her briefcase.

"I'm very confused, Mrs. Coleman. Will you tell me just exactly what happened, then? I had no idea Mrs. Mason was—was misstating the situation." She opened her briefcase.

Mrs. Coleman eyed her severely. "There's nothing to write down. Do you have to write down things? It makes me feel as if I were being investigated."

"I'm sorry," said the investigator quickly, snapping shut her briefcase. "If it would be distasteful—. I apologize again. Please go on."

"Well, there's little to tell. It all happened so quickly. My daughter was ill. My nerves were on edge. I may have said something that upset Mammy. One night she was here. The next morning she wasn't. I've been worried sick about her."

"Did you report her disappearance?"

"Her clothes were gone, too. It didn't seem a matter for the police. It was obvious that she had left of her own accord. Believe me, young woman, I was very relieved when you telephoned me." Her voice shook a little.

"I'm glad I can assure you that Mrs. Mason appears quite well. She only said she worked for you. She didn't mention your daughter. I hope she has recovered."

"My daughter is married," Mrs. Coleman said slowly. "She had a child. It was stillborn. We have not seen Mammy since. For months she had looked forward to nursing it."

"I'm sure it was a sad loss to all of you," the investigator said gently. "And old Mrs. Mason, perhaps she felt you had no further use for her. It may have unsettled her mind. Temporarily," she added hastily. "She seems quite sane."

"Of course, she is," said Mrs. Coleman with a touch of bitterness. "She's just old and contrary. She knew we would worry about her. She did it deliberately."

This was not in the investigator's province. She cleared her throat delicately.

"Would you take her back, Mrs. Coleman?"

"I want her back," cried Mrs. Coleman. "She has no one but us. She is just like one of the family."

"You're very kind," the investigator murmured. "Most people feel no responsibility for their aging servants."

"You do not know how dear a mammy is to a southerner. I nursed at Mammy's breast. I cannot remember a day in my life without her."

The investigator reached for her briefcase and rose.

"Then it is settled that she may return?"

A few hours ago there had been no doubt in her mind of old Mrs. Mason's eligibility for relief. With this surprising turn there was nothing to do but reject the case for inadequate proof of need. It was always a feather in a field worker's cap to reject a case that had been accepted for home investigation by a higher paid intake worker.

Mrs. Coleman looked at the investigator almost beseechingly.

"My child, I cannot tell you how much I will be in your debt if you can persuade Mammy to return. Can't you refuse to give her relief? She really is in need of nothing as long as I am living. Poor thing, what has she been doing for money? How has she been eating? In what sort of place is she staying?"

"She's very comfortable, really. She had three dollars when she came uptown to Harlem. She rented a room, explained her circumstances to her landlady, and is getting her meals there. I know that landlady. She has other roomers who are on relief. She trusts them until they get their relief checks. They never cheat her."

"Oh, thank God! I must give you something to give to that woman. How good Negroes are. I am so glad it was you who came. You are so sympathetic. I could not have talked so freely to a white investigator. She would not have understood."

The investigator's smile was wintry. She resented this well-meant restatement of the trusted position of the good darky.

She said civilly, however, "I'm going back to Mrs. Mason's as soon as I leave here. I hope I can persuade her to return to you tonight."

"Thank you! Mammy was happy here, believe me. She had nothing to do but a little dusting. We are a small family, myself, my daughter, and her husband. I have a girl who comes every day to do the hard work. She preferred to sleep in, but I wanted Mammy to have the maid's room. It's a lovely room with a private bath. It's next to the kitchen, which is nice for Mammy. Old people potter about so. I've lost girl after girl who felt she was meddlesome. But I've always thought of Mammy's comfort first."

"I'm sure you have," said the investigator politely, wanting to end the interview. She made a move toward departure. "Thank you again for being so cooperative."

Mrs. Coleman rose and crossed to the doorway.

"I must get my purse. Will you wait a moment?"

Shortly she reappeared. She opened her purse.

"It's been ten days. Please give that landlady this twenty dollars. No, it isn't too much. And here is a dollar for Mammy's cab fare. Please put her in the cab yourself."

"I'll do what I can." The investigator smiled candidly. "It must be nearly four, and my working day ends at five."

"Yes, of course," Mrs. Coleman said distractedly. "And now I just want you to peep in at my daughter. Mammy will want to know how she is. She's far from well, poor lambie."

The investigator followed Mrs. Coleman down the hall. At an open door they paused. A pale young girl lay on the edge of a big tossed bed. One hand was in her tangled hair, the other clutched an empty bassinet. The wheels rolled down and back, down and back. The girl glanced briefly and without interest at her mother and the investigator, then turned her face away.

"It tears my heart," Mrs. Coleman whispered in a choked voice. "Her baby, and then Mammy. She has lost all desire to live. But she is young and she will have other children. If she would only let me take away that bassinet! I am not the nurse that Mammy is. You can see how much Mammy is needed here."

They turned away and walked in silence to the outer door. The investigator was genuinely touched, and eager to be off on her errand of mercy.

Mrs. Coleman opened the door, and for a moment seemed at a loss as to how to say good-bye. Then she said quickly, "Thank you for coming," and shut the door.

The investigator stood in indecision at the elevator, half persuaded to walk down three flights of stairs. But this, she felt, was turning tail, and pressed the elevator button.

The door opened. The boy looked at her sheepishly. He swallowed and said ingratiatingly, "Step in, miss. Find your party all right?"

She faced front, staring stonily ahead of her, and felt herself trembling with indignation at this new insolence.

He went on whiningly, "That woman was in my car is mean as hell. I was just puttin' on to please her. She hates niggers 'cept when they're bowin' and scrapin'. She was the one had the old doorman fired. You see for yourself they got a white one now. With white folks needin' jobs, us niggers got to eat dirt to hang on."

The investigator's face was expressionless except for a barely perceptible wincing at his careless use of a hated word.

He pleaded, "You're colored like me. You ought to understand. I was only doing my job. I got to eat same as white folks, same as you."

They rode the rest of the way in a silence interrupted only by his heavy sighs. When they reached the ground floor, and the doors slid open, he said sorrowfully, "Good-bye, miss."

She walked down the hall and out into the street, past the glowering doorman, with her face stern, and her stomach slightly sick.

The investigator rode uptown on a northbound bus. At One Hundred and Eighteenth Street she alighted and walked east. Presently she entered a well-kept apartment house. The elevator operator deferentially greeted her and whisked her upward.

She rang the bell of number fifty-four, and visited briefly with the landlady, who was quite overcome by the unexpected payment of twenty dollars. When she could escape her profuse thanks, the investigator went to knock at Mrs. Mason's door.

"Come in," called Mrs. Mason. The investigator entered the small, square room. "Oh, it's you, dear," said Mrs. Mason, her lined brown face lighting up.

She was sitting by the window in a wide rocker. In her black, with a clean white apron tied about her waist, and a white bandana bound around her head, she looked ageless and full of remembering.

Mrs. Mason grasped her rocker by the arms and twisted around until she faced the investigator.

She explained shyly, "I just sit here for hours lookin' out at the people. I ain' seen so many colored folks at one time since I left down home. Sit down, child, on the side of the bed. Hit's softer than that straight chair yonder."

The investigator sat down on the straight chair, not because the bedspread was not scrupulously clean, but because what she had come to say needed stiff decorum.

"I'm all right here, Mrs. Mason. I won't be long."

"I was hopin' you could set awhile. My landlady's good, but she's got this big flat. Don't give her time for much settin'."

The investigator, seeing an opening, nodded understandingly.

"Yes, it must be pretty lonely for you here after being so long an intimate part of the Coleman family."

The old woman's face darkened. "Shut back in that bedroom behin' the kitchen! This here's what I like. My own kind and color. I'm too old a dog to be learnin' new tricks."

"Your duties with Mrs. Coleman were very slight. I know you are getting on in years, but you are not too feeble for light employment. You were not entirely truthful with me. I was led to believe you did all the housework."

The old woman looked furtively at the investigator. "How come you know diff'rent now?"

"I've just left Mrs. Coleman's."

Bafflement veiled the old woman's eyes. "You didn't believe what all I tol' you!"

"We always visit former employers. It's part of our job, Mrs. Mason. Sometimes an employer will rehire our applicants. Mrs. Coleman is good enough to want you back. Isn't that preferable to being a public charge?"

"I ain't-a goin' back," said the old woman vehemently.

The investigator was very exasperated. "Why, Mrs. Mason?" she asked gently.

"That's an ungodly woman," the old lady snapped. "And I'm God-fearin'. 'Tain't no room in one house for God and the devil. I'm too near the grave to be servin' two masters."

To the young investigator this was evasion by superstitious mutterings.

"You don't make yourself very clear, Mrs. Mason. Surely Mrs. Coleman didn't interfere with your religious convictions. You left her home the night after her daughter's child was born dead. Until then, apparently, you had no religious scruples."

The old woman looked at the investigator wearily. Then her head sank forward on her breast.

"That child warn't born dead."

The investigator said impatiently, "But surely the hospital—?"

"'T'warnt born in no hospital."

"But the doctor—?"

"Little sly man. Looked like he'd cut his own throat for a dollar."

"Was the child deformed?" the investigator asked helplessly.

"Hit was a beautiful baby," said the old woman bitterly.

"Why, no one would destroy a healthy child," the investigator cried indignantly. "Mrs. Coleman hopes her daughter will have more children." She paused, then asked anxiously, "Her daughter is really married, isn't she? I mean, the baby wasn't—illegitimate?"

"It's ma and pa were married down home. A church weddin'. They went to school together. They was all right till they come up N'th. Then *she* started workin' on 'em. Old ways wasn't good enough for her."

The investigator looked at her watch. It was nearly five. This last speech had been rambling gossip. Here was an old woman clearly disoriented in her northern transplanting. Her position as mammy made her part of the family. Evidently she felt that gave her a matriarchal right to arbitrate its destinies. Her small grievances against Mrs. Coleman had magnified themselves in her mind until she could make this illogical accusation of infanticide as compensation for her homesickness for the folkways of the South. Her move to Harlem bore this out. To explain her reason for establishing a separate residence, she had told a fantastic story that could not be checked, and would not be recorded, unless the welfare office was prepared to face a libel suit.

"Mrs. Mason," said the investigator, "please listen carefully. Mrs. Coleman has told me that you are not only wanted but very much needed in her home. There you will be given food and shelter in return for small services. Please understand that I sympathize with your—imaginings, but you cannot remain here without public assistance, and I cannot recommend to my superiors that public assistance be given you."

The old woman, who had listened worriedly, now said blankly, "You mean I ain't a-gonna get it?"

"No, Mrs. Mason, I'm sorry. And now it's ten to five. I'll be glad to help you pack your things, and put you in a taxi."

The old woman looked helplessly around the room as if seeking a hiding place. Then she looked back at the investigator, her mouth trembling.

"You're my own people, child. Can' you fix up a story for them white folks at the relief, so's I could get to stay here where it's nice?"

"That would be collusion, Mrs. Mason. And that would cost me my job."

The investigator rose. She was going to pack the old woman's things herself. She was heartily sick of her contrariness, and determined to see her settled once and for all.

"Now where is your bag?" she asked with forced cheerfulness. "First I'll empty these bureau drawers." She began to do so, laying things neatly on the bed. "Mrs. Coleman's daughter will be so glad to see you. She's very ill, and needs your nursing."

The old woman showed no interest. Her head had sunk forward on her breast again. She said listlessly, "Let her ma finish what she started. I won't have no time for nursin'. I'll be down on my knees rasslin' with the devil. I done tol' you the devil's done eased out God in that house."

The investigator nodded indulgently, and picked up a framed photograph that was lying face down in the drawer. She turned it over and involuntarily smiled at the smiling child in old-fashioned dress.

"This little girl," she said, "it's Mrs. Coleman, isn't it?"

"The old woman did not look up. Her voice was still listless.

"That *was* my daughter."

The investigator dropped the photograph on the bed as if it were a hot coal. Blindly she went back to the bureau, gathered up the rest of the things, and dumped them over the photograph.

She was a young investigator, and it was two minutes to five. Her job was to give or withhold relief. That was all.

"Mrs. Mason," she said, "please, please understand. This is my job."

The old woman gave no sign of having heard.

From *Opportunity: Journal of Negro Life*, October 1940

# PLUTO

PROMINENT ON MY bookcase stands a collapsible wooden image of the long-eared, sad-eyed hound known as Pluto, and immortalized by Mr. Walt Disney. There is no child, and almost never an adult, who does not, upon entering my house, immediately pick Pluto up, pull the strings that make him flop, and play happily for at least five minutes or at most to the end of the visit.

Today though, a child came to my house who did not run straightaway to Pluto. Maybe it was because he was a hungry child. And when is a child not a child? When he's hungry. This one had hollows under his eyes, and his body was too thin, and his clothing was not much comfort against the wind.

My apartment house has a prosperous exterior. Several times a week somebody comes to your door with a hard luck story. Generally it's a man, and so because I'm a woman, I simply say I'm sorry through a crack in the door, and shut the door quickly. In New York you have to be on the lookout for stick-up men.

But today it was a woman who answered my "Who is it?" There was something about her plaintive, "Me, lady," that made me open the door wider than I usually do when the voice is unknown.

I saw them both then, the thin little black boy and the thin black woman, both staring anxiously, and neither looking as if they had the strength or will to harm the most helpless female.

"Yes?" I said.

The woman swallowed hard and said, "Could you give me a quarter, missus, to buy something to eat for the boy?"

"Why aren't you on relief?" I asked suspiciously, although in my heart I was disarmed by her southern accent.

"They said I'd get a check next week," she said helpfully. "They was nice to me," she added.

My neighbor opened her door. She was smartly dressed. Her little boy ran across the hall and stared up at the ill-clad child. I was ashamed of all of us. "Come inside," I said coldly.

The boy and his mother entered and stood awkwardly in the center of my floor, the boy clinging to his mother's hand as if my sunny room were a dungeon.

"Sit down," I said.

They sat down together on the couch and Pluto was plainly visible. I saw the little boy look at it, and then he looked at me.

For a moment I started to urge him to pick it up and play with it. But then I remembered he had come begging for bread and I could not offer him a toy.

The boy's grave eyes turned back to Pluto. I wanted him to get up and go to it. It made me mad that he recognized the place of his poverty. And then I remembered again that he had come for a quarter and not for a plaything.

I didn't have a quarter to spare. I had only sufficient carfare until payday.

"I don't have a penny in the house," I lied. "But I'll be glad to give you something to eat. You like bacon and eggs?"

"Yes, missus," she said, and then reluctantly, "But I hates to put you to that bother."

"Not at all," I said shortly, because it was a bother. She had interrupted me in the middle of an excellent story. It was about poor people, too; a good proletarian short story.

I banged about the kitchenette, and after awhile the living room was fragrant with steaming coffee and sizzling bacon. I found some cold potatoes and fried them. I sliced my last tomato. I piled some slices of bread on a plate and then I felt guilty and toasted them.

All the while I was humming to myself because I did not want that woman to tell me her story. I could have told it to her myself. It would be no different from a hundred others.

It wasn't I could not hum at the table. I spooned a cup of coffee while they ate. Inevitably, the woman in return for the meal told me the facts that led up to it.

Widowed when the boy was a baby, knocking about with him from pillar to post, coming North so that he could go to a northern school, sleeping-in and sleeping-out for a string of slave-driving tyrants, farming the boy out to one indifferent slattern after another, never earning much, never saving anything, keeping body and soul together through sheer determination to survive. Now two weeks out of the hospital after a major operation, she was still too frail for domestic work, and her cousin by marriage, who was on relief, was letting her sleep in the living-room and forage for food as best as she could. The slattern who had been keeping the boy gave him back to her yesterday. She had put him to bed without any supper.

She had brought him out this morning without any breakfast. She was on her way to the relief people now to ask them if they could hurry. As for herself, she could wait, but a boy gets hungry.

The boy had already eaten more than his share of the platter, and was draining his second cup of diluted coffee. He had not said a word. He had simply looked from his mother to me during his intervals of swallowing, throughout her drab recital. It was not surprising that what she was saying evoked no response in him. He knew all about it. It was as much his life as it was hers. His life in fact was harder, for there was no way for him to know with certainty that she would come once weekly to see him, or that the slattern who beat and neglected him would be replaced by one who only neglected him.

They finished their meal, or rather the platter was clean and the coffee pot empty. Light had come into the woman's face, and the boy did not look quite so much like a wizened old man.

I got up, and the woman understood the signal. She jumped up and thanked me profusely. She prodded the boy. He did not speak, but he smiled, and suddenly he looked seven and no longer an undersized seventy.

I made a package of the odds and ends in my icebox, and after a little struggle with myself, slipped my half-dollar into the woman's hand. I could borrow carfare from a friend. Obviously she could not.

I led them to the door, but the boy broke away and ran across the room to Pluto and lovingly touched him. Pluto fell over and the boy laughed aloud. He gave him a final affectionate pat, and trotted back to his mother. He looked up at her with a face full of eager confidence.

He pronounced solemnly, "I'm gonna ask Sandy for one of them dawgs."

She looked at me almost apologetically. "He believes in Sandy Claus," she said. She hurried on proudly, defensively, "He ain't failed him yet."

"That's fine," I said and shut the door. I could hear them going down the hall, and the boy was talking volubly. I guess he was telling his mother what else he was going to ask "Sandy" for.

For a moment I wanted to believe that I had been taken in, for I am perhaps the poorest tenant in my fine apartment house. I live on the fifth floor in a tiny rear apartment, and why should she have come first to me. And then I realized that in all probability she had not.

I turned back into my room and crossed the floor to put Pluto back on his feet. It has become an automatic act when my door closes after a visitor.

The sad-eyed hound looked up at me, and his tail drooped wistfully. He did not look funny, and I did not want to laugh at him, and he is supposed to make you laugh.

I moved away and cleared the table. I was thinking that it is not right to take a child's joy away and give him hunger. I was thinking that a child's faith is too fine and precious for the dump heap of poverty. I was thinking that bread should not be bigger than a boy.

I thought about those things a lot.

228 West 22nd Street, New York City
WPA Federal Writers' Project
November 28, 1938

## THE HOUSE ACROSS THE WAY

MISS SNOWE saw her mother decently interred, came home from the funeral, locked her front door, took off her black, put on a house dress and easy shoes, sat down at the kitchen table, and wept.

They were tears of relief, and release, and hope. Miss Snowe was thirty-five. She had been her mother's handmaiden all her life. Her mother had been a semi-invalid ever since Miss Snowe's birth. The doctor had predicted she would live to be ninety. Now she was dead at sixty-five, and Miss Snowe's martyrdom was at an end. She was an old maid, but she was not an old woman.

Miss Snowe had a neighbor named Marbury Minton who lived in a run-down house across the way. To her he was a very romantic figure. He was shabby, and Miss Snowe had never had a seam out of place. His breath smelled of whiskey, and Miss Snowe had never tasted anything stronger than communion wine. He had a ruined life, and Miss Snowe had had no life at all.

Two years ago Marbury had come to live in the long vacant house of his grandfather, where he had spent the summers of his boyhood. He did not visit anybody, and nobody visited him. He had a gaunt black dog, and he took it for walks, and the dog looked hungry all the time.

Marbury was drinking himself to death, and he did not spend much money on food. He did not have much money to spend. He lived on a spasmodic subsidy from his ex-wife.

Marbury had once been married to a girl with a hidden thrush in her throat. Sometimes she sang softly to their child, and the sweetness was incomparable. Then a dark man entered her life, a dark man who waved a stick at a band. The thrush beat its wings to find a way out. It came out one night in a cocktail lounge, and soared to the ceiling, and enraptured the room. The dark man listened and muted his band, and began to make love with his brasses and strings. In no time at all he had the bird eating out of his hand. And that was the end of the happy life of Marbury Minton.

His wife ran away and took the child, and the child died. Marbury divorced his wife, and his denunciation of her kind in court blistered the ears of the listening women and broke the gavel of the judge. Marbury took to drink, and drank himself out of his newspaper job. One day he poured himself onto a train. He seesawed off when it reached the town where there was a house he could live in rent-free while he drank up his last dollar. A black mongrel puppy met him at the station. She was a dispossessed female dog. Marbury looked into the faithful eyes, and put her in his pocket.

Miss Snowe and Marbury spoke in passing, and Miss Snowe's maiden heart would burn in her breast. She was in love with Marbury. She had been in love with him since her first sight of him. He walked boldly in beauty. His features were chiseled out of cold marble. His angry blue eyes were fringed with black lashes. His hair was a mass of uncombed blond curls in which the silver of his forty-odd years vanished without a trace. His too lean body was like a boy's. He was Apollo, and Miss Snowe was blinded by the sun.

Miss Snowe dried her eyes. She felt calm and resolute. She rose, and got a large hamper from the pantry, and carried it to the refrigerator, which was crammed with covered dishes sent over by kindly neighbors. Quickly and deftly she filled the hamper, and spread one of her late mother's best linen napkins over the top. She slipped into her sweater and left the house.

She mounted Marbury's sagging back steps, as was the country custom, and rapped at the kitchen door. The dog gave an answering bark. Miss Snowe heard the sound of running feet. Then the barking stopped. The dog began to sniff along the lintel, and caught the scent of meat, and whimpered softly.

Presently the curtainless windows became diffused with soft lamplight. The door was flung open, and Marbury straddled the night. The smell of stale liquor fouled the sweet air.

"May I come in?" said Miss Snowe.

Marbury stared at her. The dog stared, too. Marbury's eyes were angry, but the dog's eyes were soft and pleading. Miss Snowe had never had a pet. She stooped to stroke the mangy fur, and did not straighten up at once, because she did not want to raise her head until Marbury gave her an answer.

Marbury slapped the side of his face. "You're letting the mosquitoes in," he said unkindly. "Come in so I can shut the door."

She sidled past him and held out the hamper. "It's food left over from the funeral," she said hurriedly. "There was so much of it, and I'd never be able to eat half of it. You being alone, and nobody to fix for you, and men not liking to fix for themselves, I thought I'd bring it over. It isn't charity or anything like that. It's just one neighbor to another. I was turning around in my kitchen, and I thought, Mr. Minton lives all alone, with nobody to fix for him—"

She covered her repetition with a little embarrassed cough, and looked about the room for a place to put the hamper. The greasy sink and grimy table were piled with soiled dishes. Empty liquor bottles had been hurled into every dusty corner. The rotting walls were streaked with wood smoke. The rat holes on the windside of the kitchen were insecurely stuffed with wadded paper to keep out the autumn chill. The coal hod was filled with empty cans. There was no sign of food anywhere.

Marbury swept some dirty underwear off a sagging chair. "You can sit down or set the basket down. Suit yourself," he said.

Miss Snowe sat down and held the heavy hamper on her lap. She was not repelled by anything she saw. This was the sort of house she had expected Marbury to keep. In her daydreams she had pictured this room and her hands transforming it.

The dog came and sat down beside Miss Snowe. Her tail thudded softly on the floor, saliva dripped from her open mouth, and her anguished eyes stared fixedly. Miss Snowe shrank back. The jagged teeth and trembling body frightened her.

"Nice dog," she said helplessly. "Now go away."

The dog did not move, but her eyes filled with tears, and her tail thumped slower and slower. She flung up her head and howled.

"Why do you torture her?" said Marbury savagely. "For God's sake give her what you've got in that basket."

Miss Snowe tingled nervously and ducked her head as if to ward off Marbury's violence. She jerked, the hamper open and picked up the first dish that met her touch, and held it out to him.

He uttered an angry snort and uncovered it. It was a sizable meat pie, aromatic with spice and onion. The dog flattened her body on the floor and crawled to her master. "All right, Blackie," Marbury said softly, and set the dish between her paws.

Miss Snowe's first emotion was horror. She did not believe in feeding a dog on a plate that came from a china closet.

Then her horror gave way to great pity. For the dog was eating with ferocious intensity. In her eagerness she could not wait to raise herself to her full height. Her legs looked boneless in their awkward sprawl. Her tail curled under her belly, her ears lay flat against her long head. The sound of her fierce mastication filled the room.

"She's starved," Miss Snowe said involuntarily.

Marbury said sullenly, "She hasn't eaten for two days."

"And you," said Miss Snowe, her eyes blinking rapidly, "what about you?"

He answered wryly, "I haven't had a drink for two days either."

"Such a thing to say with an empty stomach," Miss Snowe cried impatiently, forgetting to be afraid of him in her heartbreak over his hunger. "You need a meal more than that wicked stuff. Oh, men are such babies by themselves."

Marbury laughed. He flung back his head and sounds came out that were harsh and terrible and unreal. Miss Snowe's spine prickled. The dog stopped nosing the empty plate to look at her master. Her eyes were limpid with love. She went to him and licked his hand.

Marbury stopped laughing. He thrust his hands into his pockets, and Miss Snowe saw the bulge of his angry fists. His eyes were hot with hate.

"Do we have to hear a lecture for a plate of scraps? Did we ask for your maudlin sympathy? Get out and leave us to live how we choose."

He thrust the dog aside with his foot, and took two long strides to Miss Snowe. He glared down at her, and her clean smell came up to him, and he saw the softness of her. There was about her the mark of the maiden, the purity of brow and breast, the eyes that filled easily, the shamed cheeks, the childish curve of the mouth.

The anger left Marbury, and he was empty, and there was nothing to sustain him. The two-day dryness had weakened his defenses. Tiredness swept over him, roaring in his ears, rocking him off his feet, plunging him headlong into oblivion.

He lay at Miss Snowe's curled toes. His lashes were long on his pale cheeks, and the damp curls fringed his forehead. The dog lay beside him and licked his face. Her sad eyes pleaded with Miss Snowe.

Miss Snowe was not afraid anymore. She set her basket on the floor and slipped to her knees. Her hands were capable and strong and steady as she rolled Marbury over on his back, and stripped off her sweater to make a pillow for his head.

She felt almost happy. She knew now that she had come in answer to Marbury's need of her. It was right for her to be here. Providence had sent her.

Marbury lay in delirium for three days. On the fourth day he roused, saw a clean curtain at his window, blinked in bewilderment, and fell into quiet slumber. In the afternoon he waked, called weakly for Blackie, and saw her race into the room, with her tail like a banner, her coat clean and brushed, and her soft, shining eyes free of hunger.

Miss Snowe entered soon after, carrying a tray. She gave Marbury a radiant smile. She had only slept in snatches for the past three nights on a pallet she had made in a corner of the room, but she felt strong and alive. She had bathed Marbury, and held his hot hand, and listened to words she had not known the meaning of, and none of it had seemed unnatural.

Her own house across the way seemed strange to her now. There she had waited for a woman to die. Here she was waiting for a man to get well.

"Well, how's my patient this morning?" Miss Snowe said brightly.

Marbury stared at her, but he was still too weak for much emotion. He could not urge himself to anger.

"Have I been ill?" he asked. The bed was immaculate, his pajamas were clean and patched, the walls and carpetless floor had been washed.

"Yes, but now you're getting well. The doctor said you've been drinking too much and not eating enough." She placed the tray on the side of the bed and settled himself beside it. She picked up a spoon and said briskly, "I promised him I'd take care of the eating part."

He looked at her quizzically. "Why have you nursed me and fattened my dog? What possible use could we be to you, fat or lean, sick or well?"

"We are neighbors," she said stubbornly. She filled the spoon, and he ate obediently. He tried to speak, but the spoon clicked regularly against his teeth.

Presently his belly felt warm and full, and his mind could focus again. He pushed the spoon away.

"What is the price you have put on our heads, old maid?"

She drew a sharp breath and stared at a spot above the bed. She would not temporize. She had lived with Marbury for three days and nights in an intimacy hardly less than a wife's.

"I would like to get married," she said.

He shut his eyes wearily. "Why?"

"I'm thirty-five, but I'm not old inside. I've never stopped dreaming a young girl's dreams. I've never stopped wanting a home and a husband."

He opened one angry eye, then shut it against the exaltation in her face. He said harshly, "There are men who love women. I'm not one of them. I trust no female but my dog."

"I know what you've suffered," she said patiently. "But I'll make it up to you. I'm not like your wife. She was pretty and talented. I'm just plain folks. I'll never leave you."

"I hate human beings," Marbury said tiredly, brushing his hand across his closed eyes. "My world is no wider than my dog's devotion."

His hand found Blackie's head and caressed it. He felt her body quiver with emotion and heard the hard gulping in her throat. Her tongue licked furiously at the air, then her head twisted away from his hand, and the flame of her love ran up and down his arm.

She would miss Miss Snowe. Her belly would shrink again, her nose would be pinched and dry again, and the hunger would ride in her eyes. And she would not complain. She would not even let him see her glance toward her empty dish. Surely hers was a loyalty that deserved its reward on earth.

He opened his eyes and stared at Miss Snowe, so that she would see the hatred in him, and not be deceived, and not be expectant. But Miss Snowe could not see for the love that blinded her.

"I will marry you," Marbury said.

Miss Snowe and Marbury Minton had a bedside wedding. Miss Snowe's late mother furnished the ring. The minister's disapproving wife and her wide-eyed daughter were witnesses. Miss Snowe softly glowed in her mourning black and did not feel indecent. It would have been hypocritical to postpone the wedding in pretense that her longing was for the dead.

In the days that followed Marbury grew well enough to dress himself and sit up. He kept to his room, and spoke only when spoken to, giving incomplete and uncivil answers. The new Mrs. Minton was patience itself. She knew from the long years with her invalid mother that it was a natural thing for a convalescent to be cross.

She busied herself about the house, and scoured and scrubbed everything, but she worked no miracles. Her pride would not let her. She would neither suggest to Marbury that he move into her house or take her inheritance and renovate his. She was taking care of current needs, but that was no more than a wife should do when the wage-earner was ill. She was stubbornly confident that her love would transform her husband into a man who would work for his wife.

Mrs. Minton was still sleeping on a pallet in a corner of Marbury's room. The house had no other bed but his. The junkman and Marbury were familiar acquaintances. Blackie slept at the foot of the bed. Mrs. Minton had tried to move her during the nights of Marbury's delirium, and Blackie had bared her teeth.

To Mrs. Minton this was a minor problem that would resolve itself as soon as Marbury was completely recovered. Then she would sleep by her husband's side, and Blackie would sleep by the stove in the kitchen. However Marbury felt about women, however he felt about his dog, when he returned to vigorous health, he would make the discovery for himself that each had a place in a man's life.

The day that Mrs. Minton planned to surprise her husband with his first meal downstairs, and had bought a fine dinner to tempt his indifferent appetite, the postman brought a letter for him. Mrs. Minton got it from the mailbox. She saw that the handwriting was a woman's, and held it up to the light. A money order was plainly visible.

She carried the letter up to Marbury. She saw his hands tremble a little as he took it from her. He did not look at it. He slipped it into his pocket, and ran his tongue across his lips.

A thread of fear shuttled through her mind. She tried to speak lightly. "Aren't you going to open it and see who it's from?"

He stared at her until her cheeks flamed and her eyes were burning with tears of embarrassment. Then he said evenly, "It's conscience money from my dead child's mother. I never open it until I'm drunk. I'm always afraid I'll tear it up if I open it when I'm sober."

The tears spilled down her cheeks. "Marbury, send it back to her. Tell her you're married to me. Tell her you don't hate her anymore. Tell her you're starting life over again."

"Tell who?" said Marbury in a voice choked with loathing. "There is no woman with whom I want contact. Some creature somewhere keeps me in whiskey. You are the creature who feeds my dog."

She knew this was sickness spilling out of him. She must meet these moods with forbearance and understanding. This was the violent storm of their mating. After this would come the enduring peace.

She said with desperate urging. "You have suffered enough for her sin. Let my love heal the sores."

He put his hands to his eyes. He could not bear her stark devotion. She was a woman who stripped herself, and there was no lewdness in her. There was nothing at which to mock. He shut his eyes to the naked look that repelled him with its purity.

"Get out," he said between his stiff lips, and he shook with the fever of his anger at her indestructibility.

She slipped out quietly and went back to the kitchen to finish her preparations for dinner. She held to the hope that Marbury was wrestling with his soul. She waited for him to come and show her the torn shreds of the letter.

She heard him descend the stairs, with Blackie trailing him. She breathed very hard and sent a little prayer to heaven. But Marbury's footsteps went the other way, and the front door slammed.

She stood irresolutely. She wanted to run after him, and her fingers felt for her apron strings, then slid away. She saw him thrusting her aside to the tight-lipped satisfaction of the townspeople. Her breath expelled in a long sigh.

Blackie came into the kitchen. She advanced to her empty plate, sniffed at it, gave her mistress a mildly disappointed glance, side-stepped the out-stretched hand, and walked out of the room. In a moment or two Mrs. Minton heard the sigh of Marbury's bedsprings.

Quiet closed in on the house, and Mrs. Minton settled down at the parlor window to wait. She knew that a long dryness was in her husband. She thought it made sense to admit that fact and prepare herself for his home-coming. With Marbury she would take the long view. She would be an under-standing wife.

Day passed, and dusk fell, and Mrs. Minton lighted the parlor lamp. The room filled with frightening shadows. Upstairs the dog had not stirred. She was used to the long wait. She did not want food or female contact. All of her senses strained to separate the sounds outside and isolate the footstep of her master.

The town clock struck ten. Mrs. Minton was stiff with sitting still and her eyes ached from staring out into the darkened street. The lamp was burning low, and the shadows were stretching into shapes that were like mute monsters weaving vile words with their waving stump.

Mrs. Minton shrank in her chair, then gave herself a reproving shake. She was silly to sit here imagining things. She had not eaten since breakfast. She felt light as air and her head was floating away from her. A cup of tea would make the earth solid again.

She rose and crossed the room. The floor boards creaked, and Blackie growled softly at the alien sound that cut across her listening. Mrs. Minton paused. For a moment she wondered if the dog had forgotten that she was her mistress. Her heart thumped a little as she pictured her tearing down the stairs in search of a prowler.

Then she shook herself vigorously again. She was making the dog a monster, too. She marched out of the room, with Blackie's low growl accompanying her. The blackness at the rear of the house lay in thick folds on her nervous flesh. Mrs. Minton felt for the door jamb, and reached in her apron pocket for a match.

She stooped and struck it on the floor, reluctant to feel her way to the sandpaper she had tacked beside the stove. The match flared brightly, and a long gray rat streaked across the room.

Mrs. Minton screamed and jerked herself upright. The match winked briefly and sizzled out. The blackness scooped her up in a bag and tied a string at the top. She fought wildly, bumping along the wall, sobbing and stumbling toward the front of the house.

Blackie was barking furiously. The tortured scream, the bumping sounds, the frantic breathing frightened and infuriated her. She sprang from the bed and raced for the stairs, her fear and fury bursting from her throat like sharp explosives.

They flung Mrs. Minton against the front door, and she found herself standing outside on the stoop just as the dog lunged against the barrier between them.

Mrs. Minton leaned against the locked door and put her apron up to her eyes and cried. The monsters were secured behind her, and she was alive.

The dog had her scent now, and she was not barking, but a whine whistled softly through her nose. The familiar clean smell of her mistress was mixed with the ugly exudation of her horror, and the dog was unsure of her now. Here was a woman to keep at a distance. There was no knowing when she would turn from friend into enemy. She must watch this woman warily.

Mrs. Minton, hearing the hot breath snorting through the inquiring nose, knew that she must live with her fear of the dog. Behind the liquid eyes were the red sparks of savagery, the licking tongue hid the jagged teeth, the outstretched paw concealed the claws.

Why was she sitting here on this rotting stoop? Why was this hovel home? Was this what love was, this degradation of self, this shameless acceptance of squalor, this waiting to put a drunkard to bed, this mothering of a man's dog.

If this was love, Mrs. Minton decided, with a little bitter laugh at herself, then love was blind and dumb.

She wiped her eyes and stared at her house across the way. There were no crumbling places in its plastered walls. A finger's touch would light a room evenly, leaving no macabre shapes in shadowy corners. No dog possessed the premises.

She started slowly down the steps, vaguely aware that a neighbor's car was slowing down at the curb. A man's pale face peered out at her.

"That you, Mrs. Minton? The hospital just telephoned me to try to reach you. Your husband's been taken with a stroke. I'll drive you there."

Marbury came home from the hospital in an ambulance and was carried upstairs on a stretcher and put between the cool clean sheets of his bed, from which he would never rise again. Blackie leaped to its foot and lay with her loving head on his useless legs and licked his twisted hand.

Marbury's wife bent over him to smooth his pillow, and Marbury turned the flawless side of his face away and flaunted the ugliness of the other side. He was bound to this woman by his helplessness, but she would see his hatred of the female touch.

Mrs. Minton went downstairs with the ambulance men. She stood in the open door and watched them go.

The house across the way smiled in the morning sun. The flagstone walk and wide white porch led to the austere peace inside.

Mrs. Minton stifled a sob, and shut the door, and put on the bedside face she had worn for her mother.

Circa 1945

# MRS. MARLOWE

WHEN MR. MARLOWE died, Mrs. Marlowe retired Bella Mason from her services with a very decent pension, gave notice to the other servants, put her house in the hands of an agent and booked a passage to Europe.

She was still a beautiful woman at sixty, with much of the spirit that had been hers in the years when her youth was a match for it. But at sixty the flesh knows its limitations, and the ironic heart had no expectations.

Bella's niece, Nancy, received her aunt's letter, asking if Nancy had room for her, and read it aloud to her husband, Hank. She finished with a sigh of pity.

"Poor Aunt Bella, over forty years working for Mrs. Marlowe, and now she's been put out to pasture."

"Well," Hank asked reasonably, "what would you want Mrs. Marlowe to do?"

"Give Aunt Bella back the forty years Aunt Bella gave her. She could use them now, now that Mrs. Marlowe is through with them. She could use them to get married in, and raise a family in, for the time you need a family most, when you're old and nobody wants you."

Hank said mildly, "Well, at least your Aunt Bella can pay her own way. If you don't want her, there'll be somebody who will."

"Hank, you sound like Mrs. Marlowe. Like that pension could right the wrong. Of course, I want Aunt Bella. I want to make it up to her for all the years she spent on the fringe of the Marlowe family. I want her to feel she's part and parcel of ours."

That night Nancy wrote Aunt Bella a long and affectionate letter of welcome. In a few days Aunt Bella wired her date of departure.

She arrived with a suitcase and a small trunk, which held a few mementoes of the past.

She was a wren of a woman, whose years made a comfortable padding on her small boned body. Looking at her roundness and the trace of prettiness that lingered in her eyes and mouth, Nancy perceived that Aunt Bella had not been designed for a barren life.

During the first two weeks of her induction into the family fold, Aunt Bella came when she was called, she did what she was asked, she spoke whenever directly addressed. Otherwise she quietly kept to her room. She was like a good guest who in no way disturbed the daily routine of her hostess.

"But she's not a guest," Nancy said worriedly to Hank. "She's my aunt. It's true we never saw enough of each other to be intimate. But it's time we tried. When I start a conversation with Aunt Bella, it always dies. I want Aunt Bella to be happy here. But the way she keeps her thoughts to herself, I can't tell."

"It's a lot to ask the old to be happy," Hank said soberly. "The most you can hope for is that they're content. She's probably homesick for Mrs. Marlowe. Give her time to get over it."

"Homesick for Mrs. Marlowe," Nancy protested scornfully. "What did she and Mrs. Marlowe have in common?"

"They had the habit of living together. They knew each other's getting up and going to bed. When you're over sixty, you miss what you're used to. Even if it's just winding a clock, you miss that clock if it's taken away. It leaves an empty place in your day."

"Exactly," said Nancy triumphantly. "That's what I said from the first. "Mrs. Marlowe took away everything that Aunt Bella had taken for granted for forty years. She wiped away all the hours of Aunt Bella's day. But I disagree that Aunt Bella sits there missing her. I think she sits there hating her."

The following day Nancy decided to test her theory. If she could encourage Aunt Bella to talk about Mrs. Marlowe, the anger would come out of her, and the peace that the old cannot live without would take its place. The opening came with the postman's ring. In the mail was a letter with a foreign postmark. Nancy carried it upstairs to Aunt Bella, and wandered around the room while Aunt Bella read it.

"Was it a nice letter, Aunt Bella?" she asked finally.

"Was more a note," Aunt Bella answered politely.

"What did she have to say?"

"Just asked how I was, and said how she was. She never was a letter writer. Hated to sit still."

Nancy looked at Aunt Bella in her chair by the window with her day begun and already over for all that Aunt Bella would enter into it.

"You don't have to sit still either. You don't have to take a back seat. You've forgotten more than I'll ever know about housekeeping. Any time you want to take over, I'll be glad to learn."

Aunt Bella smiled. "You're kind and impulsive. You think I'm not happy here in my room. But you'll get used to my staying put as you never could get used to my butting in."

"But you're living a half life, while Mrs. Marlowe is still living life to the full. It's not fair!"

Aunt Bella studied Nancy's face.

"Child, would you feel easier in your mind about me if you knew that Mrs. Marlowe's life wasn't too different from mine?"

"With her husband, her children, her lovely home? Oh, Aunt Bella! Don't ask me to pity her."

Aunt Bella said in a harsh, strong voice, "Don't pity me either. I made my own bed. I ask for us both, Mrs. Marlowe and me, only your understanding."

Nancy sank down on the edge of Aunt Bella's bed. She felt frightened, as if she had thrown a small stone in a quiet pool and started a vortex seething and rolling.

Aunt Bella stared out of the window, seeing the panorama of the past unroll. Her voice was low now and toneless.

"I started in as downstairs maid for the Marlowes, just a girl with nothing much on my mind but falling in love and getting married. Then after I'd been with the Marlowes for a while, I hoped I'd meet a man who was just like Mr. Marlowe. I did meet men from time to time, but I never seemed to fancy them. The years were going by. I was made housekeeper. And I couldn't seem to meet a man I wanted to give up my job for."

Nancy said softly, "Aunt Bella, I think I know why."

"Mrs. Marlowe knew, too, before I did. She knew it the day they telephoned her that her husband had been killed in a train crash. I went to pieces worse than she did. She told me to go to my room and lie down, and she said it kind.

"Later that day they telephoned her that he was one of the survivors. She came to my room, and looked at my face full of tears and telling, and she said, Theo is alive. Not Mr. Marlowe, like always, but Theo, her special name for him. Then she said, Bella, go before your heart breaks.

"And I said, Mrs. Marlowe, it would break to go. If I stay, I'll stay in my place. If I go, I don't know what wildness might tempt me to return, what foolish words I might put to paper, what shame and sorrow I might bring myself. If I stay, I promise you he'll never know. She gave me a strange look, almost wistful. She said, 'I've never been in love like that. I married Mr. Marlowe because he loved me'."

Mrs. Marlowe had never been more than a name to Nancy, a name synonymous with money and position. The hardness her heart had felt for her slowly dissolved. The understanding Aunt Bella had asked for her began to take its place.

"Aunt Bella, did Mrs. Marlowe ever fall in love like that?"

"Yes," said Aunt Bella bleakly. "The man she fell in love with was the kind of man who was made for her. At first I couldn't see what she saw in him. He was so different from Mr. Marlowe. He was the leader of a band, unlike anyone she'd ever known.

"We were at the summer place with Mr. Marlowe just coming down weekends. This man was playing at the country club. He brought out the joy I didn't know was in her. He made her look as I had never seen her look before. She was born for him, born for his kind of life, a gypsy's life of freedom and wandering. And I knew that before summer ended she would ask Mr. Marlowe for a divorce."

Nancy knew that Mrs. Marlowe had never changed names or husbands. "He refused?"

Aunt Bella's voice was so low that Nancy had to strain to hear. "I knew that if she left Mr. Marlowe, their home would be broken up, and my life with them would be over.

"And so I went to the music maker. I told him that Mr. Marlowe was powerful enough to ruin him. That if he went on seeing Mr. Marlowe's wife, he would never get another job anywhere. And I asked him what he could give Mrs. Marlowe in exchange for what he would take her away from."

Nancy asked almost reluctantly, "What did he do, Aunt Bella?"

"That weekend he married the girl who sang with his band."

Involuntarily Nancy said, "Oh, poor Mrs. Marlowe."

"Did I do wrong?" Aunt Bella said suddenly, in the same strong, harsh voice as before. "I sit here and ask myself over and over, did I do wrong?"

"I don't know," said Nancy. She wanted to cry. "I don't know."

Circa 1950

# THE STAIRS

THE GRANDMOTHER stood on the front porch, feeling summer's softness on her face. It was good to be back in the country, in her own cottage, after so many months of being shut up in a city flat.

This was the morning the carpenter was coming to fix the porch steps. All of them were weak, and some of them were wobbly. They were treacherous to the old. The grandmother's bones were growing too brittle to chance a fall.

A neighbor's dog trotted up the road to pay her respects, in the manner of country dogs, who make no unkind distinction between themselves and people.

"Good morning, Brownie," the grandmother said. "You couldn't ask for a better one. But I haven't time to entertain you. I'm expecting Mr. Hathaway. Look, there's his truck coming now. You come back later. I may have a bone."

The dog had listened intelligently, understanding all the important words like "come back" and "bone." He grinned, wagged his tail agreeably and ambled off, not flustering her by coming up for a pat, knowing by animal instinct that she was too old to be confused by dogs and trucks dividing her attention.

Mr. Hathaway braked his little truck, scrambled down, and smiled at the grandmother. He was seasoned with living and daily labor. A countryman who had had a long spell in the city, with a sizable business, a wife who wore furs, and a house with all the conveniences. When they were gone, the wife deceased, the business sold because there was no one for whom to buy furs, and the house sold, too, because it was too big for a widower, he came back to where his roots were.

He had money in the bank, but he could not live out all his days on money alone. So he worked at his trade, working without a helper, because a younger man beside him made him do foolish, reckless things, like climbing a ladder too fast, making too long a reach from a scaffold, carrying too many things at once, just to prove that he still had more go than a young whippersnapper.

"Mornin', Mrs. Edwards," he said, "I'm here."

"I see you are," she said brightly, with no attempt at sarcasm. "Couldn't ask for a better day to start a job. But could I get you a cup of coffee before you start?"

It was a common courtesy. Everybody was on the same footing, dog and man, servant and those he served. Besides, Mrs. Edwards could trust Mr. Hathaway. He wouldn't add her cup of kindness to his working hour.

"Well, thank you. I'd like that fine."

"You come sit while I get it. Walk with care! Those steps have seen a lot of wear. So many children over so many summers have bumped up and down them with their bicycles and tricycles. But those days are gone now. I've already got a married granddaughter. And the rest of my grands are up in their teens. Old enough to find the country too quiet. They like to go where it's lively. They don't stay children forever. It isn't fair to wish they could." She gave herself a little shake. "Well that's not getting the coffee. I'll be back soon."

She was back quite too soon with coffee and buns on a tray. She settled the tray on the rail and dispensed her hospitality.

"My," said Mr. Hathaway, after a long satisfying swallow, "there's nothing beats a good cup of coffee except the company of a good soul."

"Well," said Mrs. Edwards, "I always say if we haven't got time to take time with each other, we'll have plenty of time to be sorry."

Mr. Hathaway pondered this sage observation. "Say what you will, dog or cat, hunting or fishing, there's nothing the same as human talk."

Mrs. Edwards poured more coffee into his waiting cup and steered another sugared bun into his reaching hand. She sighed, not sadly, but routinely, as one who knew that the best was behind her.

"Every once in a while I think of the many echoes of children's voices. None of my family has been here for over five years. Oh, I see them through the winter. But summer's when I have the most hankering. I guess that's because in summer there's more beauty in the country than you can bear alone."

Mr. Hathaway nodded agreement. "There's no place like here for soaking in love for everything the eye takes in. I wouldn't change my boyhood for anybody's. All those years I was away, I always knew I was coming back. I always knew that a countryman must walk a dirt road before he dies."

Mrs. Edwards said softly, "A child who sees the heart of summer in growing things and greening things has a store of memories to last him through the lean years of his life."

A station wagon drove up the road and parked behind Mr. Hathaway's truck. A young blond mother poked her head out of the driver's window. Three little girls leaned forward from the rear seat to crowd their own fair heads around hers.

"Good morning Mrs. Edwards, Mr. Hathaway," the young mother called, and the children chorused after her. She felt some envy of the two old people. They were past life's harassments, and had only themselves to please. What bliss to look forward to, thought the young mother, my children grown, and my time my own.

"Won't you come up and have some coffee, dear?" Mrs. Edwards asked. She had already poured the last of it into Mr. Hathaway's cup, but you offered kindness anyway, and if it was accepted, you pretended it wasn't putting you to any trouble. "Maybe the children would like a cookie."

The little girls opened their eager mouths to answer, but their mother said firmly, "Thank you, but we only stopped to bring you your mail."

"I'll come get it," said Mrs. Edwards. She explained to Mr. Hathaway, "This dear child gets my mail every day. Time was I used to enjoy the walk to the post office, but now the way there and back gets longer every year."

"Let me," said Mr. Hathaway, rising. "I can save you those few steps anyway."

He got the letter, and everybody said good-by until everybody had given and received this gentle benediction. The young mother drove away, with her children's hands fluttering out of the window like banners waving in the breeze.

Mrs. Edwards thanked Mr. Hathaway, and made a great show of gathering up cups and trays, so that Mr. Hathaway would not take offense because she was going indoors to read her letter in private.

"Well, time to get started," Mr. Hathaway said, getting started. "Thank you for my repast."

Mrs. Edwards stood by the kitchen window and examined her letter. It was from her married granddaughter. The return address, the handwriting told her that much. But she couldn't imagine what Laurie had to say. Like all young people she never wrote unless there was a special reason.

But what could be special when it wasn't her birthday? Oh dear, was it trouble? Was somebody sick? If she had any sense, she'd open the letter and see.

She opened the letter and read it, read it twice to be sure her old eyes weren't fooling her. Tears wet her lashes. The miracle of life had begun in her granddaughter. Laurie was going to have a child.

The news was too good to keep to herself. She went to the front door. Mr. Hathaway was measuring and putting marks on paper. She really shouldn't interrupt him.

"Mr. Hathaway, I really shouldn't interrupt you, but I'll burst if I don't tell somebody. I'm going to be a great grandmother. Come March. And my granddaughter and the baby will spend next summer here, and many more. That's what her letter said. She wants her baby to have the happy times she still remembers. So make those steps solid, Mr. Hathaway. It might be a boy."

Mr. Hathaway was something of a practical man. "And it might be another boy after that. This porch could stand a few new boards. You walking ladylike over it is one thing, boys stomping over it another. You think about it, I'll quote you a fair price."

"You do what has to be done. I'll find the money. Right now I feel like everything's possible. Next summer you may see me pushing a baby buggy to the post office. A baby keeps you stepping. They don't give you time to feel old.

My granddaughter's only got two hands. Mine will make the four she has to have."

The stoop in her shoulders seemed to vanish. She felt strong and special and needed.

From the *New York Daily News*, December 11, 1961

*Chapter One*

JENNIE ELLIS was raking her backyard and surveying the return of spring with the swollen satisfaction of one who had been instrumental in accomplishing it. She felt no older than she had felt the spring before. She knew that Bea would say she looked no older. She was certain that she could return the compliment. But the same could never be said about Bit. There were a good many things in the world that wanted doing—Jennie raked vigorously to confirm this opinion—and if you were too old to do them, you were old enough to die.

She had drawn a magic circle around herself and her best friend, Bea. If her sister, Bit, were excluded, it was because Bit had let herself look her age. Jennie and Bea could pass for fifty—or so. Bit showed every day of her sixty-four years. But poor Bit had never been a beauty. And maybe it didn't matter how you looked when you were old if you hadn't been much to look at when you were young.

So Jennie Ellis discoursed with herself as she raked her back yard, knowing quite well that Bit was at the bedroom window watching, and not once looking up to smile. She had never liked old people, and she guessed it was too late to learn to like them now. Even if she and Bit were only three years apart.

A squirrel stopped running along the fence and stared at her. He looked very comical, sitting up straight, with his paws clasped over his heart, and his tail going six ways for Sunday. Jennie leaned on her rake and stared back at him.

"I suppose you think I look comical, too," she said. "That's because there's nobody here." She raised her voice so that Bit, who was looking, could listen, too, if she liked. "When Bea comes, I'll get dolled up. When Bea isn't here, I might as well be living by myself."

The squirrel scampered away. His conversational powers were less than Bit's. But before he leaped from the fence to the oak, he looked back at Jennie. He saw a rather tall woman of splendid build, whose easy movements suggested strength and vitality. Her costume was a navy blue sweater, shapeless with age, rusty with wear and sun, whose original buttons had been replaced from time to time with buttons that never quite matched in color or shape. Under it was a clean but faded housedress, a combination of two housedresses which had conveniently and respectively worn themselves out top and bottom.

They had been identically made, thriftily bought at a sale. The thing was, though, Jennie had bought different colors, and now, in a subdued sort of way, they clashed. On her feet were a pair of scuffed shoes, once summer white, now streakily dyed brown.

Jennie was the color of honey, and her smooth unlined skin showed the pink of health and cleanliness. Her dark eyes were as clear and candid as a child's. Her curly dark hair, cut short for easy doing, was threaded with glinting silver. She was still a handsome woman, and she still remembered with satisfaction that she and Bea had been the beauties of brown Boston.

"I'm going in now," she said to the squirrel. "Time to get dinner."

He raced up the tree. He was going to get his dinner, too. Nuts, he said to her.

Bit was peeping out of the window at Jennie. Jennie was raking leaves, and more than anything in the world Bit wished she was raking leaves, too. She had always wanted to do everything that Jennie did except get married. And she had never done any of the things that Jennie had done, including getting married. At least she had thought they would grow old together. And now it appeared they were not even going to do that.

If only she had a little more strength. If only she had a little of Jennie's. She was only three years older, but she might as well be Jennie's mother. Once a stranger had thought she was. One day last summer. Of course, that was only six months after It happened, when she couldn't walk and talk the way she could now. The stranger had asked her where Carlson House was. For the life of her she couldn't tell him. Her tongue would not straighten out the right words. She was mortified to death. Jennie heard her gabbling and came to the door. The stranger said with a changed voice and a changed face, as if he were now addressing his equal, I was asking your mother where Carlson House was. Jennie told him. That was all. Not a word to correct his mistake. That was the day Bit figured out that Jennie was ashamed of her sickness. After that she didn't sit outdoors much.

She could smell Jennie's stew. It sent up a heavenly meat smell. Papa used to say meat made strength. Papa used to insist on plenty of meat on his table. But, of course, things were different now from what they were in Papa's time. The money that used to feed a whole family would hardly feed one. And Jennie was, by rights, the one.

The screen door slammed. Bit scuttled away from the window, and though the lame sound of her walking was perfectly audible, and the jarring thump as she settled in the rocker, she assumed a look of long concentration as she opened her Bible at the place where she had shut it to go and watch Jennie. She loved to watch Jennie working. The beautiful rhythm of Jennie's body made Bit's small frame tremble with vicarious motion. If only she could do the things that Jennie did. It only she had the strength to do them.

Her copper brown face bent over the Bible, with the glasses slipping down her nose a little, was full of belief as her mouth, miraculously straight again, shaped the words of the halt made whole. Illness had aged her face with lines and lost flesh, but suffering had filled in the hollows with sweetness. Her hair caught in a sparse knot—for she had lost a good deal of it in the weeks that she had lain in bed—was entirely white. She had once been called a plump little body, but in the past year, with her will to walk and her daily hunger, she had shrunk to thinness, and everything she wore was too large.

But she was so glad to be alive that her heart was forever throbbing with happiness. She could use her bad hand well enough to help her good hand keep her person clean. She could help herself in every way. All she could possibly pray for was a little more strength to help Jennie.

"Bit!"

"You want me, Jennie?" Her tongue was a little awry in her eagerness. She knew to the moment when mealtime came, for minutes beforehand her stomach and mind were sending wild distress signals to each other.

"Of course, I want you," floated up the reproach. "I always have to call you when it's time to eat. I don't know why you never know."

But they both knew why. It was just a fiction they maintained. Jennie always ate a little something first. On the few occasions in the past when Bit had come down to dinner without being summoned, Jennie had been swallowing fast and looking flustered.

Now Bit never came into the kitchen before she was called. Though this permitted Jennie as many secret snacks as her vigorous appetite demanded, the enjoyment was no longer there. She felt guilty, she felt greedy. And she was unaccustomed to begrudging food. But she was finding it hard to cope with the high cost of living. The monthly check from her husband's small estate was inadequate for two. When Bit was well and able to help, there had been money enough for everything.

But then Bit began to fail, getting one worry headache after another from fretting about her work, and losing days at a time from being half sick. She had been a dressmaker, and for many good years she had worked for the wealthy. But there came a time when no one wanted her faithful reproductions of the fashions. The exclusive shops had exclusive labels that were more impressive than the imprint of her skilled hands.

Her families dwindled to a handful whose mending was the only sewing assigned to her. And she became unsure of herself. Her fingers slowed and sometimes fumbled on the delicate silks and satins. Her stitches were no longer invisible, she left snaps where there had been smoothness. The more she worried about it, the heavier grew her sewing hand, and the blinding headaches began. Regularly she drew on her savings to pay her part of the household expenses.

Jennie, whose clothes had been made by Bit, discovered what a difference there was between the cost of material and the cost of a finished garment. As is inevitable, when more is going out of a purse than coming in, her wardrobe wore itself out just when Bit's sewing hand lay paralyzed on a hospital bed.

Bit's hospitalization was long and expensive. When she was able to return home there was still the specialist, and presently the masseuse, and after awhile the wheelchair. Bit, who had learned to make a fairly legible scrawl with her left hand, drew out the last of her never large savings.

Then it was spring. The doctor consented to Jennie's taking Bit to the island. It might be good for her to go. He had heard of the salubrious powers attributed to the place. By mid-summer Bit was out of the wheelchair. By fall she discarded her cane.

Jennie's best friend Bea was the last summer lingerer to leave. In late October she went back to Boston, taking the keys to Jennie's flat. She was to send down Jennie's winter coat and Bit's, for it was now too cool for thin-blooded Bit to travel in a spring coat. But when they came, Jennie thought hers looked shabbier than ever. She didn't see how she could go back to Boston in that old rag. And the worst of it was, there wasn't a way in the world to buy a new one. She and Bea went everywhere together, and Bea took pride in looking just right. Jennie knew how she would feel if she were Bea. She would be ashamed to go around with a fleabag.

There was only one way to solve her problem. She would give up her flat for the winter, and every month she would put something by just as if she were paying rent. Next fall would find her in a very different boat. Poor Bit would be dead by then, and no longer a burden.

She would rent another flat and ask Bea to share it. And Bea could stop ruining her stomach in cheap restaurants. Since her husband's death she had turned her back on all domesticity and taken a room without kitchen privileges. If they shared expenses next winter, Bea would be able to dress without punishing her stomach in the process. Jennie would do the cooking and get some regular meals under Bea's belt. Why should Bea be blessed with a girl's figure anyway. If she were a comfortable size like Jennie, she'd be better off.

Jennie wrote Bea to see her landlord and put her furniture in storage. When these matters were settled, Jennie found that a dozen things had to be done to tighten a summer house for winter. All of them required material and workmen. Instead of being able to put something by, she would have to take part of her check for months to pay the bills that had piled up.

It made her feel somewhat resentful toward Bit. If it weren't for Bit's being old and sick, all these precautions against the cold would not be necessary. Jennie's blood ran swift enough to keep her warm. But if Bit were going to die before the winter was over, it was little enough to let her die decently.

But spring came, and Bit was still alive.

## Chapter Two

Bit limped into the sunny kitchen from which all winter traces of smoke and grime had been scrubbed away for spring. She looked at Jennie. Jennie had an apron on. There was nothing unusual about that. Jennie put an apron on three times a day. And three times a day Bit limped into the kitchen and looked at that apron with longing. If only she could put it on and peel the potatoes, or slice the onions, or dish up the stew.

Her tongue licked out before she could stop it. The stew sent out such a strengthening smell. She wished she had a plate of it as big as the moon. Slyly she cast a sidelong glance at the table to see what size dish Jennie had put at her place. Her mouth quivered a little. It was the small one that was always there, and she shouldn't have been surprised. She had chosen it herself months before when it was so tormenting to eat with her left hand that her appetite vanished as she tried. But when she had taught her left hand to manage, and her bad hand, too, was catching on, Jennie had got used to serving her on a small plate.

Of course, all winter there'd been the bills to pay, and fuel to buy. Now there were only one or two small bills still owing, coal was no longer needed, and kerosene was only bought for cooking. Jennie would have more money for food. She would set a Sunday table every day for Bea. And Bit would sit at that table and eat a second helping of everything.

This was her fine fantasy as she looked at her little plate and saw a cornucopia in its place, and herself made strong as an ox by its plenty. She went to her chair with the funny hopping movements she made when she hurried. She knew that Jennie wished she walked like other people. But if you are foolish enough to fall ill after you are sixty, you are resigned to being different. The important thing, the wonderful thing is to still be alive.

As Jennie served the stew, Bit's lips began to move, though she was not aware of how often her mouth moved with her mind. She was counting the pieces of meat on her plate. There were four. She wished she could count the pieces on Jennie's. She took a quick look. Oh, there were hundreds of lovely pieces. If only she could know exactly, she would know how many it took to make a person strong. She stole another look. One . . . two . . . three . . . four . . . five . . .

"Bit," said Jennie sharply, "will you stop that staring and mumbling, and eat. You make a body nervous."

Bit's head jerked up, and the too hasty action confused her. Her tongue and mind could find no meeting ground. "I— I—" she looked at Jennie helplessly, her eyes filling with tears.

Jennie's tone softened. "Pick up your spoon. Now eat. You never do anything until you're told."

Jennie was treating her as if she weren't bright, and who could blame her?

How could Jennie know there was nothing wrong with her head if she acted as if there was at the least provocation. The mouthful of stew was spreading its warmth and strength all through her body. As soon as she took a few more spoonfuls Jennie would see how straight she could talk.

But she couldn't stop spooning the lovely stew. It was like the wine of life. She had just been lightheaded from emptiness. Now her head felt as clear as a bell.

"Bit," Jennie chided, "take your time. When I said eat, I didn't mean you weren't to come up for breath. You remind me of Bea's Chad when he was a little boy. If he didn't like his dinner, he'd gobble it up to get through with it. If he liked it, he'd linger over it to make it last."

"I like my dinner," Bit said distinctly. "I don't know when anything's tasted so good."

"Then have some more."

Bit began to breathe rapidly. She couldn't remember when she'd been offered a second helping. But, of course, it was spring. There was more of everything in the spring, more sun, more kindness, more stew.

But she said modestly, "I guess we ought to save it for tomorrow."

"Bea's coming," Jennie reminded her. "I wouldn't give her leftovers on her first day. Besides, I bet she hasn't had a decent meal all winter with me not there to invite her over for one. I believe I'll get a nice fryer. Bea says nobody can fry chicken like me. Though to tell the truth I think she likes a lamb chop better than anything. But, of course, nothing beats a steak when it's cooked just right. What do you think?" she asked generously.

She was thinking about the second helping. "If it was me, I'd be satisfied with stew. I don't know when anything's tasted so good."

"Well, it's not you. It's Bea. I think I'll decide on a fryer. I saw some nice ones in Central Market. Guess I'd better get started." She rose, picked up her plate, and reached for Bit's.

Bit clung to her spoon and said desperately, "A fryer's fine tomorrow. It's just today I'd rather have stew. My, I don't know when anything's tasted so good."

"Bit," said Jennie shakily, "if you say that one more time, I'll go out of my mind, and then we'll both be crazy. If it tastes so good, why in the name of thunder don't you have a second helping. I asked you once. I'll ask you twice. But I'll swallow my tongue before I ask you a third time."

"I'll have a second helping," Bit said gratefully. "I don't know when anything's tasted so good."

Jennie picked up Bit's plate and gripped it hard to keep it from flying out of her hand. With the greatest difficulty she resisted flinging the filled plate in Bit's face. She went to the sink and slapped the dishpan down hard. She threw the silver hit or miss into it, and let the soap powder flow in a reckless stream. She gave a vicious turn to the hot water tap. Her violence eased, and pity took its place.

Poor Bit. She had never wanted a second helping before. Was she feeding death? The old folks used to say that when people were getting ready to die, they ate like a house afire. Was Bit getting ready to die? Was it in sight, Bit's release from her wretchedness? Was her own release in sight, too? Would she be with Bea next winter?

Bit slurped noisily and slowly, savoring each bit of meat in her mouth. She was filled with happiness. "Jennie," she said, "don't you think Bea will be surprised to see me?"

Jennie started. Did Bit feel, too, that her death was imminent? A little shiver of fear coursed through her. Without turning to look at Bit she said nervously, "Why should she be surprised? Why shouldn't she expect to see you?"

"I—I mean," Bit stammered in her pride and eagerness, "I was sick when she saw me last. She'll be surprised to see me so well."

Jennie turned now, torn between relief and exasperation. "Bit I'm waiting for your plate. First you eat too fast, then you eat too slow. I want to get the eggs from Old Ma and get downtown before the mail closes."

"Jennie," Bit said boldly, "You get the eggs. I'll finish the dishes."

Jennie was disturbed again. There was Bit acting strangely once more, just the way the old folks used to say, gaining new strength in the time of going.

"All I want you to do, Bit, is get through." She didn't want to have to remember the day Bit washed the dishes and died that night.

"I wouldn't break them, Jennie. You'd be surprised how strong I feel."

"I'm not surprised at all," Jennie said soberly. "But you haven't got an apron on. Maybe some other time."

Bit swallowed the last morsels of meat, and they were nothing but lumps in her throat. That was what you said to children, some other time. It might mean tomorrow, but mostly it meant never. She looked at Jennie's apron, that badge of ability. If she had had an apron on, Jennie would have had to look far for an excuse.

## Chapter Three

Jennie's cottage had been her husband's gift to her on her twenty-first birthday. He knew that she wanted the children that were to come to spend their school vacations where she had spent hers. She had come to the island as Bea's guest when she and Bea were seven. Bea's father could not refuse his only child's pleas that her best friend be invited to go with her on this first trip to a far place called an island; an enchanting but awesome word.

There were no other colored children of their acquaintance on the island that summer. Besides the family with whom they boarded, there were only two other cottagers from the Boston circle of their parents. One boarded white only, the other made the daily rounds to the homes of the rich as a manicurist and hairdresser. These three families used the front door whenever they entered the homes of whites, and thereby settled their status in the community.

Occasionally Jennie and Bea saw a colored child and looked away because she was helping her washlady mother pull a wagon piled with white people's clothes. They knew she was a back door child, who lived in a shack on the edge of Portygee town, itself a place of pigs and shanties. They felt ashamed of the woolly-headed, dark-skinned pair, and they knew this feeling of shame was recognition of kinship.

They played with the children in the neighboring cottages. They were a very pleasing pair in the expensive outfits supplied by Bea's father. Most of the time their new friends forgot that they were colored. Jennie's rose tan was considered a wholly summer achievement. Bea was pearly-skinned, with light brown curls shot with golden strands, and dark blue eyes. A delicate finger had lightly traced a dusting of soot just under her eyes. It added enchantment to her face. But when she was sick, against the pallor of sickness, it was a tell-tale mark of pain. For the rest she was a willowy child, with the exquisite features of her French grandmother, and the love for fine clothes.

In the next few years the colored colony gradually expanded to a dozen or so Boston families, who purchased property wherever there were houses that suited their modest means and requirements. They were too few in number and too scattered in locations to excite any prejudice. Those who took paying guests selected them with a microscope that detected any flaw that might offend their white neighbors. Those who could purchase houses without the help of strangers invited their nicest friends to visit them. The price of their stay was called "chipping in."

To these first Boston settlers life on the island was ideal. Discrimination was not encountered, though, being careful with money, it never occurred to them to storm any costly ramparts. At the turn of the century simplicity was the island's charm. The beach, the woods, the ice cream parlors were all that beckoned the majority. Manners were modest, dress unobtrusive, jewels were left in a city vault. Liquor was never served, and cards were played for prizes.

The Boston Negro learned his vacation manners, which he handed down to his heirs, in this atmosphere and in this age of innocence. Because he was hidebound by acquired tradition and daily exposure to the original, his vacation pattern was set. Any behavior that deviated from his own was considered ignorance of proper conduct.

When Bea was twelve, her father died. As a brilliant and popular district attorney married to a woman whose father had been a judge, he and his wife had had many obligations to entertain on a scale beyond their prudence. They moved in two worlds, their own black world which had their allegiance and affection, and the white world with which they shared many special interests. The upkeep of maintaining a place of importance in both left no backlog but insurance.

Though Bea's mother could manage her daughter's vacation expenses, it was no longer possible to undertake Jennie's. Jennie cried for a week at the thought of being left behind. And Mama could not bear to see her pretty daughter cry. Every time Mama looked at Jennie she was reminded of her late and still lamented husband. He had been a very handsome man who had looked superb in his headwaiter's uniform. He had worn a dress suit as if he had been born in it. His eminence in brown society was very largely due to his ability to look and act like gentry at a time when a certain segment of colored Boston was coalescing into an upper class. At his death Mama transferred her admiration to Jennie, and spent most of her moderate earnings as a milliner's assistant on Jennie's indulgence.

She went to the island as usual that summer. Bit, at fifteen, was already clever with the needle. She made Jennie's vacation clothes with such professional skill that Mama spoke to the madam of the milliner shop. As she had hoped, the madam did know a dressmaker who could use a fifteen-year-old assistant at a fifteen-year-old's scale of pay. The sum, though small, was a great help with Jennie's board and spending money.

When fall came the dressmaker was so delighted with Bit that she hated to see her leave to return to school. She offered Bit a raise. She could take home seven dollars a week instead of six. Bit, who had always been frightened by textbooks and was not at all hopeful of ever graduating from high school, needed only her mother's consent to give her own to the dressmaker.

Another summer came, and with Bit now earning ten dollars weekly, and bringing home enough lovely and sizable scraps to make several outfits for Jennie, Jennie's vacation was assured. If Bit ever wished she was in Jennie's shoes, she knew it could never be a reality. In her shop there were no vacations with pay, and she could not go on a vacation without it.

Everyone said that Jennie and Bea acted more like sisters than Jennie and Bit. Bit had been christened Eleanor. But when she was a toddler her teasing father would ask her for a bit of sugar when he wanted a kiss. When she demanded one back, she was too small to say anything but "bit." She loved her big gay father, and demanded his kisses so often that the nickname naturally followed. And it suited her. For she had no more than a bit of any of the charms with which Jennie and Bea were generously blessed.

The three had been christened in a mid-town church, and were all Sunday school members until Jennie and Bea acquired a pleasant consciousness of boys. They swore Bit to secrecy and transferred their piety to a colored church in Cambridge. The minute Bit was told their motive, she declined their invitation to join them. The thought of being stared at by boys frightened sixteen-year-old Bit as much as it intrigued the self-assured thirteen-year-old Jennie and Bea. The God in her church was familiar to Bit from the many years of her meeting Him there. She did not have the imagination to picture Him in a colored setting.

In time she became the sole survivor of the original band of brown worshippers who had scattered to colored churches when the changing times brought changing attitudes in the successive men of God who outgrew the abolitionist fervor of the founders. But Bit, who went her unnoted way in her own group, did not expect recognition from another. It was God's grace she wanted, not man's. And she obtained it when Mama fell ill.

The doctor told her that Mama had six months to live. She had worn out her heart after ten years of ignoring her doctor's warning that she must stop work for a rest. Mama read her doom in Jennie's scared face. And Mama begged Bit not to let her die.

Bit took Mama's trouble to God. People shouldn't work and die. There should be a time in life for sitting in the sun. If only Mama could live a few years longer. Jennie was soon to graduate from high school. Mama had been good to her. She would want to be good to Mama. She would want to work for Mama. The two of them would do everything to make Mama happy, if God would only let her live.

In her extremity Bit went to her rector, to whom she had never murmured more than a gulped greeting. He prayed with her. This mighty spokesman of the Lord knelt with her humble spirit, and asked God's mercy on her mother. As he prayed, he felt her faith in his power to intercede. It quickened his own faith. He believed with Bit that God had heard and would make Himself manifest in a miracle.

The miracle was that Mama lived twenty years longer. Though she spent those years in bed, she was happy to be alive. The flesh can bear pain if the mind does not add to its torment. And Mama had peace of mind. She found it in loving Bit. She saw, as she could not see when she was up, and working, and harried that Bit had stood by her right hand ever since her husband's death, that now, too, she was standing by. She saw the gentle beauty of Bit's spirit and was more awed than she had ever been by Jennie's radiant prettiness. That she came to this knowledge when she was a burden on Bit and could give in no measure what she received was just one of life's many ironies. But Bit never knew that Mama was a burden. Mama's face filled with expectancy whenever Bit entered her room. She hung on to Bit's every word. Bit's shy tongue ran away with itself. She talked and talked. Mama was Bit's company.

Jennie couldn't talk at all. She was afraid of Mama. She had not prayed for Mama to live. She had prayed that Mama would not suffer long. She did not think Mama's life had been miraculously spared. With her splendid health she had a horror of chronic illness. To her there was no difference between being dead and being only half alive. The shadow of death lay on Mama's face, and Jennie could not bear to look at it. She could not bear to live with it. She ran away and got married. She persuaded Bea to run away, too. They eloped with the two young men who had been squiring them for a year. Jennie's new husband was a court stenographer, able to give her a very decent living. Bea married a dentist, whose practice and ability were not impressive, but whose family tree had several educated people hanging on it. Though the marriages were made in haste, they were never repented.

It never mattered to Bea that she did not have an island cottage of her own. She found it hard enough to take care of a city flat. Housekeeping was an art that eluded her. Though in time she was able to bring some semblance of order to a room and a fairly recognizable taste to a table, she was not at her best in domestic endeavors.

Her summers were spent with Jennie, who preferred this arrangement to Bea's having a house, which might have created the problem of divided popularity. With both of them living under one roof, there was no question that Jennie's porch was the most sat upon in the colony. Every day she and Jennie kept faithful count of their visitors, one of the colony's curious pastimes, and by bedtime their total had exceeded anyone else's.

Jennie never quite forgave God for blessing Bea with a little boy, while she was denied any child at all. Still Bea was perfectly willing for her to take Chad in charge every summer. She could always blame Bea's winter training when Chad got out of hand. And Bea would always agree that she would have made a better mother, which was a handsome consolation prize.

The summers grew more enchanted because of Chad. Jennie and Bea delighted in taking him over all the old trails of their own childhood. Nothing had changed. The island's pace had not quickened. An evening's adventure was still a hayride, with young voices singing innocently of innocent love, or a moonlight sail with the captain's familiar cry, "Is everybody happy?" making every heart shed its load of winter leftovers, or a beach party on a balmy night with each invited guest chipping in for the weinie-roast, and the root beer to wash it down.

The brown Bostonians, with impartial access to these inexpensive pleasures, saw themselves as welcome citizens with full rights. Their dignity was never challenged. Their children's feelings were never hurt. The island was their Eden. And then they found themselves furiously fighting an incoming wave. Finally it swept over them. The New Yorkers had arrived.

*Chapter Four*

Jennie was dressed and ready to leave. She looked quite presentable in her spring dress and coat. Though they were not of recent style, they were of good material and make. Jennie had never had Bea's enthusiasm for the fashions mostly because she had never had Bea's ability to wear them.

She was bareheaded. Hats were impossible to wear except in summer when nobody wore them. In other seasons the wind mocked anything more citified than a cap or kerchief. In summer, when the island was overrun with city people, the wind conceded their right to the temperate breeze they were paying for.

Jennie had her shopping bag over her arm. In one hand she carried a bowl for the eggs, in the other her unstamped letter to Essie Carlson. It was Bit's job and joy to stamp all outgoing mail. This she had taught her bad hand to do, and though the stamp was sometimes a little askew, it was a triumphant accomplishment to maneuver so small an object to its proper place.

She had been waiting with some agitation in the front room where the stamps were kept, fearful that in her haste to be gone Jennie might stamp the letter herself. The room was ready for Bea's coming. The sprawling wicker desk, the wicker settee and chairs, all somewhat creaky with age but held together by the sturdy construction of their vintage year, the occasional chairs, bought second-hand for a song forty years ago, and now exquisite period pieces, the two ladder-back rockers, the low couch piled high with pillows, the round tier table and the square one, all had fresh covers or gleaming surfaces. The bric-a-brac had been dusted. The braided rug had been washed by Jennie's strong hands. Spring flowers from the vases and the big jardinière.

There was a good deal of furniture in the room, but there had been a time when Jennie and Bea had had a good deal of company, and there had to be places for people to sit and surfaces from which to serve the fragile sandwiches, shaped with the cookie cutter, the heart shape flavored, the punch with its floating bits of limp fruit and its grape juice base, the homemade ice-cream and cake, the salted nuts and mints.

Though there was no longer need for so many chairs, and an ice-cream and cake party was an anachronism, the impress of Jennie's vitality made the room one for remembering youth instead of regretting old age. Only when Bit was present did one know that Jennie, for all her resistance to time's destruction, must wither, too.

"Jennie, you-you got the letter," Bit said shrilly, though she knew Jennie knew she was looking straight at it.

"Here, Bit," said Jennie, passing it to her, so that she could have one free hand to hold her patience.

Bit went so limp with relief that even her good hand began to shake as she turned to the desk, and she dropped the little stamp box as she drew it out of the drawer. The lid flew open. The half dozen stamps fell out. Bit lifted an agonized face to Jennie.

"Waste some more of my time," Jennie said pleasantly. "Pick them up."

She stooped. She was not aware of the struggle. Indeed at any other time she would have been proud to show Jennie that she could bend down. But the stamps would not let her pick them up. They clung to the polished floor. In desperation she moistened her thumb and gathered them up in a bunch. She rose and held out the useless wet wad. She was speechless with horror.

"Eighteen cents worth of stamps," said Jennie bitterly. Her eyes widened. "And, oh, dear God, look what you've done to my letter."

It was clutched in Bit's bad hand, the hand with which she had steadied herself on the floor. It was crumpled and dirt-streaked.

Jennie snatched it from her. "I'll buy another envelope in the post-office. If I stay in this house another second, I'll die of apoplexy."

Some of the bric-a-brac shivered a little as the door slammed after her.

Bit wept like an abandoned child. She took off her glasses to weep better. She was not sorry for herself. She was sorry for Jennie who had to put up with her helplessness. She, who used to pick up pins without thinking as she fitted her ladies, couldn't pick up a stamp that was ten times bigger.

She cried her way back to the kitchen to get away from the scene of her disaster. She always stayed downstairs when Jennie was out, so that she could get to the door as quickly as possible if anyone rapped, and usually she sat by the front room window watching for Jennie to come up the road. But today she was in disgrace, and she did not want Jennie to see her when she returned from Old Ma's with the eggs. She would leave the eggs in the front room, as was her custom, and continue on her way downtown. Bit, of course, knew better than to touch the fragile things. Jennie would carry them back to the kitchen on her return. As well she might, Bit thought bleakly.

She closed the kitchen door to be doubly sure of being out of sight. As the door swung to, there was Jennie's apron hanging from the hook, swaying before her widening eyes in a tantalizing way.

Abruptly her sobbing stopped. She dried her eyes and put her glasses on again. What a thing of delight that apron was. She stroked it gently, and her fascination grew. It would only take a minute to slip it on and off. There was nothing easier than putting on an apron, and nothing she could think of that she wanted to do more.

She took it off the hook, her lips moving rapidly as she told herself not to be nervous. Then the loop was over her head, and her good hand and her bad hand took an apron string apiece and slowly and carefully tied them together. She could tie things in back! Oh, if only she could tell Jennie of her great accomplishment. Maybe in a few more weeks she could stop saying her good hand and her bad hand. She could just say *my hands* like everybody else.

A dog barked. There was always a dog barking somewhere. But the sound made her jump. He might be barking at Jennie on her way back. She had better take the apron off to be on the safe side. She reached in back and pulled. And the strings did not separate. She pulled again, and they still held fast. She began to pluck feverishly at the mulish knot. She tugged until her hands shook too much for another try. The apron was on her to stay.

Jennie walked up the road to Old Ma's, feeling the gentle wind cool her heated face. The country road was beautiful with spring, with the glistening new leaves on the great and small trees, the slender young grass sprinkled with spring flowers, the apple blossoms against the blue sky, the scent of honeysuckle and lilac, the blackberry brambles blossoming white, a startled bluebird taking flight, a gold finch following in mild alarm, trailing beauty in the wake of beauty, the unafraid robin preferring to watch, and the sparrows dressing for summer, too used to Jennie to stop. Here in the wooded highlands the sea seemed far away, though the sound of it was part of the murmur of spring, and the shortest walk would bring it in sight.

The houses Jennie passed were still unoccupied, but the lonely winter look had been carted off by the caretakers, which pretentious title was applied to whatever grumbling islander would give a Sunday or a supper hour to opening up or shutting up for an arriving or departing cottager. Blinds had been removed, leaves raked away, shrubs freed from winter wrappings, and a leak discovered and patched, a cook stove cleaned of winter rust, a fence that had fallen in a fierce northeaster put back in place, about which unexpected chores the caretaker and doubting cottager would argue for weeks.

In the very long ago Jennie had had white neighbors exclusively. But now the circle in which she lived was entirely populated by colored. For in the years of Jennie's early occupancy, whenever a nearby house was offered for sale, a colored purchaser took possession, knowing by Jennie's established residence that he would meet no prejudice. Ironically those early inhabitants, who had made such a point of living apart, were now the unwilling elders of small negro settlements.

As the road turned, Old Ma's house came in sight. Beyond it stood Carlson House on its great stretch of cleared land. The original house was now quarters for the two chambermaids, the two waitresses, the assistant cook, the chauffeur, and Essie Carlson who, at sixty-eight, still did most of her excellent cooking, including the baking of the Saturday beans, which to her New England clientele was the one disputed dish of the week. But Essie Carlson had never eaten anything but beans on Saturday in her whole life. She would never serve anything else in the time that remained to her.

The Colonial type main house, built in the period of wild prosperity before the Great Depression, had fifteen double rooms, four baths, a dining room that would seat fifty in excess of its listed guests, a flagstone patio, onto which one of the doors of the dining room opened and one of the doors of the great living room.

An arrow pointed to a parking space where, at the season's height, expensive cars would hardly have walking space between them. A clay tennis court had already been rolled to beautiful perfection. The impressive lawn, yearly tended by a landscape gardener, was dotted with handsome outdoor furniture that had been set out a few days before by the caretaker, who was several cuts above the others in that his sole occupation was the year round superintendence of fine houses.

Essie Carlson's original house had had no more formal name than Essie Carlson's cottage before the arrival of the New Yorkers. It was they who began calling it Carlson House in their winter boasting to friends who could not afford vacations. It was Bea who innocently started Boston-born Essie Carlson on her profitable career.

The first New Yorker to stop at Essie Carlson's had been a distinguished addition to the Boston colony. His considerable fame in the field of serious music had crossed an even broader surface of the Atlantic than the stretch between the mainland and the island. The polish acquired in his years of travel and wide acquaintance with prominent whites took away the taint of his New York address. These uncelebrated Bostonians accepted this celebrity as one of theirs. Besides, he was Bea's godfather. Though this was not a blood tie, it was a tie with Boston.

Essie Carlson's husband had died before her house was paid for. For a summer or two she had rented her bedrooms to Bostonians, and slept on a cot in her front room. But the sum the Bostonians were willing to pay scarcely paid her for the trouble of keeping their rooms in order. She was quietly but desperately in danger of losing her house the summer Bea asked her if she would board her godfather. There was not enough privacy in Jennie's popular house for a seasoned bachelor, who, in any case, would have wanted more quiet to work and relax than would have been possible with active little Chad.

When Essie Carlson timidly told him how much she would like for bed and board, he refused to rob her and doubled her figure. At summer's end she was completely hopeful of saving her house and putting in electricity. Next season, with Bea's godfather helping again, the house was almost wholly hers, and she could think about putting in a bathroom. The following spring, on her return to the island, she found a half dozen letters from other New Yorkers requesting two-week reservations, and recommending themselves as friends of Bea's godfather. More letters followed the first. Essie Carlson replied favorably to them all. With New York money other improvements were possible.

That was the year the New Yorkers began their infiltration. Though one swallow does not make a summer, a dozen foreigners do seem to constitute a swarm. When they show color their number is multiplied ten times over in that strange arithmetic applied to dark minorities. One of the longest and loveliest beaches had, by its location, become the almost exclusive property of the wealthier whites and the colored Bostonians, who considered themselves in the same scale of society even if the same yardstick could not be applied as a measure.

To this sacred strand came the colored New Yorkers with the natural assumption that they were no different from colored Bostonians. But they were. They made their daily assault on the beach with lunches, liquor, and loud joviality. The women wore diamonds with bathing dress. Cigarettes glowed in painted mouths. Men passed liquor in paper cups, and sometimes the ladies took a bold sip. Chicken bones littered the sand. Slang was used like speech. Stag party stories had to be shouted to reach all the ears of so noisy a group. A little light love play was always in progress. A card game was started with money in sight.

They were freedom drunk, these brown New Yorkers. Like the Bostonians they had never found so fair a place. But their reactions were dissimilar. They felt, with some justification, that you only live once. To them the Bostonians did not look as if they were living at all.

Carlson House became a little oasis of late-burning lights in a desert of sleeping cottages, as the New York crowd refused to bed down early in vacation. They tried to make their own nightlife on this island where there was nowhere to go in formal dress unless one had country club or yacht club memberships. These success symbols were not yet included in the colored vacationer's achievements. It was still enough that he could take a two-week holiday. When he came complete with tennis rackets he stood out in modest splendor as a man whose background had not been all hard work. On the town courts, before a mixed gallery, he played hard and well because there were white people watching the race in one man.

Though no Bostonian ever owned to accepting an invitation to Carlson House, every Bostonian knew all about the fast living that went on there. It was said that Essie Carlson had to buy a separate trash can to accommodate the liquor bottles. Poker was played as if whist had never been heard of. In the small hours of the morning when the New Yorkers retired, after keeping the neighborhood awake with a gramophone blaring out the loud and vulgar laments of the blues singers, it was said that they did not always get in the bed that belonged to them.

At the end of the season the beleaguered Bostonians held a protest meeting in Jennie's house. Bea's godfather had left in mid-July to spend the rest of the summer in the south of France, swearing his intention never to return to the island. From him, in the heat of his departure with his unfinished scores, Jennie and Bea had amassed a good deal of misinformation, and had become the official detractors of the New York crowd.

At the meeting Jennie took the floor. She was eloquent. The New Yorkers, she pointed out, had no home sites to protect. They were like people despoiling a picnic ground. It wasn't their park. But the Bostonians had everything to lose: their welcome on the island. Massachusetts laws might defend a man's rights but they could not safeguard his feelings. The lovely beach might be lost to them by subtle ill-will. Then they would have to bathe with two-week whites from the rooming houses and cheap hotels on the other side of town, where there were no nurses and governesses and pony carts to give the beach an aura of elegance.

Take little Chad for a very good example. He had gone to no other beach in all of his six summers. He didn't know there was any difference between himself and the children with whom he played so nicely. To deprive him of these contacts and send him to the beach on the other side of town, where the colored servants' children bathed and felt inferior to the common white children who bathed beside them, might warp Chad's whole life.

Something should be done about the situation before the better whites took action. Already there was a growing division on the beach. The whites had begun to separate themselves from both colored groups, and the brown Bostonians were separating themselves from the brown New Yorkers. The friendliness that had been so prevalent on the beach was beginning to freeze into a very stiff appearance of tolerance.

It was true that the behavior of the New York crowd was not exemplary by local custom. Still the child has to crawl before it can walk. Only Bostonians are born to do the right thing. It was also true that their coming had increased the colored population. But however they had behaved their numbers would have weighed against them. For white people and the negroes who belong to them live under the constant fear of being ploughed under by black outsiders.

The little group of crusaders decided that Jennie and Bea should call on Essie Carlson. They were to ask her in a nice way to accept no New Yorkers as guests next summer, to give her house back to the Bostonians.

Essie Carlson was sorry but firm. She did not have a man to take care of her like Jennie and Bea. Her dear husband had left her nothing but debts. She was, therefore, not in business to please the Bostonians. Already she had received several paid reservations for next summer, and she couldn't be expected to return all that money. In this world you had to live and let live.

Jennie and Bea reported the failure of their mission. Essie Carlson had gone over to the camp of the enemy. But she would suffer for her unwisdom. The New Yorkers were only a flight of migrants. Who knew where they would light in other summers. One day Essie Carlson would be begging the Bostonians to rent her empty rooms, and the town would take her house for taxes.

But Essie Carlson had prospered despite this prophecy. Jennie and Bea were the only ones left of the old Bostonians who had snubbed Essie Carlson's first New York guests. They alone remembered the alarm their coming had spread through the colony. Though they now gave grudging admiration to Essie Carlson for knowing how to make a dollar, they were still disdainful of Carlson House and had never recanted their vow to ignore the New Yorkers. When the present-day New Yorkers smiled and spoke in passing, Jennie and Bea responded with stiff little nods. The New Yorkers were a grandiose sight, the women sleek and handsome and sophisticated, the men with a newer, coarser look of success. The two Boston ladies out of a past of which they had no knowledge, and in which they had no interest, were part of the pleasant island picture to them. In the Great Age of Gush they liked their simple nods of greeting. Jennie and Bea would have been quite outdone to know how often these young New Yorkers had considered stopping for a chat, except that there never seemed to be time between going some place and rushing home to change for some place else.

Now Jennie had turned renegade. She had succumbed to New York money as had all the other Bostonians who rented rooms to other Bostonians only when there was no prospect of anything better. Say what you would about the New Yorkers, they knew how to take vacations. They came to spend their vacation money and they spent it. The Bostonians tried to see how much of theirs they could take back home.

For several summers Essie Carlson had had to find rooms outside of Carlson House for her overflow. She preferred rooms nearby, so that her guests would not have far to come for meals. Jennie's house was ideally situated. Frequently Essie Carlson had asked her to accommodate one of her couples, and regularly Jennie had refused. As far as she could see the New Yorkers still drank liquor and stayed up late. She certainly would not countenance any such carousing under her roof. And now she had written a letter to Essie Carlson, asking her to put her first if she needed an extra room.

Bea would die when she was told, for Bea would forever hold the New Yorkers responsible for the Bostonian's loss of the beach on the best side of town, for her own loss of Chad. But she would be mollified when Jennie explained that she had to have a winter coat. Renting a room to New Yorkers would bring her that much nearer to living with Bea in Boston.

Though the completion of this plan depended on Bit's dying, she hoped Bit would manage to last through the summer. For, of course, no roomer could be expected to stay if there was a death in the house.


*Chapter Five*

Jennie turned into Old Ma's yard. Old Ma had been Jennie's first caller when Jennie, as young Mrs. Ellis, was a newcomer in the little community. Now Old Ma was the last survivor of the original settlement. Years ago twenty-one-year-old Jennie had been very grateful for the friendliness shown her by Mrs. Aldridge, who was a pretty woman of forty-five, in her energetic prime, at the time of their meeting. Jennie had constantly sought her advice. Every day a new house presented a new problem to an inexperienced girl who had always lived in flats. As the years advanced, and colored cottagers began to surround her, Jennie liked them to see her going in and out of Mrs. Aldridge's house with easy familiarity. But suddenly Mrs. Aldridge was sixty, and Jennie, who was thirty-six, began thinking of her as old. Her visits gradually dwindled to the time it took to buy a dozen eggs. She could never think of anything to say to old people.

Old Ma had become a permanent resident when she was sixty-three. She had always wanted to keep chickens. In her widowhood there was no reason why she shouldn't. There was nothing to keep her in the city. One summer she came down to stay.

The year she was eighty her son lost his wife. When he came to spend his summer vacation with his mother, the thought of death was still in his mind, and he was sadly aware that his mother was very old. He saw her dying alone in winter and he tried to persuade her to return to the city with him. But she would not leave her chickens. And he could not bring himself to leave her in what surely must be her last year of life.

He arranged for a year's leave of absence from his job, sublet his city house, and went to work for the railway agency on the island. Now five years later he was still with the railway agency, had long since resigned his former job, and sold his city property. Jennie, shooing the chickens out of her path, felt very sorry for a man, scarcely more than sixty, who was tied down by a foolish old woman's refusal to die.

She went to the back door, in the way of winter neighbors. She had not seen Old Ma since the first of winter, when the cost of coal had forced her to cut eggs off her breakfast menu. Occasionally she had seen Old Ma's son on his way to or from work. When she asked him how his mother was, he would say rather doubtfully that he guessed she was holding her own. Jennie had felt guilty about her unneighborliness, but had given herself and Old Ma's son the excuse that she never left her sister alone except to go to the store.

Jennie rapped once and entered the kitchen. Old Ma had grown too old to be left behind a locked door. She was sitting in her rocker by the stove, and for a moment Jennie stood very still. Old Ma had not won her battle with winter. All of her eighty-odd years were grooved in her skeletal face. Her skin was as dry and yellow as parchment, her snow-white hair grown so thin that her scalp showed through, and her gums so shrunken that her false teeth, which her pride never permitted her to be seen without, slipped whenever she spoke. The flesh of her throat was in folds, her back now so bent that she constantly leaned forward a little. In her lap was a small sewing basket. She was mending a sock. Her knuckles were knobs, her fingers so stiff and claw-like that the stitch she was drawing as Jennie entered took as long to emerge as if it were going through stone. Jennie thought suddenly, why, I bet Bit could do better than that with her bad hand. Some day I'll tell her to try.

The sound of Old Ma's breathing was very distinct. It was a little gasping sound, but not harsh, not unrhythmic. Jennie, after her first feeling of shock, had a curious feeling of calm. Old Ma had been a fine looking woman in her day. Then, to Jennie, she had grown old and ugly. But now and strangely, for all winter's destruction, Jennie saw something in Old Ma's wasted face that moved her more than beauty. She saw tranquility.

"How are you feeling, Ma?" Jennie said, using the name by which everyone called her now. And she heard herself saying it with tenderness, her mind no longer mocking the word.

"Nothing hurts," Old Ma answered with quiet pride. "Get a chair, Jennie, and come to the fire. It's been a cold spring."

It was a warm spring. The kitchen was too hot for comfort. But Jennie got a chair and carried it to a place by the fire. "I would have come before," she said, and faltered. She did not feel like lying.

"Son told me about your sister," Old Ma said with sympathy. "But you won't lose her. She'll get a new lease of life on this island. You tell her I lived to be eighty-five."

The sound of the past tense echoed in Jennie's ears, but she said cheerfully, because she thought Old Ma wanted her to, "I'll be sending you a card when you're eighty-six."

Old Ma shook her head solemnly. "I've used up my borrowed time. The doctor won't say, but I know. Time before last when he was here, he asked me my age, and my middle name, and so on. And after he left I started worrying. I've got two middle names, and I only gave him one. I knew he would want everything just right. I knew it was for my death certificate."

"Oh, no, Ma," Jennie protested in distress.

"That's just what he said," Old Ma said composedly. "Last time he came I asked him. Oh, no, he said, he was fixing up his records. He was fixing them up for all his patients. But he's a young man. He doesn't fool me. Young men can't hide their pity. So I got it straight about my two names. I don't want to cause him any extra bother when it comes time to bury me."

Old Ma's voice was so free of grieving that Jennie knew there was no need for evasion. "You've had a rich life, Ma. And you haven't left any goodness undone. No wonder you don't mind knowing."

"I guess if it wasn't for Son, I'd have gone this winter. It took all my grit to stay awhile longer. But it didn't seem right to leave him in the lonely time of year. Now it's turned spring, it'll be easier on him. The days are longer. He won't miss the light. I guess that was most on my mind this winter. How he'd hate to come home to a dark house."

Jennie had the sharp realization that she, too, had drawn comfort from Old Ma's winter lights. Every night they winked on she had felt a contact established between the two lighted cottages, that, in a sense, they had narrowed the distance of darkness between them, and were looking after each other. When Old Ma's lights had winked out, she, too, had gone to bed, as if to sit up any longer would have been to sit up alone.

"I guess I've used your lights to live by, Ma, more than I knew."

"It's a natural thing in the Highlands, where most of the houses are closed all winter. There's a loneliness around. Son won't stay up here in the hills when I'm gone. He'll move into town or he'll go back to Boston. Once you start living here year round, you can't leave. Seems there's a spell that makes you stay."

"I'm immune to it," Jennie said emphatically. Suddenly she wanted to tell her secret to Ma. "Ma," she said, her words tumbling out like a child's, "I'll be back in Boston next winter. Just like you know about yourself, I know about my sister, Bit."

"I'm sorry, Jennie," Old Ma said, her voice full of pitying.

"Don't be sorry for Bit, Ma. She'd say herself she's ready to lay down the burden her body's been to her."

"It's you I'm sorry for, child. Like I'm sorry for Son. It's the living that's left with the loneliness. It's a funny thing about the sick and the old. They're a care. Take me. I've been a burden this winter. Son's had to cook and clean. Best I can do is the dishes with a chair drawn up to the sink. And the money I'm costing, with the doctor coming in, and the wash going out. And Son always wondering, though he doesn't say, if he'll find me dead inside a dark house. But the thing about the sick and the old is they're always there to be company. And when they're gone, you forget the care. You're lonely for their company."

For the first time in all the years since Mama's death Jennie understood why Bit had taken on so when Mama died. She had thought Bit would be glad to be free of Mama's sickness, as she had been glad to be free of the thought of it. But Bit had sorrowed as if Mama had been whole, as if her invalid years had been worth living. Now Jennie knew why. Bit had missed Mama's company.

There had been nothing Jennie could do about poor Bit's living alone in Boston. The spare room was Mr. Ellis' den. And men hated to be evicted for their in-laws. But there was room in the cottage for Bit, and after Labor Day was the nicest time. The weather was loveliest, the crowd had gone, and Bit could enjoy a two-week holiday without having to be bothered with seeing people. The time was ideal for Jennie, too. For Bit could do some altering on her fall clothes that were always a little too tight when she tried them on at the end of summer. She could mend the sheets and whatever else had collected a rip or two. She could make a new couch cover and some matching curtains.

Bit did not feel put upon. She felt useful and important. She had never learned what to do with leisure, for she had never had enough of it to accustom herself to its tempo. She would have felt lazy and ashamed with her hands lying idle in her lap.

When Mr. Ellis died, ten years after Mama, Jennie was able at last to invite Bit to share her flat. But Bit was reluctant to move. She was past fifty. She hated to sell the things she had lived with all her life. The trolley stop was at her corner. Sometimes her legs bothered her, and Jennie's flat was quite a walk from the carline.

But Jennie finally made her see that people would think it was queer for two sisters both alone in the world to live apart in the same city. Particularly since, if Bit didn't move in, Jennie would have to rent a room for the money it would mean. And when you rented to strangers, your house never felt like home. Two sisters chipping in was quite a different thing.

Bea's husband died two years later. Though Jennie didn't mention it to Bea, it did seem a pity that he couldn't have died two years earlier. Then it would have been Bea in Mr. Ellis' den. And Bea for company.

"Ma," she said, "you don't have to feel sorry for me. I won't be alone in Boston. I'll be living with Bea. She's coming tomorrow. That's one of the reasons I'm here. Bea thinks your eggs are the best on the island. I'll take a dozen today, and a dozen a week for the rest of the summer."

Old Ma set her basket aside, grasped the arms of her rocker, and slowly and painfully drew herself to her feet. Jennie knew she did not want to be helped.

"Give me your bowl, Jennie. I want to pick out the biggest one. I remember well you were my first customer. And now you're my last. Son's done all my work all winter. With the rush already started at the express company, it's too much to expect him to keep on with my outside chores. Farmer Maitland's coming down island this Saturday. I'm selling him my chickens."

Now Jennie knew that Old Ma was ready to die. She watched her slow progress to the lean-to where the eggs were kept. Old Ma walked very carefully, as if the floor were glass. Finally she crossed the threshold, and presently Jennie could hear her placing the eggs in the bowl. It seemed to Jennie it took her five minutes to pick up each one. She longed to go in and do it herself. The sick and the old exacted so much patience.

Old Ma started back, the bowl in her hands, and Jennie got up nervously. Why didn't Old Ma just stand still and let her come and get them? But if she moved toward her, Old Ma would only get stubborn, and try to meet Jennie half way. And if she dropped that bowl, there'd not only be all those beautiful eggs gone, there'd be all the mess for Jennie to clean up. She had already stayed longer than she meant to stay. With Bit holding her up because she thought it was something wonderful to put a stamp on a letter, and now with Old Ma holding her up because she thought it was wonderful to carry a bowl of eggs, it would be tomorrow before she got downtown. Some kind of medal ought to be struck for the strong and well who had to deal with those who weren't.

"Here you are, Jennie," said Old Ma, smiling and showing her slipping teeth, and plainly wanting praise for taking all day.

Jennie tightened her lips and opened her purse. She couldn't trust herself to speak without betraying her irritation.

"Jennie, I don't want money for your last bowl of eggs. These are for you to have. I put in better than a dozen. You make a custard for your sister with the extra ones. It'll give her strength. I was sorry I wasn't able to help with her this winter, if only to sit with her, so you could have got out more."

Jennie's eyes filled with tears. "I don't know how to thank you, Ma, for the eggs, for everything."

"Why, child, I thank you for letting me keep you so long. And don't let me keep you any longer. I know you've got things to do, and time is a precious thing."

Jennie went to the door. "I'll be going, Ma." She closed the door quickly behind her. She did not want to say good-by, nor see the lonesome word on Old Ma's lips.

She reached her own yard, crossed the porch, and entered her front room. Bit was sitting in her waiting chair, her eyes blinking fast behind her glasses, her breath coming jerkily, her good hand and her bad hand still trembling from exertion. She had decided not to hide. Jennie might as well see her now as later. This way she might cool off on the way downtown. To be closeted with Jennie's anger when she came back was a worse affliction.

Jennie looked at her. Jennie saw the apron because she certainly wasn't blind. And Jennie said, "Bit, Old Ma sent some of these eggs special for you. I'll make you a custard for supper. You want to carry this bowl to the kitchen?"

Bit jumped up and hopped across to Jennie in no seconds flat.

"You want me to carry the eggs, Jennie?" She clapped a hand to her mouth to catch the words back, for she knew how Jennie hated fool questions.

But Jennie just said, "Yes."

Bit took the bowl of eggs. Her hands were as steady as if she had never had a day's sickness. She backed up to Jennie, and said with dignity, "Will you untie this apron, please? I guess I put it on."

"I guess you can wait till I come back."

And Bit was alone with an apron on and a bowl of fragile eggs in her hands. She carried them back to the kitchen. She knew that she would not drop them. When she had set them down, she knew she could untie the apron. Slowly and surely she did. She put it back on its hook. Then she pressed her lips against it. It was a magic apron. If Jennie would let her wear it again, she could perform another miracle. She could wash the dishes. She could sweep a floor. She could sew.

She took off her glasses, for she was crying again. But her tears were of joy and thanksgiving. She thought she could feel Samson's strength flowing through her. And if you think it, it's so.

Chapter Six

"Whew!" said Jennie, plopping down on the porch glider and fanning briskly with her hand. "I guess we've tramped our legs off. We tried to see it all in one day." She settled back against the plump pillows. "How'd you like the house that New York doctor bought? I think he paid more for it than it's worth. I wonder how much he paid for it. Bet that section will be colored in a few years' time." She sighed. "The colored man moves a step up, and the white man moves a step away." But it was a morning for gossip not gloom. She said bossily, "The Baxters would have done better to leave well enough alone. One coat of cheap white paint looks worse than no paint at all. If it was me, I'd have put that money in a new porch. Did you see how some of those boards were rotting?" The disapproval remained on her face. "Didn't you think the new room the Thayers added to the south side of their house makes the north side look skimpy? If it'd been me, I'd have built a room both sides for balance. But I suppose they built according to their pocketbook. I hear he doesn't make the money he used to. Oh, my, I'm hungry as a horse. How about you, Bea?"

"Let me catch my breath," said Bea. She had listened to this monolog from the foot of the porch steps. Now she grasped the rail and reluctantly climbed them. Carefully she lowered herself into her favorite rocker and leaned back against it, panting a little.

Jennie looked at her critically and said comfortably, "Your feet hurt. You're rusty. You've been riding around in streetcars all winter. I've been hoofing it. I've toughened up. You're still soft."

They had been on their annual rubberneck tour of the colony. In addition they had walked into town, for Jennie had been secretly anxious to see if there was a letter from Essie Carlson. It now burned a hole in her pocket, its contents still unknown. If she'd had an sense she'd have sent Bea home to wait for her, and gone into town alone, and read her letter in peace and privacy.

For certainly Bea was not the good walker she was last summer. Or maybe she still felt a little weak from being so sick the day she arrived. Which was odd when you thought about it, for Bea had been a good sailor for more than fifty summers. In the two days since she had eaten as lightly as a bird. Even this morning, though she knew she was going on a long walk, she had taken only coffee and toast, despite the beguiling smell of sizzling bacon and the hiss and pop of Old Ma's eggs frying sunny side up. If it wasn't for Bit, who was still feeding death, a lot of good food would go to waste.

No wonder Bea gave out so easily. Even a camel had sense enough to eat himself a bellyful before he made a journey. It took time and trouble to plan a meal. The least you could expect from people was appreciation.

"Bea," she said indignantly, "you got your breath back yet?"

Bea smiled. She was still a beautiful woman. She had a look of flawlessness. Her pearly skin was soft and unlined, her hair was free of gray, and the golden strands still glinted in the sun. Though her dress and topcoat were suitably simple, their lines were as revealing of cost as the exclusive labels inside them. When she made her expensive emergence from the taxi, Jennie had felt very fat and homespun beside her. But her brief jealousy had been submerged by her greater delight at having someone in the house who didn't have one foot in the grave and the other on a banana peel.

She smiled at Bea because she was so much better company than Bit, but she left a little reproach in her eyes so that Bea could see she was not entirely restored to grace.

"No wonder you get winded," she scolded. "The way you eat, I wonder you aren't dead. There's nothing takes the place of food, not even a stylish shape. It's natural for women our age to thicken. It's nothing to be ashamed of. You may look better thin, but I bet you'd feel better fat."

Bea was wounded to the heart. "Jennie, you know it's my nature to be thin. And you know how much I have to live on. I can't afford to dress and eat, too. And I never think about eating if there's nobody to make me. I missed you this winter, Jennie. I didn't feel like food."

Jennie wanted to say something affectionate, but she and Bea had been brought up in the Boston school of suppressed emotions. They had not displayed their devotion openly since childhood. Reaching for the Boston paper she had flung down beside her, she said casually, "Here, Bea, you look over the headlines while I look at this letter I've got in my pocket." And to appease the gods she added, "It probably isn't anything."

But when Bea was behind the headlines, Jennie tore open the letter with the nervous haste she despised in Bit. Her eyes raced across the rambling first page with increasing impatience. There was nothing on it of any importance to anybody but Essie Carlson. Who had asked her about her rheumatism? Who cared how well she'd been otherwise? Who was interested in hearing about some friend of hers that had died? Who wanted to know how eager she was to get back on the island? If she'd stayed here all winter, she'd be even more eager to get off. Why didn't Essie Carlson come to the point?

She turned the page. Slowly, carefully, she read and reread every word. When she had finished, her eyes were shining with happiness. "Bea," she said softly, "put down that paper. Bea, I'll be back in Boston next winter. Next winter I'll see you don't miss any meals."

Bea's smile was unsteady, but its bliss was unmistakable. "Oh, Jennie, I've been scared to ask you about next winter. I didn't know what you'd answer. I know you could live cheaper here than in Boston, and I just didn't think you'd ever come back. Why didn't you tell me before?"

"I didn't know before. I didn't know until just now. This letter's from Essie Carlson. She wants me to take a young man and his wife from June until September. She'll feed them, of course. I'll just sleep them. I'm going back to Boston on Essie Carlson's money."

Bea said innocently, "I didn't know she ever boarded Bostonians."

Jennie said diffidently, "I think she said something about them being New Yorkers."

"Well, Essie Carlson has some nerve," Bea exclaimed indignantly, and she looked at her heretofore like-minded friend for confirmation.

"Now wait, Bea," Jennie said firmly, "this is the first piece of good luck that's come my way in a year. Don't act like you don't care."

"But they sound like racketeers to me. Anybody who can afford a three months' vacation, with times what they are, is earning his living dishonestly. They may be coming here to hide from the law. Essie Carlson should have said how they make their money."

"If you'll hold your horses, I'll tell you. She says the man's a writer."

"A what?" Bea asked in a startled voice.

"Just what I said. A writer. That's why Essie Carlson is sending him to me instead of keeping him herself. He has to have peace and quiet, and he wouldn't have it at Carlson House." She paused and looked rather wistful. "My goodness, the sun do move. I remember when we sent your godfather to Essie Carlson because ours was the liveliest house around here. Now it's the quietest. We were the youngest in the married group. Now we're the oldest."

But Bea was not concerned with reminiscences. "This writer," she asked mistrustfully, "does he write about colored people? I never read books by writers who write about colored people. They write about things you're better off not knowing. I hope he won't talk about those things, too."

Jennie, who was made of less squeamish stuff, regarded Bea coldly. "Then stopper your ears when he opens his mouth. How do you know he can talk? Maybe he's deaf and dumb. All I know is his name's Pierce Hunter, and his wife's name is Carol. All I care is they're making it possible for me to get back to Boston."

"Jennie," Bea said softly in surrender. "I'm glad you're coming back."

"Well," said Jennie briskly to hide her pleasure, "I say we go and see what's to eat."

"You go eat. I just want to sit here." She felt in her pocket. "And take this candy bar to Bit. I got it while you were buying the paper. I felt kind of hungry. But after I bought it, I didn't want it, so I stuck it in my pocket for Bit."

There was a sudden mad scramble in the front room. The screen door banged open, and Bit hopped quickly to Bea's side, trying very hard not to hold out her hand. "Here I am, Bea," she said breathlessly.

"Where were you?" demanded Jennie. "You were quiet as a mouse."

"In there," said Bit, nodding back toward the spot where she always sat to watch for Jennie to come up the road.

"Spying," Jennie spat, though she knew that Bit knew better than to speak before she was spoken to.

"Here, Bit" Bea said quickly, handing over the candy bar. "Sit down and eat it," she added kindly. "I guess you were glad to hear you're going back to Boston."

Bit began to unwrap the candy bar. It was nice of Bea to ask her to sit down, but Bea wasn't the one who had the authority to tell her what to do. Because she was busy with the wrapping, and didn't have to meet anybody's eyes, she said definitely, "I don't want to go back to Boston. I like it better here."

All of the nervous tension Jennie had felt during her suspenseful and solitary wait for Essie Carlson's letter suddenly exploded. "Don't you worry about going back," she cried wildly to Bit. "You may never go back except in a coffin." Tears began to course down her cheeks. "And I may not either if it's left to you and Bea. Go on and act uppity with the Hunters, Bea, and, Bit, you sit in there and spy on them. Run them away if you want to. It's me who hasn't had anything new since God knows when. It's me who's lost a winter of my life here. And neither of you care enough to help."

Bit had not raised her eyes from the candy bar, but she no longer saw it. The sound of Jennie's sobs aroused a deeper emotion than greed. She felt pity. She couldn't remember the last time she had heard Jennie cry. It was too long ago. Jennie had to be awful hard hit to give way like this. Oh, she wished she could make Jennie a fine new winter wardrobe. She wished her sewing hand could hold a needle. But if she couldn't help, she wouldn't hinder. She raised her eyes to her sister's.

"Jennie, you don't have to worry about me. Those young people won't hardly know I'm here. If they say 'good morning' to me, I'll say 'good morning' back. But the rest of the time I'll stay far away."

Jennie dried her disgraceful tears. She was genuinely sorry and ashamed that she had let her emotional steam scald Bit and Bea. She must learn to rein her tongue when she talked to Bit. Bit had so little time left for forgetting and forgiving, while she and Bea had all the years ahead to make up for this moment.

She put the blame for her outburst squarely on Pierce Hunter. "You suit yourself about staying out of that writer's way, but I think you'll be happier if you do. It's already kind of unnerved me just knowing he's coming. I won't see him either any oftener than I have to. Writers are kind of crazy. They write about anything that comes into their minds. If he was to see a lot of you, that Pierce Hunter would have you limping all over his typewriter."

"Oh, my goodness," gasped Bit. "Oh, my stars." But suddenly a look of defiance crossed her face. "Well, let him write about my limp. Before he leaves, he'll have to cross it out and write how I'm hardly limping at all." In her spirited stiffening to the challenge, she tightened her hold on the candy bar, and the chocolate spread between her fingers.

Jennie uttered a loud, long-suffering sigh. Then she remembered her resolution. She said sweetly, "You better go eat that candy over the kitchen sink. Then nobody has to worry if it drips."

"And while I'm back there," Bit asked stoutly, "you want me to start the lunch? I can cut up those cold potatoes, if you want me to. And what else you want me to do?"

"I want you to wash that mess off your hands before you do anything else. Bea, next time you bring home candy, you'll please me if you bring home the hard kind."

"And after I wash my hands," Bit went on doggedly, "can I put on your apron to peal the potatoes in?"

"You can put it on and keep it on until it drops off," Jennie snapped along with her resolution. "God knows you make me nervous staring at me every time I wear it. What you see in that old apron. From now on consider it yours. It'd give me the creeps to wear it again."

"Oh, Jennie, thank you!" Her face filled with dignity. "Well, I guess I better go in and get busy."

When the screen door had shut behind her, Bea said warmly, "That was kind of you, Jennie."

"Oh, well," said Jennie modestly. "If I let her keep busy back in the kitchen, she'll be out of those young folks' way. I know from myself and Mama how young people feel skittish of sickness."

Bea stared at the spreading hydrangea that Jennie had planted last fall. Had it stood transplanting well enough to bloom this summer? Jennie had a green thumb. Already the hydrangea was twice the size it had been when Jennie uprooted it from the weeds of neglect. Jennie had said it wasn't stealing to take a plant that had nobody to care for it. She had rushed back home for her spade. Bea had sat on the rotting steps of the abandoned house to wait for her. The sun had been warm on her back. There had been no sound but the humming earth. She had been filled with quiet content. And she had wondered idly if this was what old age was, just this peaceful sitting in the sun. If so, it was nothing to fight against. It was not the worst part or life. It might even be the best. Then Jennie had come back, and Bea had watched her without words, wanting the quiet peace to continue, wishing she need never leave this moment in time, somehow fearful of leaving it.

"Jennie, you still don't like sick people, do you?"

"Well, who does?" asked Jennie in honest surprise. "I'll always appreciate the way Milton went. No lingering like Mama and Bit. Got acute indigestion at his brother's in Chicago, died right a way, and when they brought him home, he was all ready to be put in the ground. And it was all over with no fuss or bother. I'll always remember Milton as a kind and considerate husband. He always did the right thing."

"Well, I guess that's a nice way to go," Bea agreed. "Quick."

"It's the only considerate way," Jennie said emphatically. "If you linger you spoil somebody's life, like Mama spoiled Bit's, like nobody's going to spoil mine."

Chapter Seven

June lay on the land. The dusk-pink roses were thick as thieves along Jennie's back fence. The scarlet hollyhocks stood almost shoulder to shoulder with the back porch. The honeysuckle was in flower, blanketing the side fence, burdening the air with its sharp sweet scent. The Shasta daisy and showy dianthus bedded together, the delphiniums were in magnificent bloom, and the lilies had unfolded to flaming orange. In the unfenced front yard the annuals were already easily distinguishable from weeds, almost distinguishable from each other, and by July would separate themselves into petunias and balsam and cosmos. In the center of the lawn the hydrangea had begun to bud.

Jennie stood in the front bedroom that was to be the young Hunters, thrusting down the front of her dress the fine sum that Essie Carlson had just handed her for their first week's rent. The whole of summer stretched ahead of her. This was only the start of this weekly munificence that meant the difference between waiting for death on the island with Bit and living a full life in Boston with Bea.

"I know he'll be pleased," said Essie Carlson, giving one last, disinterested look at Jennie's special endeavor. "I can see Mr. Hunter just writing away by that window." But she couldn't really, for Essie Carlson had too much energy to picture anybody, particularly a healthy young man just sitting by a window putting words on paper.

"Well, I did what I could," said Jennie complacently.

She had been pretty certain for a while that Mr. Hunter would put her in the book he was writing. And staring into her looking glass, she had wondered if it would seem too vain to show him some pictures of herself when she was younger and not so stout. Her life could make a real nice story if he left out the parts about Mama and Bit. But then she remembered what Bea had said about colored writers. She remembered what she, herself, had said about Bit. That fool young writer would probably choose a poor lame thing like Bit to write about and leave out the parts about her whole and able sister. But before she arrived at this bleak conclusion, she had arranged a writing corner, and it would have been too much trouble to shift everything around again.

She had divided the room into what she called "his half" and "her half." His area was on the north side where there were two windows for light and air. By one she had placed a worktable and chair, and a small cupboard with four open shelves for whatever a writer packed as paraphernalia. By the other window were a vast armchair and an old-fashioned smoking stand. She had spent half a morning plotting the unwieldy armchair up the narrow stairway, with Bit and Bea fluttering about below in unhelpful alarm. On "her side" Jennie had cramped the four poster bed and night table, the boudoir chair, the bureau and chest of drawers in as small a space as possible so that there would be enough room left over for Mr. Hunter to pace the floor if that was what writers had to do for inspiration.

"I appreciate your taking the Hunters," said Essie Carlson. "June's my quiet month, and I could have slept them until July. But I said to myself, If Jennie takes them in June, they won't be strangers in July."

"Well, I appreciate your sending them to me. With Bit on my hands, and more going out than coming in, it wasn't an easy winter. I stayed here because I had to. But I'll never do it again."

"Well, you won't have to stay here again on your sister's account," Essie Carlson said heartily. "She'll be able to go back good as you. I think she steps around something wonderful, considering. I never saw anyone improve so fast, with what she had, at the age she had it. I believe this place had a lot to do with it. Why," she admitted magnanimously, "Bit looks as good as I do, and I've never been sick abed in my life."

Jennie thought blackly that if one more person implied that Bit was going to live to a ripe old age, she would lie down and die herself. Essie Carlson could afford to be cheerful about Bit. If she had an afflicted sister, she could stick her in a nursing home, and go on her merry way. Money could do everything. It was keeping Essie Carlson alive. She couldn't bear to die and leave it. And what if Bit did look as good as she did? Anybody who didn't look any better than Essie Carlson was ready to give up the ghost.

To Jennie, who was sixty-one, Essie Carlson, at seventy-one seemed enormously older. But Essie Carlson was not bowed down with her years. She was erect and wiry and tough. Though her pale-yellow face was grooved with a thousand lines, they were the marks of her endurance. She believed that hard work was the secret of long life. She worked herself like a dog, and it was her superstition that she must never stop.

It was not known how much money she had, but it was thought that she had a great deal, for she had neither chick nor child to spend it on, and she didn't spend it on herself. Everybody who knew Essie Carlson knew her "dark blue" and her "best black." For the past several years she had never gone anywhere to wear out her clothes except to funerals. And those she attended mostly for the pleasure of quietly rejoicing that she had survived her contemporary in the coffin. To postpone her own departure she had created a second career for herself. For several winters she had been a Boston caterer, with her summer help continuing in her employ.

She lived alone in two rooms in a private house that had once belonged to her best friend. Her friend had been dead many years now, the house had changed hands twice. Though the successive owners had seen no reason to unsettle Essie Carlson, who always paid her rent on time, neither of them knew, nor would have cared, that her original reason for moving to this address was to be near someone who would take an interest in something besides her money.

"Well, Essie," Jennie said jealously, "I guess you'll get rich again this summer. You'll be jam packed, as always. And every cottage around here will be sleeping some of your overflow. I can remember when Bea and I knew everybody in every house. Now we can sit on the porch and count on one hand the people we know to speak to."

"That's because you and Bea and me are old timers," Essie Carlson said wryly. "Most of the people we know have gone on. All my best friends have gone on. You and Bea are still together. You ought to call yourselves lucky. At our time of life we've got to resign ourselves to knowing fewer and fewer folks. But that don't mean a new face is a different manner of face. All of my guests came highly recommended. I've never slept a hoodlum under my roof."

"And what about the people you put out to sleep?" Jennie probed. She was certainly not going to be less choosy than Essie Carlson, who had hardly had cold beans to eat when Jennie was eating cold lobster.

Essie Carlson stared Jennie down. "I've always been fair and square. I've never put a cutthroat in anybody's bed. If it's the Hunters you're hinting about, Dr. Clyde Harris wrote a beautiful letter of recommendation. Seems like Pierce Hunter is pretty important. But don't ask me what he wrote. I don't have time to read except my newspaper."

"Well, take the time to sit down a minute," Jennie urged in a mollifying voice. "The way you're always on the go, I never think to ask you."

Essie Carlson perched on the edge of the straight chair so that she would be ready when her nervous energy pulled her to her feet. Jennie sat down in the armchair because she had no such old folks' ailments as rheumatism that made soft sitting hard rising.

"This Dr. Harris," she asked disarmingly, "he's the one with the white wife, isn't he?"

But Essie Carlson was not disarmed. "White or no, you couldn't ask for a nicer person than Mrs. Harris," she said firmly. "She married Dr. Harris when he was poor and struggling, when colored women were passing right by him, because, God knows, he's not nothing to stop and look at. I bet they're standing in line to get next to him now. And I hope he's got sense enough to hold on to his money and hold on to his wife."

She rose and peered out of the window at the rooftop of Carlson House. Whenever she was near a window that brought Carlson House within view, she always reassured herself that it was still standing. There had once been a minor fire in her kitchen. Though the sparks had been extinguished years ago, she had got in the habit of looking to see if an ember was still in the ash.

She turned back to Jennie. "I guess I better get going if I want to look in at Old Ma. I told one of the girls to take lunch to her, and I'll pick up the dishes. I've been sending down lunch to her, and dinner for her and him both ever since I found her so low when I came. It gives him more time to sit side of her if he don't have to stop and fix food. And it rests his mind to know there's somebody from the House looking in on his mother while he's at work. It's little enough to do for a good neighbor in the little time left to do for her. I knew something wasn't right when I didn't see her chickens."

They both sighed, for those who are over sixty know only too well that the death of an old acquaintance means that the number of those who remember their youth has dwindled again, and more and more they are being surrounded by people who cannot imagine what they were like when they were young. Why, Old Ma remembered Jennie when she was a bride, remembered Essie Carlson when she had a husband. It is a good feeling not to be the one chosen when the reaper comes, but it is a sad feeling to know that the one who is will never again recall old times.

In this mood of melancholy Essie resumed her tentative perch, lowered her voice, and said gloomily, "Bea looks thin, don't she?"

Jennie flushed. "I hadn't noticed Bea looks thin," she said defensively.

"I give her credit for keeping her figure. She's better off. This hot weather, I feel my fat."

"Well, something about her ain't right to me," Essie Carlson insisted. "She always was a looker, but seems like this summer she's prettier than a picture. Puts me in mind of the way people look when they're getting ready to leave this world. You think she pines for her boy? When you get on in years it's hard to be without blood kin nearby. You're blessed you've got Bit. You think Bea ever thinks about going to California to be with Chad?"

"My goodness, no," Jennie cried in alarm. "She'd never leave Boston with me going back there this fall. That's what's wrong with her. She missed me last winter. It took her appetite. It'll take a little time for her to get it back. But there's nothing wrong with Bea that food won't fix. She'll outlive a lot of people."

Essie Carlson pursed her mouth, but then she preferred to speak her mind. "I've been in this world longer than you," she had to admit to make her point. "I know the signs of death where I see them. I don't say Bea is going to die, but I do say she's sicker than you know."

"I know she was heartsick for me, that's all. But now that I've told her I'm coming back to Boston, you watch her put on some flesh."

"If her boy wrote her that he was coming back, I bet she'd bloom like a rose. Blood's thicker than water."

"We couldn't be any closer than sisters," Jennie protested hotly. "I think more of Bea than I do of Bit. I know she feels nearer to me than she does to Chad. Why, it's nearly twenty years since she set eyes on him. He's not a boy any more. He's a man, a white man, a stranger. Bea's got grandchildren she's never seen, and never will. It's like she and Chad lived in different worlds."

"All the same, it's hard for a mother."

Why did people always talk as if mothers had more feelings than everybody else? Jennie thought resentfully. She had loved Chad every bit as much as Bea. Bea used to say herself that she would have made a better mother. Chad had been the same as her own son, but she wasn't heartsick for him. Most of the time she forgot he was on earth.

"I don't believe Bea thinks about Chad one year to the next. They stopped writing each other years back. He didn't want to hear about his old colored friends. And she didn't want to hear about his new white ones. I don't know when was the last time she mentioned his name to me. Twenty years is a long time to grieve."

"All the same, a mother's heart holds a heap of tears."

She made a sound of sadness for Bea. She remembered that Chad had been such a dear little boy. Before she got busy with her New York boarders, he often came to her cottage to keep her company. After that, she just got glimpses of him going past on his way to the beach. When he started going to the other beach, she scarcely saw him at all. She lost track of the kind of boy he was growing up to be. Still it had been hard to believe the news when it sifted from rumor to fact that Chadwick Jennings, calling himself C. Emory Jennings, was practicing law in California and living as white. His grandfather and great-grandfather had practiced law without having to pass, had risen to district attorney and judge. What had got into Chad to make him turn his back on his heritage and on his race?

Essie Carlson said grimly, "It was a bitter day for both races when the white man drew the color line. Made our people think he had something wonderful his side of it. Made some of them deny their own mothers so they could get to see."

She rose and peered out of the window once more, then briskly shook off her sadness, as Negroes learned how long ago. She said, as she almost invariably said, "Well, I better get back while I still have a house to get back to."

Bea was sitting in her favorite rocker when they came out on the porch. She hitched her chair around until she faced them. It was the sort of graceless act that was never associated with Bea, and she was immediately aware of it. She looked embarrassed.

"I guess you and Essie think I'm glued to this rocker. But I feel too good to move. It's just heavenly like in the sun. I used to think about this all winter. I yearned for summer to come. I wanted to see that hydrangea bloom. It just stayed on my mind. You think funny things in the winter when you aren't what you used to be."

"I don't give myself time to think, winter or summer," Essie Carlson said. "Except sometimes I think I'm crazy to work myself so hard. And then I turn around and think it's hard work keeps me going. I tell you one thing," she gave opinion, "Growing old isn't easy, and I sometimes wonder why God gave us old folks such a hard thing to do." She shrugged away the grievous thought.

"And I'll tell you another thing," she said, taking the steps one at a time, and talking over her shoulder, "this time I'm really going, and you won't see me for dust."

Jennie settled herself on the porch railing, watched Essie Carlson out of earshot, then said quarrelsomely, "What does she mean 'us old folks'? She keeps trying to put us in her class. Essie Carlson's seventy, if she's a day. We're barely sixty, and we don't even look it. I hate people who try to make you out as old as they are. That's why Essie Carlson says you seem so thin. She wants to think you're shriveling up like she is. I as good as told her you'd dance on her grave."

Bea said tranquilly, "It isn't so bad growing old. I think that's what's happening to me. And most of the time it's kind of nice and peaceful. All I want is to do it without being a bother."

"Well, what I want," said Jennie vigorously, "is for you to put some fat on. With me renting a room for the first time in my life, and Essie Carlson going around saying you look thin, people'll think we don't have enough to eat in this house. I can remember when we were on top, and Essie Carlson was way down at the bottom. Many a summer I wondered how Essie Carlson was making it. I don't want her wondering about us."

Bea laughed. "Oh, Jennie," she demurred, "Essie Carlson just said she kept too busy to think. She's got too much to do to mind our business. How did she like the way you fixed up the room? I think you did wonders. And, Jennie, about the Hunters, I want you to know I'll be civil to them for your sake. I just won't promise to like them." The years raced backward along her mind. "Their kind cost me my son."

Jennie, too, went back in time, seeing with her mind's eye the footpath behind Essie Carlson's first cottage, a trail that wandered through a quiet wood, emerged among the houses of the rich, and gently sloped to the sea. Chad was walking ahead of her and Bea, carrying his pail and shovel and water wings. The pants of his bathing suit came down to his knees, his sleeves ended just above the elbow. But this one-piece suit was so much less than what he had changed from that to his elders, in bathing stockings and bloomers and billowy skirts, he had next to nothing between him and the beneficial sun.

The footpath met the concrete road that ran horizontal to it. On the other side of the road the lovely beach again. Chad, dashing across, turned round to flash an impish grin that plainly said he was getting too big to wait for a grown-up's hand. Then he was running again, shouting excited greetings to his friends. In a moment he had melted into a group of little boys from the big houses, and Jennie and Bea really had to look hard to determine which bright head was his.

Bea said in a dull, drained voice, "All the nice people, white and colored, bathed together on the best beach before that New York crowd came and carried on so. When that rich white group leased the beach, and fenced it in, and formed a club, we couldn't say we hadn't seen it coming. But it was like a slap in the face the first time we saw that fence that as good as told us which side to stay on."

Color surged under Jennie's skin as if she were again extracting the meaning implied in the words, Members Only. *Colored people, keep out. If you worm your way in by due process of Massachusetts law, you'll be treated like a worm all right.*

She said roughly, "The white man even draws a line in the undivided ocean. I remember Chad started to race across the street, like he always did, and we screamed at him to stop, as if we thought he was running into a cage of lions that would tear him apart. You and I stood there like we had turned to stone, with Chad looking back at us like we had lost our minds. Then some children he knew drove up in their pony cart and called him to come on over. That kind of brought us back to our senses. We grabbed him and dragged him off like the devil himself was after us."

A mother sparrow was scratching around the hydrangea bush. A baby sparrow followed close behind her, his fledgling state attested to by his ceaseless fluttering of his new wings that still seemed a strange part of him. As the succulent morsel of the earth went into her mouth instead of his he bitterly complained with bitter cheeps. But she was teaching him that the world was wider than the nest. Though every time she found a tidbit, he opened his beak to receive it, her mother love, her protective instinct would not let her yield. If he did not learn this first lesson of survival, how would she prepare him for the rest of life's harshness? He would let himself be swallowed by a cat.

But Bea was not looking toward the hydrangea. The remembered humiliation that had reddened Jennie's face now whitened hers. The shadows deepened under her eyes, stood out sharply against her pallor. The helplessness she had felt that day surged in her again like sickness. Her stomach shuddered, and pain set it afire, as if the white-skinned child she had once carried in her womb was seeking to destroy the last trace of his black beginning.

"It makes me sick to think about it," she said numbly.

"You look sick," Jennie agreed heartily. "And I'll never forget how poor little Chad looked when we reached the beach where everybody bathed. Maybe we shouldn't have fooled him about how he'd like it better. The water wasn't near as clear, there wasn't near as much nice sand, and what there was of it was crowded. But we had to tell him something. And he was only seven. We couldn't tell him the truth without starting him thinking about being colored. And you see what happened when he did. It ruined his whole life."

The baby bird began to scratch around the hydrangea. He did not know the earth sounds. He was only imitating his mother. And suddenly there was food before his eyes, in his belly, filling the emptiness his mother had ignored. His senses began to perceive the movement under the earth. His tiny breast swelled with this important knowledge. The ways of the air-borne had been as strange to him hitherto as the ways of the earth-bound. He knew no more about the other living creatures, but that was not his present concern. He had grasped the tremendous truth about himself. In his pride at this self-identity he did not believe there was anything more wonderful than being what he was.

But Jennie was not looking toward the hydrangea, either. She blinked her eyes, but she could not shut out the small stranded figure who had only had herself and Bea for company all that long summer.

"I guess that was the loneliest summer Chad ever spent. He didn't belong. He didn't have anybody to be with. The white children were passable. They weren't bluebloods like those others, but their fathers could afford to give them vacations, so they weren't trash. But the colored children were from the washerwomen's shanties. They were just dirt. You couldn't let him be with them and you couldn't let him be with the white ones, or the colored ones would have thought he was trying to be white, and they'd have picked fights with him. If there'd been somebody near his age among our friends' children, he wouldn't have been so by himself. But the next under Chad was a toddler, and the next over was a boy about eleven or twelve, who didn't want Chad tagging after him. When we lost that beach on the other side, we lost Chad. After that summer he was never the same."

Bea said convulsively, "If that New York crowd had left us alone, they would never have fenced in that beach, and Chad would never have grown up thinking he was on the wrong side of it."

"Bea," Jennie said gently, her conscience troubled by those telltale marks of pain, "I'm not saying we're getting any older, but we're not getting any younger. It's plain something eating away inside you. Is it heartache? Chad's your own flesh. Maybe you ought to try to get in touch with him. Maybe you ought to consider going to visit him next winter. People rave about California's climate, say it's summer all year round, say food's way cheaper. You could dress and eat both, and put on some fat. And maybe you'd like it well enough to stay. I don't know but what you ought to give it serious thought."

Bea said coldly, proudly, "You forget Chad must have a white mother. My blood is black. I'd die before I denied it. When Chad denied his, he denied me. I have no son. And now let's talk about something else."

"That's all right with me," said Jennie thankfully. *You were wrong, Essie Carlson, she triumphed. It was me on her mind last winter, not Chad. She says herself she wants no part of him. There's nothing wrong with Bea that my cooking won't cure.*

She got to her feet. "Come on, Bea. You say nobody can fry chicken like me. Let's be extravagant for once and have our fryer for an in-between snack. And I wish the wind would carry the smell straight to Carlson House."

"All right," said Bea, because Jennie's pride was still smarting, and she would have felt mean if she hadn't been acquiescent.

"Well, goodness," said Jennie happily, "That's the first time since you've been here you haven't made a fuss about eating. I should have bet Essie Carlson it'll be the same with you as it is with Bit. A year ago she ate like a bird. Now she's eating like a dog." But she suddenly remembered why Bit was eating like a dog. She added anxiously to whatever laughing gods might be listening, "But I didn't bet."

## Chapter Eight

After their meal, Jennie fidgeted with a fold of her dress, as Bea talked.

"I don't scorn peace and quiet any more," her oldest, dearest friend went on calmly. "My dancing days are over. You wouldn't believe how much I stayed at home last winter, how many days I didn't speak to a living soul. Sometimes I didn't even leave my room to walk to the corner to get a bite to eat. I just don't walk any more unless I have to. I even hate to get on a streetcar unless I'm sure of a seat. I'm too tired when I get where I'm going if I have to stand till I get there. I know how you hate to hear about age, but I don't mind admitting I feel old."

Bea was making Jennie nervous with all this talk about breaking health. Anybody carrying Bea's few pounds should feel like a million dollars. She wasn't hauling around the extra fat that everybody said was so dangerous to people no longer young. For all Bea knew she, Jennie, could drop dead of heart disease any time at all. It had killed her mother. It could kill her.

Quickly she shied away from this disquieting thought, and sought comfort in a calming one. On the other hand, fat was a base to build on when sickness laid you low. If you were skin and bones like Bea, you'd better do your best to stay well. If you ever got sick, God help you. If Bea ever got sick . . . . God, help her! God, help Bea!

Panic roared in Jennie's ears, raced her pulse, choked her lungs, but she forgot to be frightened by these violent symptoms of heart disease in her greater fear of the nameless thing that threatened Bea.

For now the dread image that Jennie had been averting her eyes from for days dragged itself into the open, forced her to follow its trail of slime until it reared and spat upon Bea's face.

Bea was in decline. It could no longer be ignored. Her beauty was imbedded in fragile bone, the pearly skin stretched taut. The violet smudges under her eyes were deeper and darker than ever before. Her eyes looked enormous in this setting. Laughter would drown in their depths. Between the slender body and its skeleton was only a delicate breath.

Jennie jumped up to run away from the horror she felt. She erupted so violently from her chair that it continued to sway back and forth after she reached the screen door. And hearing that creak above all the others, like screws being turned in a coffin, she remembered how the old folks used to say that a chair that rocked with no one in it was a certain sign of death. The chill of the grave turned the beads of perspiration on Jennie's brow to drops of ice.

It was Bit who helped Jennie get ready for the trip to Boston. For the first time since her sickness she sewed, sewed the black dress for Jennie to wear to Bea's funeral.

Jennie could still hear Bit's thin quaver rising in "Beulah Land." Bit sang because her heart was full of thanksgiving, as old hearts always are when someone else is chosen to die. She sang a hymn of the radiant life on the other side of the sky, because she rejoiced that the one chosen was worthy to be united with God.

Now, in the stillness, the sisters moved calmly in their rockers. They were growing old in the peace and health and quiet, which the island offers to those who want it. Jennie was surprised that instead of feeling dismay that Bit, too, would complicate her plans, she felt a curious relief.

Circa 1950

# WINTER ON MARTHA'S VINEYARD

WINTER WAS an enemy of the old. Through the savage months of its stay there were no fiercer adversaries. And no two more unmatched, no struggle more uneven. When winter won, it was an easy victory. But when an old, beleaguered heart, abused for sixty years or more by sorrow and sickness, terror and hate, passion and pain, outwitted winter, survived its thrusts, and limped to spring and healing, the victory was won with stubborn will. Marshaled against the weaponless heart had been winter's battalions, snow and ice and cold and wind.

On the island snow was not the chief slaughterer. The salt air magically melted it, and the white loveliness of the woods lasted no longer than a day. But when the clouds refused to break and the sun was unable to warm the sea, the mounting beauty of the snow was touched with treachery. For a shovel had to be put to it. To the old the path was unending, the task Herculean. In the night the outraged heart hammered against the imprisoning flesh. The terror of death stalked the darkness. And the anguished foghorn, guiding the snow-blinded ships over the moonless sea, sounded a dirge in the sleepless ear. Only dawn and clearing skies restored the weary heart to its regular beat.

Ice laid a trap for the old. The walk to town, the worry of it starting just outside the front door with a snail-like descent of each step, was like a journey on the rim of the world. The old have a fear of falling. They know the brittleness of their bones. They know that once they fall they have measured themselves for their coffins. The hospital door shuts after them, never to let them out the way they came in.

When the ice endured, the immobile white-bellied gulls hungered on the frozen harbor, rows of them staring toward shore, admitting man's almightiness, begging for bread. The birds cheeped bitterly at night, and in the morning complained on back porches, eating their weight in seeds and suet to compensate for the body's cold. The dirt roads were like macadam, as if they could never again sift to summer's sand. The froth had frozen along the shores, a spellbound wave that would not roll back to sea. The red-cheeked children, fresh from skating, ate to bursting. And the old ate sparingly to make their store of food last until the streets were safer.

The wind was the cruelest scourge. Blowing north, with nothing to stop its sweep from the sea, it hurled itself across the unsheltered island. Snatching off shingles, swooshing down chimneys, churning glowing coals into comfortless ash, rubbing the tree tops against the roof, scraping them back and forth, back and forth, screech, scraw, screeech, scraaw, overturning everything that wasn't battened down, slamming and banging at windows and doors wherever it found one not storm-tightened, goading rain or hail or sleet into the fury of stampeding horses, so that the tormented summer houses shook and swayed on their slender supports, penetrating unplastered walls, sucking under every lintel and ledge that had not been braced with weather stripping, blowing an icy breath wherever tongue and groove had widened, the wind played every mean trick in its bag.

The lamps were always kept ready with oil. In a windstorm the lines went down. The old lit their lamps in advance that there need not be even a moment of fumbling terror. For the noises of the furious night tore the nerves apart, and the old imagined the worst. They had seen too much of death not to seek its face everywhere. In a great storm there was always one who died in directionless flight, believing the walls would cave in and crush her, only to fall in the path of a crashing tree, and lie pinned to earth's bosom that in winter was earth's bier, with the spade put to it for planting deep, not for planting shallow; or one who ran from one room to another, searching some place where the sound of the wind would not follow, carrying her destruction in the old and beautiful lamp, and freeing one hand to pull a shade that the wind had flung up, to keep the blackness from coming in, the other palsied hand could not support a lamp unaided, nor catch the ball of fire that ran up the curtain. And a summer house that had withstood a thousand winter storms, of whose antiquity its owner would have boasted on an August day, became a blazing pyre.

Still the old could die sitting unmoving in a chair, the lamp quite safe and steady on a table, the house clear of trees that might crash. The old could die from the act of not moving to rekindle a fire that the wind had devoured, not caring to stick match to kindling lest the wind snatch a spark. When the tide turned the wind's face away from the land, the old were then too numb with cold to move. And in the unguarded hours of early morning, when death finds its victims most accessible, an old heart slowed and stopped.

When the cold was a still cold, however bitter the night became, it could be borne. There was the moon's benignity. The world outside was white with its light. The neighbors seemed nearer. The paths to their houses were clear and comforting. A dog's bark had the windless sky for a sounding board. And a dog's bark is a fine night noise in a place where dogs go visiting like people, and are just as well known by name and nature as the folks they let live with them. The motor horns were like friendly halloos on the highway. The old thought gratefully, I am not the only one not sleeping. There is someone who has been somewhere and is going somewhere, and where he was, they are still awake, and where he is going, they will wake to welcome him. And the awareness of all these voices in the night was like shaping friendly faces to put to them.

The old, whether island born or island loving, whoever watched the windless night, gave thanks that the ships were riding on calm seas. No one lives on an island who does not love the steamer that sails to her, who does not pray for her when the seas are high.

The steamer is the core of island life, the link with the mainland, with "America," as islanders say in solemn jest. There are just two kinds of people in an islander's thinking, islanders and off-islanders. There are just two designations of places, the island and off-island. America is broken up into states and cities in his mind only because when you buy a ticket, you have to name a destination. But he tells his friends he is going off-island or to America, and it's up to them to guess, from his known opinion of the summer people and their winter habitations, what unimportant part.

In summer the steamer is a turncoat that brings the summer swarm who think that islanders are a different breed of men, which they don't mind admitting if allowed to say so to the visitors' disfavor. The steamer, gliding smoothly over glass, arriving on schedule with no trouble docking is just a convenience for the summer people, who don't know her stem from her stern, and maybe don't know their own.

But in winter the steamer is listened for as anxiously as a lover. The minutes are counted for her coming. There is no one on the streets. They are all indoors, waiting to plan the day after she comes. As the hours pass impatience turns to uneasiness. When it is known that she will not touch port that day, that she has put an impassable sea between herself and those who wait for her, that day is lost out of an islander's life.

There is no mocking of the mainland then. There is bitterness at the isolation of an island. The invisible Cape, so clear on clear days, about which the islanders hold the summer opinion that its railway reach of the great eastern cities is more a blemish than anything else, the shrouded Cape is considered a blessed abode, and the island the misbegotten spawn of the Atlantic.

Then the seas quiet and the steamer comes. In her holds are milk for the young, bread for the old, meat for the toilers, and printed matter for the mind. And even more than these there is the mail. In the six towns every post-office fills with expectant faces. An island can hold only so many souls, and the young will always seek a larger world than the one they are born into. Those who are busy with jobs and careers cannot chance a winter's sea. The island is a dot on the map, unimportant to city timekeepers. Letters keep the love coming through a winter of waiting.

To the old who waited in summer cottages letters were the mainstay of the long day. For the summer settlements were far from the snug areas of winter living, and the surrounding shuttered houses were for those whose lights shone out on still roads. And the lighted houses were limited within themselves to a small sphere of movement. The kitchen stove was the principal source of heat. As winter progressed, whatever rooms were outside of its radius were closed off and their keyholes padded. The kitchen became the heart the house. The bedroom above it was the one chosen for winter sleeping. The portable oil stove, without which no cottage was complete, took the chill off the bedroom in the morning before the kitchen stove had been shaken free of slumbering ashes.

New Englanders expect to be cold in winter, and all they ask of a heating agent is that it takes the chill off. A hot house keeps the hand in the pocket. Coal is something you must constantly buy only to burn it up as soon as you buy it. Oil has the same disadvantage. A good wool sweater and a change of wool underwear, if not washed too often, will last for years. A brick will last a lifetime. And what is better than a hot brick to warm a cold bed?

A seasoned New Englander doesn't spoil himself. He is nurtured on making out. He can make out till spring on what coal he has on hand. No need to buy more with winter half gone. Look at all the signs of early spring. And what did God make trees for? Wood didn't cost anything but the time it took to saw it into chunks. And the time it took to keep the fire stoked. Let the witless argue that a coal fire saved bother, and the man of sense retorted that a wood fire saved money. The smart and thrifty course was to burn wood in the waking hours and throw on a sprinkle of coal at night to protect the pipes.

In summer water was just a tepid stream from a tap that nobody gave a thought to or even drank without a spot of whiskey and ice. Nobody came to an island that was known up and down the eastern seaboard for its wonderful salt water bathing, which any selectman would testify to as truth, to show any interest in a faucet except to be annoyed when it wouldn't run hot enough for a bath.

But in winter, in the summer houses without cellars, where the pipes were above ground instead of buried in it, the morning greeting of the old women was the inquiry, "Did your water freeze? Mine got caught, but I put a hot cloth to it. Hope this cold snap breaks today. I'd like to sleep sound tonight without keeping an ear out for the water."

On zero nights, from the taps in kitchen and bathroom, little silver streams glistened and plopped, and the anxious ear was alert for any cessation of the life sound.

When water ran free, the winter day could be endured. The little rituals that used up the long hours, the washing up, the morning coffee, the friendly kettle spilling singing drops on the stove, the cozy cup of tea, the piece or two to rinse out, the window plants demanding a drink, soapsuds sparkling in the dish pan, all these small occupations made the old competent of their ability to take care of themselves.

If the water froze, they were dependent on a neighbor's facilities. They felt like ill-mannered children asking to go to a neighbor's bathroom, and like the homeless, asking for a kettle of water, when every roof worthy of the name had water under it. There was nothing to do with the day but wait for the plumber who wouldn't come anyway until tomorrow. The dishes stood in the sink, there was not enough water for a real wash, the unemptied chamber shamed them. They were robbed of their dignity. They imagined that the outside world was saying they needed looking after. Water was a symbol of their independence.

In winter the young neighbors interfered with their independence anyway, spying on their houses to see if the shades were up when it was day, and if the lights were on when it was night, asking as many questions as a doctor whenever they met, coming round with food as if there was somebody sick. And if anything seemed amiss on their prowls, they knocked softly as if to knock loudly would disturb the dead. When they gained entrance, they acted surprised that the old were still alive.

Of course they were alive. They were not going to die in the allotted time of man. There was a magic in island living. You had simply to look at the gravestones to see it. No one died but the ancients. Only the foolish say seventy is old. Eighty is just about right for elderly. Ninety is time enough to make room.

And when they did die what better place to sleep than where every pebble on the beach felt familiar to the hand. What better place to sit in the sun when the time came for remembering. This was the place they had loved best when their world was young. This was homecoming, not in the way of the boy from college, or the man with his bride, but in the way of those who come home to die.

In the New England cities of their origins, they had moved from house to house as a father's income increased or decreased, as a family shrunk or spread. As wives they had moved many times, from flat to city house to suburb. As widows they had gone here and there and everywhere in ceaseless treks to married children.

They had lived in many houses in many places in their winters. But summer had found them returning to the island from however far their winter's search had taken them. They knew the smell of salt air better than city smoke. They knew the length and breadth of the island as they could never know the extent of a complex city. And they knew, a knowing they cherished as life assailed them with lost youth, lost husbands, lost friends, lost income, lost health, they knew that on the island time stood still.

The island, with its changelessness, held the best of their remembering. If they looked backward long enough they would see their children searching for the singing shells, and themselves in bathing dresses and stockings, their long hair tucked in frilly rubber caps, joining hands with other laughing bathers and bobbing up and down, up and down in the gentle ripples, as if it were no feat to bend the knees; or they would see their young husbands coming on holidays, the five-pound box of chocolates tucked under their arms, and the sight of their striding maleness would bring the blood to their cheeks as they wondered if the thin bedroom walls would keep their love inside the room, and then the blood deepened as they wondered if a really good woman would have such thoughts, not knowing that time would take care of their thinking; or they would see themselves seated on the grass beyond the lighted bandstand in the park, eating hot buttered popcorn out of their own bags and sticky sweet molasses popcorn out of their best friend's, such a wonderful feeling to eat out of a bag and know it was not an inelegant act on a summer night in a park by the sea, as if good teeth and good digestions and bones that did not creak in night air were not reason enough for this simple pleasure.

Best of all the remembering back was the reliving of the opening of the cottage. The children shooed from underfoot, with no fear for their wanderings on an island that cherished all swift small wild life. Last year's newspapers taken down from the windows. The red pepper that had kept the mice away swept out of corners. The blankets aired, the rugs unrolled. The furniture that had been carefully piled in the center of each room, as if doing so was a more housewifely act than leaving it in place—pushed back to its original position, the exact spot carefully located, lest an inch or two out of the way would indicate an indifference to doing things right. And then the inventory. Papa would have to be sent a list of things to post down from the city. And then Granny, interfering, getting in the way. How sad, how lonely, how useless it was to be seventy. I hope, the younger heart said fervently, I hope I die before I'm old, before I have nothing to live for.

And then came their time to be old. And they were not ready to die. They were content with a flower's unfolding, a bird on a bough, the sun riding out of the sea. The miracles of daily living were well worth waiting over for another showing. And they felt that God's world looked best in an island setting. One summer's end they settled down to stay.

In this unaltered place they, too, might be spared time's changes. Summer after summer the island remained the same in substance. Rounding the bend the steamer saw the panorama its parent steamers had seen for years out of memory. The lighthouse on the Chop, the white spires of churches, the gleaming sand, the dunes, gingerbread cottages, the island sky, none bluer nor more serene, and none overspreading a richer vineyard.

Here was the abundant sea, but the land it bound was as abundant. The wild grape twined by every tinkling stream, blueberries and huckleberries were thick on up-island bushes, blackberries and strawberries grew wherever grass would grow, the beech plums waited to be jelly, cranberries reddened in the bogs, fruit hung heavy on gnarled trees. The earth was good to seed, yielded a harvest to every man who put his hand to planting. Cows and sheep grazed in the pastures, goats chewed calmly in backyards, chickens made the morning loud. Game birds wandered in the woods.

This was the land of milk and honey to which the old returned to taste its elixir on their tongues.

Circa 1950

## ELEPHANT'S DANCE
### A Memoir of Wallace Thurman

IN 1925 he came hopefully from the West Coast. He was 25, and the Negro literary renaissance was in its full swing. He wanted to get in on the ground floor, and not get off the crowded lift till it banged the roof off and skyrocketed him, and such others as had his ballast of self-assurance and talent, to a fixed place in the stars. He died on Welfare Island 10 years later, with none of his dreams of greatness fulfilled. Yet there is no other name that typifies that period as does that of Wallace Thurman.

He was Wallie to his friends, and his sycophants were legion. He could "dish it out," and there was no tongue that could return it. Perhaps if Harlem had produced a dozen contemporary minds as keen as his, he would not have drowned his disillusion in drink, and under his leadership something better might have come of that period than the hysterical hosannas that faded on the subsequently stilly night.

Thurman was a slight, nearly Black boy with the most agreeable smile in Harlem and a rich infectious laugh. His voice was without accent, deep and resonant. That voice was the most memorable thing about him, welling up out of his too frail body and wasting its richness in unprintable recountings.

He had just received his A.B. degree from the University of Southern California when wind of what was called the Negro Renaissance blew West. He was writing a column called "Inklings" in a Los Angeles newspaper, a Negro sheet, doing pieces of topical interest on mildly controversial subjects. He read about the goings-on in New York, where Negroes and whites were mingling socially to discuss that elephant's dance, Negro writing, remarkable not so much because it was writing but because it was Negro writing.

He got very excited about it and he was young enough to feel inspired. There in New York people like Carl Van Vechten, H. L. Mencken, Fannie Hurst, the Van Dorens, and others equally well known, were talking shop with newly arrived young Negroes no older and maybe no wiser than himself. Their works were being published and hailed as masterpieces. Contests were in progress and hotels heretofore closed to Negroes were hired for the award presentations.

Thurman tried to organize a literary group in Los Angeles. But his associates had not followed the eastern activities with his interest. He plunged his insufficient savings into a literary publication in an abortive attempt to revolutionize the West. Nobody was really stirred. Thurman headed East.

Countee Cullen, Langston Hughes, Zora Neale Hurston, Bruce Nugent, Rudolph (Bud) Fisher, Jean Toomer, Eric Walrond were the new names. A few older writers—Claude McKay, Walter White, George Schuyler—had preceded the Renaissance but their age and activities set them apart from this group whose youth and high spirits kept them on a continual round of gayeties. When the dawn came up like thunder, most of them were still posturing.

Thurman fitted into this crowd like a cap on a bottle of fizz. Only Cullen looked at him askance because Cullen was a lyricist, far removed from the primal earthiness Thurman often extolled.

There were a brief three months after his arrival when Thurman had no job and very little money. It did not matter, for that was the great sponge era, too, and you ate at anyone's mealtime and conveniently got too tight to go home at your host's bedtime. There were other stratagems. Downtown whites were more than generous. You opened your hand and it closed over a five-spot. Or you invited a crowd of people to your studio, charged them admission, got your bootlegger to trust you for a gallon or two of gin, sold it at fifteen cents a paper cup, and cleared enough from the evening's proceedings to pay your back rent and your bootlegger and still had sufficient money left to lay in a week's supply of liquor and some crackers and sardines.

Thurman's first job in New York was on a Negro newspaper that folded after his arrival. It lasted long enough, however, to print his review of *The New Negro*, Alain Locke's analysis of the flourishing period. Of this book, which, by the way, does not mention Thurman so lately arrived on the New York scene, Thurman wrote, "In it (*The New Negro*) are exemplified all of the virtues and all of the faults of this new movement, even to a hint of its preciousness. Many have wondered what this Negro literary renaissance has accomplished other than providing white publishers with a new source of revenue, affording the white intellectuals with a 'different' fad and bringing a half dozen Negro artists out of obscurity."

He was acquiring cynicism already and biting the hand that was feeding him. For to him there were only one or two whites who did not patronize. The rest were exploiters, and since they were the important people, one must either wrap a handkerchief around one's head or steadily insult them. This last, which was Thurman's way, they found amusing, for the Negro was a childish creature not to be taken seriously. He, Thurman, was a bad boy, and therefore doubly endearing. Where the others were sometimes too docile, he was full of delightful surprises.

His attitude was no deterrent to job-getting and, although he continued to sponge on his friends, he was rarely unemployed. It was his way to carry a check for days, invite a succession of friends out for the evening, show them the check and bewail his inability to identify himself to the waiter, and leave them with the bill to pay. He was always stimulating, and neither party was the loser. He rarely tried this trick with his own contemporaries. Rather, he would invite a string of them to join him as his guests, and an unsuspecting downtowner would foot the bill for the lot of them and expand with simple kindliness while Thurman and his coterie went into peals of laughter which the benefactor imagined was peculiar to Negroes after a heavy meal.

Thurman was writing steadily, but his life was as steadily growing more hectic, and his philosophy more confused. It was his nature to rebel and to pull the pedestal out from under the plaster gods of other people.

He hated Negro society, and since dark skins were never the fashion among Negro upper classes, the feeling was occasionally mutual. In his book, *The Blacker the Berry*, whose dedication reads, "To Beulah [his mother], the goose who laid the not so golden egg," his dark-skinned heroine suffered many of the small humiliations he would not have admitted suffering himself. For he was never humble or apologetic, and he laughed very hard when things hurt him most.

Negro society was taking itself very seriously in those days. Carl Van Vechten had revealed its inner workings in the pages of his *Nigger Heaven*, and Harlem had become a mecca for the smart set thrill-seekers. Downtowners sought any means to gain *entrée* to uptown parties. Van Vechten could hardly lead the throng, for his unfortunate choice of title for his book, the exotic types he had chosen as typifying Negro society, the whole exposé, made him outcast to all but the close friends from whom he had drawn his chief characters.

Harlem, however, had had the taste of white patronage and found it sweet to the palate. There was no party which did not have its quota of white guests who were distinguishable from the fairest Negroes only by their northern accents, the majority of fair-skinned Negroes having southern accents. The artists were the liaison group. They were not exactly an exemplary lot, but they knew the downtowners, and a carefully worded note instructing them to bring a friend, any friend, was read between the lines. The young artist showed up slightly drunk, having been paid in the preferred coin of alcohol by a grateful white, and proceeded to lap up his hostess' liquor as further payment for providing her the privilege of sending another important name to the society columns of the Negro papers.

It was Thurman's delight to take a whole entourage of whites, some of them sleazy, to these parties. He earned the enmity of many hostesses by his companions' silly behavior and his own inability not to pass out and be carried bodily from a party. The conservative group disinherited him. Though he despised them for their insularity and their aping of privileged whites, still he allowed himself to grow extremely sensitive following their changed attitude and to believe that it was his black skin that made him *déclassé*. He mocked their manners and their bastard beginnings, and divorced himself completely from a conventional way of life.

He began to surround himself with a queer assortment of the "lost generation" of Blacks and whites. They clung to him like leeches, and although he saw them clearly and could evaluate them in a half-dozen brutal words, he chose to allow them to waste the valuable hours of his ripening maturity.

He had no privacy except on the infrequent occasions when he literally pushed his companions out of his quarters and wrote for a stretch of 48 hours or else escaped to the suburban home of a married friend, where he lived in peace and normalcy until his writing stint was finished. In the suburban home his sanity returned, and he always came back to the city with a sense of something lost. There was a child there, and Thurman loved it. He wanted a child, but he knew that he had wasted his energies and might never reproduce himself. The knowledge frightened him. He wanted to be thoroughly male and was afraid that he was not. He looked about his narrowing circle, and of the few women on the fringe of that group, there was none whom he would have married.

Inevitably he married the first fresh face that pierced the pea-soup fog of his horizon. His wife was chaste and saffron-colored, a former schoolteacher lately arrived in New York. Like any other young married man, Thurman wanted to establish a home with his bride. It was the way a man put down roots. He forsook his old haunts and attempted the transition from bachelorhood and bohemianism to the life of a conventional family man by going eagerly to a new address with his wife and also his mother-in-law, for whom he had real affection. His achievements—*The Blacker the Berry* had been widely acclaimed, he had been chosen editor of the short-lived but much-touted Negro Magazine, *Fire*, his place on the editorial staff of MacFadden Publications— were solid enough to convince his wife that she could reform him. Other women were marrying artists and thereby firmly entrenching themselves in Negro society by giving typical parties of the time. Thurman's wife tried it, and on all occasions came to grief through the absence of her husband or his tardy and reluctant appearance.

Their marriage, which was ill-fated from the start, lasted about six months. Thurman had long wanted to be a father, but he had not taken into consideration that he must first be a husband. When he realized that insurmountable handicap, it was too late to unlearn his oft-repeated philosophy of doing everything once before he died. Habits had taken hold of him that heretofore he would not have admitted were habits. He missed the drinking sessions, the allnight talk fests, the queer assortment of queer people, and the general disregard for established customs.

Under the announcement of his marriage in his scrapbook is penned, "Proof that even the best of us have weak moments." That was braggadocio. With the failure of his marriage, Thurman, for the first time, became unsure of himself. Scandalous things were said about the disunion. The people who aligned themselves with him were the people to whom nothing was scandalous. To them Thurman was not the marrying kind. This proved it. The disastrous interlude was over and better forgotten. Yet Thurman had been in love and had found that he was as vulnerable to its dissolution as any man who plans a future around his wife, a home, a child.

His wife left his home the night before his collaborated play, *Harlem*, opened on Broadway. The night the play opened, he went around to the flat of some friends with his tie and collar in his hand. He had wanted his wife to share in what he had hoped would be his triumph, or to go out with him and get drunk in the event of a cold reception. The fact that she could desert him at a crucial hour did not make him see that she was as much a failure as a writer's wife as he was as a conventional husband.

Mrs. Thurman took very seriously the embarrassment of the breakup and went through a period of utter instability. Later, she made a complete about-face and replaced her old gods, perhaps in unconscious determination to right, to the fullest extent of her energies, those conditions that first bred the cynicism that corroded her husband's mind and led finally to his physical destruction. She became an active worker in the field of labor organization.

Thurman had had a super's role in the Theater Guild's Negro drama, *Porgy*, and had gone into this play in the hope of learning the rudiments of stagecraft, with *Harlem* already in the back of his mind. His was a walk-on part, and his salary was $16.50 weekly. He fought vigorously for an increase in pay for the supers, and the fight was won one week before he quit the company to sit in at the rehearsals of *Harlem*. Some months later, his own cast made capital of this fight when they waged one of their own.

The late Elisabeth Marbury was one of the few whites who met with Thurman's wholehearted approval. He met her one afternoon when he went with a group of writing friends to her home in Sutton Place. She received them like Queen Victoria on her throne, and Thurman was not amused. She was more nearly genuine than anyone he had lately met, and her tongue was as sharp as his. She liked him best, though he made no effort to outshine the others, and wanted a hand in his writing career. She believed enough in his talent to advance him a generous sum to keep him in food and rent while he completed a novel. The novel was *Infants of the Spring*. His tribute is that she is nowhere in those satirical pages.

*Infants of the Spring* is wholly autobiographical. In it is summed up Thurman's disillusion with the New York years. He writes of a typical party: " . . . the drunken revelry began to sicken him. The insanity of the party, the insanity of its implications, threatened his own sanity. It is going to be necessary, he thought, to have another emancipation to deliver the emancipated Negro from a new kind of slavery." The anger with which Thurman wrote in this novel was directed as much toward his own vacillation as toward the foibles of his fellows.

Of whites he wrote: " . . . they have regimented their sympathies and fawn around Negroes with a cry in their hearts and a superiority bug in their heads. It's a new way to get a thrill, a new way to merit distinction in the community . . . this cultivating Negroes. It's a sure way to bolster up their own weak egos and cut a figure. Negroes being what they are make this sort of person possible."

With this complete lack of illusion about anything, sacred or profane, Thurman could be almost brutally objective. At one point in *Infants of the Spring* he ponders the one-time appearances of Negro writers, the "splurges" as he called them. He wondered if the single appearance were the result of "some deep rooted complex," or if they betokened a lack of talent. Fundamentally, however, he identified himself with his writing colleagues and argued in less objective moments that these "splurges" had no fixed relation to talent, or lack of it. He recognized the attitude of patronage wherever he saw it, and he despised it. The traditional attitude of white America, despite its shift in emphasis during that turbulent period, was still such as to discourage the most honest and energetic of creative impulses.

*Infants of the Spring* was published in Thurman's thirty-second year, two years before his unnecessary death. He knew now very definitely that he did not have the elements of genius. He did not even know whether or not he was a first-rate writer. At one time the character who is himself says, "I don't expect to be a great writer." He not only understood himself but he also understood his period. He recognized its artificiality, its high-blown divorce from reality, and speaking further he said, "I don't think the Negro race can produce one [a great writer] now, any more than can America." He felt that Jean Toomer was the only Negro writer who had the elements of greatness. The others were "journeymen, planting seed for someone else to harvest. . . . We younger ones are mired in decadence. We're a curiosity, even to ourselves."

He felt, however, that his critical judgment was sound, and as a critic of his colleagues, he was as much prophet as contemporary observer. He realized that his field was magazine editing, but there were now fewer and fewer indulgent whites to sponsor a literary publication, and previous ventures had proved that Negroes in numbers would not subscribe.

Thurman was sincere in wanting to tear off the tinsel of the literary scene in Harlem, and for a while he tried to get at fundamentals. In *Fire*, of which he was the guiding light, he declared editorially that the superfluities of the Renaissance should be torn away and the worthwhile elements preserved. Despite his general scorn for the achievements of the Renaissance, he felt, and said, that it had done more in six years for the benefit of the race than W. E. B. Du Bois and the late James Weldon Johnson had done "in a generation." He attributed to those older men the virtue of tolerance where the younger group was concerned. As for the attitude of the infants toward those elders, he said, " . . . we laugh at them . . . we don't feel the old urge to get out and harangue for social justice." Yet his urge to tear away the tinsel, to expose the exploitation that went on under the guise of friendship, to show up and refuse humiliating patronage where- and whenever it existed were toward the end of equality with all writers.

The first issue of *Fire* cost a dollar a copy, and the several hundred copies were sold immediately. But they were sold to the friends and well-wishers of the editorial staff, whose members included Langston Hughes, Zora Neale Hurston, Aaron Douglas, and others less well known. It would appear that the magazine had set out to be shocking, for much of the material was sensational. Where the friends of this group could regard these outpourings with indulgence, the wide audience which the magazine needed for its support rejected them because they were too far removed from ordinary, conventional experience. Thurman, as chief editor, had mistaken the shadow for the substance, and after its initial appearance *Fire* was extinguished.

After a two-year interval, *Harlem: A Forum of Negro Life* appeared. It was soberer than its predecessor, but it did not last beyond the second issue. With sufficient financial support to make its appearance and to carry it over, if it was not immediately self-supporting, Thurman decided to run it on a large scale. He established an office on Seventh Avenue, and called in several young writers without commitments to help with the business of running the magazine. Aware now that any successful magazine must of necessity draw its support from a wide audience rather than from a select group, *Harlem* was less esoteric than *Fire* had been, closer to earth, and its appeal was broader. It was 25 cents a copy, a concession to the proposition that a literate mass might exist, and it included older writers among its contributors. While these changes were for the better, and were not lacking in response from readers, expenses increased disproportionately with returns on distribution, and after the second issue, the magazine folded.

In the winter of 1934, Thurman was working as chief editor of the staff at Macaulay's. With A. L. Furman, lawyer-brother of the publishers, he had collaborated on a novel, *Interne*. It was Furman's first novel and Thurman's last printed work. The book had little to offer save its over-sensational exposé of conditions on Welfare Island. It was cheap and poorly written. The characters were white, and of a class of which Thurman could know very little. There were many who did not believe he had a hand in writing the book, but his scrapbook gives mute testimony to material collected. He visited Welfare Island and, for the first time in his New York years, was shocked and horrified. He came away loud and bitter in his denunciation, and with the avowal never to set foot again in the place.

It was Furman who introduced Thurman to Bryan Foy, who had lately arrived from Hollywood where he was engaged in the making of class "B" pictures. Thurman's work with MacFadden Publications had taught him what a large part of the public wanted. He was editor at Macaulay's, successfully turning out "popular" fiction. These facts, with Thurman's engaging personality, sold him to Foy. They talked about a contract over dinner in a downtown restaurant. It amused Thurman very much that, although the late John Barrymore's profile was on prominent display at a nearby table, it was he who was the object of all the ogling.

He left New York in February with a contract with Foy Productions, Ltd., in his pocket. His first scenario was *High School Girl* which had a fair run at the Astor. His second was *Tomorrow's Children*, a film on sterilization which was generally banned in New York. The story sessions were mad, and Thurman's nerves were shot. He hated the long, drawn out, senseless discussions. On one occasion he became violently ill through sheer physical revolt at the antics of his colleagues.

It was June when a doctor on the West Coast cautioned him about his health. He was losing weight and a cold he had caught one night on the beach persisted. He and the joy-seekers who comprised his new crowd were inclined to bathe and imbibe, and more often than not fall asleep on the beach in their wet bathing suits and wake in a chilly dawn to a dismal regard of a circle of blue lips.

Thurman did not want to take the doctor seriously, but he knew that he was dying, and he wanted it to be short and even merry. He had been advised that he must give up all his indulgences, and reasoned that if he didn't death would come quickly and without bother. Twice before he had attempted melodramatic suicides, and they had been fun rather than funereal. This time there was no one to snatch him back from a theatrical finish.

He flew to New York, determined that his end should be spectacular. He arrived on a hot summer day in a flamboyant Hollywoodian costume. He sounded an alarm on Seventh Avenue and rounded up his friends, laughing more loudly than he ever had before, telling unprintable tales of the cinema city, and refusing to be left alone for a minute.

He was frightened and determined not to admit it. He got drunk, and stayed drunk, and talked very much, and would not sleep alone, nor say one serious thing.

Suddenly he collapsed, and found himself recovered from unconsciousness, and not dead. On a hot July 1, he lay in the incurable ward on Welfare Island. For six long months he lay there. They were the bitterest months of his life. Death was to be drawn out, and that riotous month was only making it harder. He was too weak for anything but contemplation, and there was no one with whom to exchange *bon mots*.

Mercifully, he died in late December, and on Christmas Eve his wasted body lay in a Harlem funeral parlor. It was the first break in the ranks of the "New Negro." They assembled in solemn silence, older, hardly wiser, and reminded for the first time of their lack of immortality.

So Thurman lived and died, leaving no memorable record of his writing, but perhaps the most symbolic figure of the Literary Renaissance in Harlem.

Circa 1945
From *Black World*, November 1970

# THE INROADS OF TIME

THE UNJOYS of growing older could easily fill a sizable portion of this page. Fortunately for the squeamish, I am only allowed the length of a column. Which is just as well. To go beyond that length would only give me license to exaggerate.

I remember coming across a picture some years ago that had been taken some years before the day of its reappearance. It was a group picture, 20 young men and women on shipboard. Europe bound, and I knew that I had been along. But I could not find myself in the picture. Had I balked at being included, perhaps not liking how I looked that day? Had nobody noticed I wasn't there, and nobody had scoured the ship for me?

And who was that girl in the front row, that intruder smiling straight at the camera as if she had every right to share this indelible moment? I stared hard at her and felt crazy. She was a total stranger, and yet I was beginning to feel I had seen her some place before.

Then I gave a little gasp, not so much of dismay as of disbelief. I was looking at myself. Though that face was familiar, I could not juxtapose it with mine and see the slightest resemblance. I remember saying softly, Now I am that girl's mother. And now, so many more years later, I am that girl's grandmother.

It took me a long time to accustom myself to accepting the inroads of time. It is not a joy to behold my face at an early hour in the morning. But that unjoy is easily dissolved when I think of the fledglings of my family and of my friends, all so dear to me, who would never have been born to make their mark if the world had stopped at some given point to accommodate my vanity.

I remember the day my seven-year-old dog, a wire-haired terrier, who could outrun every dog he challenged to a race, who took great joy in being the winner, fell into step with a new, neighborhood dog, no more than two, if two, by the look of him, and off they went, running as fast as flung arrows, with my dog leading, and the young dog gaining, and my dog falling back, and the young dog outrunning him, running out of sight, and my dog coming back, coming back to me, looking up at me, his puzzled face, his puzzled eyes asking me what happened.

I still remember the pain and shame in his eyes. And I remember patting him and telling him softly that everyone grows older, that everyone slows down. The saving grace is to do it with grace.

That I am winding down, that my house and yard grow bigger every year, that a walk from one place to another takes minutes longer, that an incline has become a hill, that it takes two hands to do what one could do with ease are inconveniences, not catastrophes. If I can do what must be done with grace, whatever form unjoy parades, I am ready to rout.

From the *Vineyard Gazette*, October 26, 1984

## SELECTED LETTERS

IRONICALLY, DOROTHY WEST'S work has hitherto rarely been included in anthologies on the Harlem Renaissance although, as these letters indicate, she enjoyed a lively correspondence about art, literature, life, and politics with Zora Neale Hurston, Langston Hughes, Countee Cullen, Helene Johnson, Wallace Thurman, James Weldon Johnson, and particularly Claude McKay. They praised and encouraged her work and clearly expected her to find literary success. She labored valiantly to meet those expectations. About her aspirations, she declared candidly in a 1933 letter, "I want to be a great Negro writer."

From the letters it becomes clear that Dorothy West was center stage during the Renaissance and closely involved literarily, intellectually, politically, and socially. She shared an apartment with Zora Neale Hurston, traveled to London with *Porgy*, watched Alberta Hunter sing in smoky speakeasies, attended rent parties with Wallace Thurman, and dated Langston Hughes and Countee Cullen. She was also involved romantically with the writer Marian Minus, her co-editor for *New Challenge*, and with the striking visual artist Mildred Jones, whom Langston Hughes dubbed, "the beauty-sensation of the season."

The correspondence spans the period from 1926, when West was eighteen and recently arrived in New York City, to 1966, when she was, in her words, living quietly on the island of Martha's Vineyard, but still writing. These fascinating letters not only shed light on West's personal and professional life, but they help us to contextualize and more fully understand her art. They offer, moreover, fresh insights into some of the more prominent figures of the twentieth century.

# OPPORTUNITY

JOURNAL  OF  NEGRO  LIFE

PUBLISHED BY THE NATIONAL URBAN LEAGUE

127 EAST 23RD STREET, NEW YORK CITY

OFFICE OF

CHARLES S. JOHNSON

EDITOR

May 4,
1 9 2 6.

Dear Miss West:

I offer my congratulations to you on your success in the Second OPPORTUNITY Contest and my
genuine commendations on the superior quality
of your entry, "The Typewriter," in the Short
Story Section of the contest. I am taking
this occasion also to enclose your check for
prize money, which represents one half of the
second prize offered for short stories.

The enthusiasm this year has been more intense
both on the part of the contestants and those
of the general public interested in letters.
We see a measurable advancement both in substance and technique, even over last year, and
it would be quite proper for you to begin now
the careful preparation of entries for next
year.

This is more than a mere awarding of prizes; it
is to our minds, the evolution of a literature.

Some of the entries will be published in OPPOR-
TUNITY and probably in some other medium that
will bring them to the attention of the public.
Of these plans you will hear more.

Letter from Charles Johnson, editor, *Opportunity: Journal of Negro Life*, to Dorothy
West, May 4, 1926. (Schlesinger Library, Radcliffe Institute, Harvard University.)

Will you let me have promptly a photograph and
a brief sketch of yourself to accompany the
story about the contest in the June issue?
These pictures should be in possibly before the
12th.

With best wishes, believe me to be,

Sincerely yours,

*[signature]*

Charles S. Johnson,
EDITOR.

CSJ/WLW
Enclosure (1)

Miss Dorothy West,
470 Brookline Avenue,
Back Bay, Massachusetts.

---

### The Short Story

First Prize of $100.00 to *Symphonesque* by Arthur Huff Fauset, of Philadelphia, Pa.

Second Prize of $50.00 to *Muttsy* by Zora Neale Hurston, of New York City, and to *The Typewriter* by Dorothy West, of Back Bay, Mass.

Third Prize of $25.00 to *The Heritage of the Heathen* by Lee Wallace, of Topeka, Kansas.

Fourth Prize of $15.00 to *Rootbound* by Eugene Gordon, of Boston, Mass.

to *Rootbound* by Eugene Gordon, of Boston, Mass.

For Honorable Mention to 1. *Clay*, by John Matheus, of Institute, West Virginia. 2. *High-Ball*, by Claude McKay, of Paris, France. 3. *Polly*, by Carol Carson, of Washington, D. C. 4. *Waters of Megara* by John Davis, of Lewiston, Maine. 5. *General Drums* by John Matheus, of Institute, West Virginia. 6. *A Matter of Inches* by Warren A. McDonald, of Philadelphia, Pa. *Falutin'* by Pearl Fisher, of New York City. 8. *Black Gum*, by William V. Kelley, of St. Louis, Mo.

Judges for Short Stories: Zona Gale, Novelist and Playwright; Stuart Sherman, Editor of *Books*, Author and Critic; Jean Toomer, Short Story Writer; Carl Van Doren, Literary Editor *Century Magazine*, Author; Blanche Colton Williams, Author, Columbia University and Hunter College.

*[handwritten note]* It was pleasant to meet you. I hope the various meetings of the Contest proved valuable.

From: Charles S. Johnson, 127 East 23rd Street, NYC
To: Dorothy West, 470 Brookline Avenue, Back Bay, MA
May 4, 1926

Dear Miss West:

I offer my congratulations to you on your success in the Second OPPORTU-
NITY Contest and my genuine commendations on the superior quality of your
entry, "The Typewriter," in the Short Story Section of the contest. I am taking
this occasion also to enclose your check for prize money, which represents one
half of the second prize offered for short stories.

The enthusiasm this year has been more intense both on the part of the
contestants and those of the general public interested in letters. We see a
measurable advancement both in substance and technique, even over last
year, and it would be quite proper for you to begin now the careful preparation of entries for next year.

This is more than a mere awarding of prizes; it is to our minds, the evolution of a literature.

Some of the entries will be published in OPPORTUNITY and probably in
some other medium that will bring them to the attention of the public. Of
these plans you will hear more.

Will you let me have promptly a photograph and a brief sketch of yourself
to accompany the story about the contest in the June issue? These pictures
should be in possibly before the 12th.

With best wishes, believe me to be,

> Sincerely yours,
> Charles S. Johnson,
> EDITOR.

CSJ/WLW
Enclosure (1)

From: Zora Neale Hurston, General Delivery, Sanford, FL
To: Dorothy West and Helene Johnson, 137th Street YWCA[?], NYC
[Sunday] May 22, 1927

Dear Little Sisters D & H—

Yes, I'm married now, Mrs. Herbert Arnold Sheen, if you please.[1] He is in his
last year at the U. of Chicago Med. school, but is going to stay out until we get
a good start. We are all quite happy now. But write me still by my maiden name
as I dont want my mail balled up.

Darlings, see can you find me a copy of Elmer Gantry. I am submerged down
here in this wilderness, where such books are not for sale.

1. Hurston and Sheen were married in St. Augustine, Florida, on May 19, 1927.

Things going dull down here. Working hard, but the people are impossible—all except my husband. The scenery is gorgeous, though.

I have given up writing things until the expedition is over. Then I shall try again. By the way, I hope you two ran away with the "O" contest. I *know* you did even though I have heard nor seen a thing down here in the swamps.

Tired and full of indigestion so I shall not write at length. My love to all the bunch.

Lovingly your sister, Zora

P.S. Do you girls want my apartment for 3 months? You can keep it cheaper than you can your present quarters besides greater comfort insured.[2] I shall not return until Sept & by that time, I might be able to get a front apartment and let you keep it, having a hubby to look out for me, now.

Any way, let me hear from you at once as I know several people who want it, and I cannot afford to keep it vacant. The man who had it is ill in Chicago, and had to give it up.

Lovingly
Zora.

From: Dorothy West, 43 West 66th Street, NYC
To: Rachel West, 470 Brookline Avenue, Boston
Tuesday [March 12, 1929]

Dearest Mother,

Cheryl Crawford called me up this morning and told me I can go abroad. Isn't that wonderful! We are sailing the 26th. To-night I must see the stage manager and company manager about my passport. In the morning I must go down to see Cheryl.[3]

This is so sudden because someone backed out at the last moment, and Cheryl immediately thought of me.

Tommy says earnestly that I must tell you that she will take really excellent care of me.[4] And Cheryl will be along, too.

2. West and her cousin the poet Helene Johnson accepted Hurston's offer and moved from the Harlem YWCA to Hurston's 43 West Sixty-sixth Street apartment.
3. Crawford (1902–86) was assistant stage director for the Theater Guild's 1929 London production of *Porgy*. She went on to enjoy a stellar career as a director and producer, culminating with a Tony for her 1951 production of Tennessee Williams's play *The Rose Tattoo*.
4. Tommy is Edna Lewis Thomas (1886–1974)—an actress, pianist, singer, and good friend of Dorothy West's mother, Rachel, whom she met while living in Boston. When in New York, West and Helene Johnson frequently shared a room in Thomas and her husband, Lloyd's, Seventh Avenue apartment.

It is a pity that Helen cannot go but it seems impossible. Perhaps you and Jinny[5] had better come and stay with her until I'm back.

I'm afraid I shall need a few things. Tommy says I may use her trunk. Don't you think you had better come to New York to help me get ready? Perhaps you can coax more money from father than I can, and perhaps he can get some of John's money for me out of the bank.

As soon as I get the fare I'll send it to you. I have only two weeks in which to get ready.

Are you glad I'm going? It's probably the opportunity of a lifetime. I don't know just how long we will be gone, and our first, and perhaps only stop is London.

Do you think I should tell my father? Or shall I wait until you come?

Answer this at once, will you?

Will send money as soon as I get it.

Much love,<br>
Dot

From: Rachel West, 43 West 66th Street, NYC
To: Dorothy West, London
Sunday May 5 [1929]

My dear Dot—

This card has just come from Zora. If she comes home this summer, will she take this flat? Don't you think you had better write to her so you will know just where you stand. Lloyd called up yesterday said you and Edna had a very nice flat. I am so glad. I know you will be happy now all alone. Mr. West had a very bad cold but is better. I think Virginia is out with Eugene.[6] If you write to Eugene Gordon tell him to send me 2 or 3 of the Quill Club copies.[7] Tell me just how you are. Don't get too thin it is not wise. Eat at least two good meals each day.

Lots of love to Edna

Love

Mother

5. Johnson and West's maternal first cousin, Virginia Ayer Crockett (1918–1995).

6. Mr. West is Dorothy West's father, Isaac Christopher West (1860–1933). Virginia Ayer was her cousin and Eugene Benson her uncle.

7. Eugene Gordon, originally from Oviedo, Florida, was a World War I veteran, a writer for the *Boston Post*, and president of Boston's Saturday Evening Quill Club. Some of Dorothy West's and Helene Johnson's earliest work appeared in the club's annual, the *Saturday Evening Quill*.

From: Wallace Thurman, 308 East 9th South Street, Salt Lake City
To: Dorothy West and Helene Johnson, Oak Bluffs, MA
August 30, Friday [1929]

Dear Dot and Helene:

It is measly writing you a single note for two, but I have been quite ill for the past month, and am now in no mood to write or even think consecutive or coherent thoughts.[8]

I am worried about you Helene. The leg? How on earth did it happen? Is that all Harlem could do for you?[9]

And Dot, so cosmopolitan now. A traveled lady planning to spend the winter in Paris. The idea of a colony intrigues me although such things generally turn out to be stupid unless colorful personality abounds, and then it grows tedious and unproductive. However should I be able I too shall flee to Europe this fall.

I await the story. I am all eager to see it. Shoot it to me.

And Helene? What new poems are written or conceived. I would enjoy receiving some copies of recent effusions.

Have finished a book of essays entitled: Aunt Hagar's Children. It contains essays on Negro writers, Du Bois, Garvey, Washington, Douglass, and divers other subjects. And my new novel is progressing nicely if slowly, and I am writing a talking movie. Please write to me both of you. I promise to write individual letters next time. Much love,

> As always,
> Wallie

From: Dorothy West, 1890 Seventh Avenue, NYC
To: Mrs. Grace Nail Johnson, 187 West 135th Sreet, NYC
March 8, 1931

Dear Mrs. Johnson,[10]

I cannot resist writing you this note to tell you how warming our conversation was this morning. Just when I was beginning to think, oh dear, I shall never finish this wretched novel, and certainly it will never be published, your

---

8. Thurman (1902–1934) was in Salt Lake City (his birthplace) visiting his maternal grandparents. He edited the short-lived journals Fire (1926) and Harlem (1928) and authored two novels, The Blacker the Berry (1929) and Infants of the Spring (1932).
9. Johnson hurt her leg while on tour understudying dancers in Thurman's play Harlem. She traveled with the group to Detroit and Chicago.
10. Mrs. James Weldon Johnson.

encouraging voice came over the telephone, and I am actually inspired to work hard and long until my blessed book is ended in beauty. Thank you very much! It's such seemingly small things that matter most to me. Yours was the kind word I needed to rekindle the spark. There is a lively flame in my heart.

Dorothy West

From: Dorothy West, Meschrabpom Film Corporation, Moscow, USSR
To: Rachel West, NYC
June 29, 1932
Wednesday

Dearest Mummy,

I would have cabled you the moment I arrived—Monday—but it was very expensive and I was afraid a cable might frighten you.

Already we have received 60 roubles apiece as advance, so I am getting on fine and need nothing.

I cannot write you how marvellous the trip has been. I will have to wait and tell you. We were two days on the Baltic Sea and a day and night in Berlin. And in Berlin and on the Baltic the sun never sets. It is dusk and then it is dawn again. It is clear as day at three in the morning. I shall never forget that trip up the Baltic. The sun never setting, always on the horizon the pink flush of dawn.

I loved Berlin. I want to go back before I go home. All of us do. It's a thrilling and beautiful city. Marvellous buildings, night life, everything enchanting.

From Berlin we went to Helsingfors, Finland, where we stayed the day until the boat came for the trip up the Baltic.

In Helsingfors I had my first ride in a buggy wagon. Langston and I rode for an hour, and stopped at an inn and had tea and pastries, and when I came back to the hotel, I went riding again with Mildred Jones.

We are staying in the Grand Hotel in Moscow. It is really a grand hotel. Mildred and I share a big room. I like her so much. She is intelligent and very fine.[11] I don't know how long this arrangement will last. We may move to rooms with different families. I'd like to stay on here. There are no inconveniences. We can have a bath almost every day, and the food is good, though it costs a lot. But there's nothing else for me to do with all my roubles.

Sweets are delicacies. I pay two roubles for a small portion of cake. The

11. Mildred Jones was a visual artist who studied art at Virginia's Hampton Institute. After returning to the United States, she designed the covers and layout for most issues of West's literary magazine, *Challenge*. West referred to her, as late as 1988, as "a woman whom I loved very much" (qtd. in Dalsgård 36).

strawberries are delicious. We buy them from street venders and they sell them in a cone twisted out of newspapers.

I think I start work tomorrow. The director seems sensitive and intelligent. I am eager to begin.

[ . . . ] We stopped in Leningrad before we came to Moscow. Leningrad is one of the most beautiful cities I have ever seen. We went in a bus on a sight-seeing tour. It is a city of magnificent palaces. We were given a fine dinner costing $7.00 apiece. Soup, chicken and rice, ice cream, and coffee, worth 75 cents in an American restaurant.

It is possible to get ice water. We have it every day at dinner. But there is no such thing as toilet paper. I have a little of my own, and when that goes, I'll buy some sort of paper. By the way, could you possibly—if you're still in New York—send me an iron comb. Mollie's is no good. Send me one like the one I had at home, small. Send a new one if you can.

Lots of love dear Mums.

Dot

From: Dorothy West, Meschrabpom Film Corporation, Moscow, USSR
To: Rachel West
[Early July 1932]
Sunday

Darling, dearest Mums,

I hope you and Ikey and Jinny[12] and all the rest are well. I'm just grand. Some of the others are finding it difficult to get acclimated, but I haven't had a day's sickness. For one thing, I don't eat much of this Russian food. I have so many roubles and no reason to save them, so I go almost daily to one of the four or five really magnificent hotels here, and there I order recklessly and have a grand meal. These restaurants are left over from the old regime of the Czar, and are therefore gorgeous with fine French cooking and excellent service and a soft orchestra. It's grand to go into a place and know you are welcome. The head waiters know us now and greet us with such heartwarming bows.

We are still living in the Grand Hotel. I'd rather stay here than go into a Russian home. Everything is so convenient, and we are so central.

In a few days we will be able to join the various clubs and begin meeting interesting people. Tonight some six of us are going to a party where I dare say will make some worthwhile contacts. I want to join the writers' club, one of the finest here, and also the theatrical club, I am eligible for both.

12. West's father, Isaac West, and cousin Virginia Ayer.

Langston Hughes is awfully nice to me. He brought me a bottle of champagne last night. He's working with the director on the scenario, so I've seen very little of him the past week. I've been mostly with Mildred Jones who continues to be a lovely kid. I want you to meet and like her. She's a more suitable companion than Mollie.[13] More serious-minded, intelligent, very fine. Fortunately, Mollie likes her a lot, too, so she hasn't minded the threeesomes, and Mollie likes Leonard Hill very much, so she isn't lonely.[14]

I'm not lonely either. It is definitely certain that we'll stay four months. That's in our contracts, and if we choose, we may stay longer. I think I'd like to if it is agreeable to you. You have no money worries with me here, and perhaps you can have a little for yourself.

It rains a lot in Moscow. I don't mind it but my hair does. It's almost in complete rebellion. I intend to wash it tomorrow. It got so full of train dirt I can't do anything with it.

There are more people in Moscow than anywhere in the world, I think. It's amazing. I've never seen anything like it. The streets are crowded continuously.

The strawberries and cherries and tomatoes here are delicious. Mildred and I buy them about every day. I had strawberries and milk and bread and butter for my supper here in my room last night. I feel like a little girl again when I eat cornflakes and milk at my table.

There is a colored woman here—Emma—who has been here thirty-odd years. She's going to be in the picture, too. She came here years ago as an actress, I believe, and then she lost her passport or something and had to stay on here having no American money to purchase another. What I intend to say about her is that she does our laundry so I keep as clean here as I do in America with much less bother.

I really have nothing to complain of. I expected very little, and am agreeably surprised with a whole lot. I'm just laying low, not even writing. I think we start working on the picture in a few days, and then I shall be extremely busy, no doubt. And if I can't write often, I'll send cables, so don't be frightened when you get one.

If you haven't yet gone to the beach, will you send me a large bottle—60 or 70 cents—of Hind's honey and almond cream, and an iron comb? It may cost you two dollars for duty, so if it's too expensive, don't bother. I can get along.

13. Langston Hughes (1902–1967), the most famous of the Harlem Renaissance writers, published more than three dozen books and enjoyed an influential career as a poet, short story writer, playwright, novelist, autobiographer, translator, essayist, and critic. Mollie Lewis (1907–1990), originally from Hattiesburg, Mississippi, and later Mrs. Henry Lee Moon, was a social worker and longtime board member of the National Urban League.
14. Leonard Hill was a social worker and a graduate of Howard University.

Darling Mums, keep well. Do be the same and look the same when I see you. Love to Jin and Ike. Lots to you

Dot

From: Dorothy West, Meschrabpom Film Corporation, Moscow, USSR
To: Langston Hughes
October 27, 1932

Lang, my very dear,

I didn't get your card until the twenty-third, because I joined the group in Baku[15] the thirteenth. Lang, it was too awful lying there missing you all, and thinking very straight. And after many days I was better and then began my impatient waiting for the telegram. I wanted terribly to see Mil and you, and I did not know whom I wanted to see most.

Well the telegram did come. And I left with such eagerness. If I had come ten minutes later to Baku, their train would have left me. Mil came running to me, and it was such a happy meeting, but my breathlessness did not abate, and my eyes searched everywhere for you. And then someone told me they had left you behind. Nothing in the world seemed to matter quite so much. I felt I could not bear it. I stood alone at the window and no one could have consoled me. Something was happening to me. Lang, will it sound awfully trite if I call it love. My emotions were many. Remorse, the realization of your constancy—are you made of finer stuff than most people, and is your understanding so profound? Did you know this moment would come? Do you forgive me my folly? That brightness that was beginning with us, can I make it shine again?

Oh, Lang, I want to crawl. I feel so unworthy! What I have done is not unforgivable. But what I have missed of you—three months in this marvelous country!—I shall regret as long as I live.

I had planned to leave, but they told me you were returning to Moscow in December. My feet felt clamped. I would stay on until I could see you and say to you clearly and sincerely, I never stopped loving you, not for one moment, and after my first feeling for M. had passed, my love for you grew very steadily and sturdily, and it was like a sudden flood of light when I found you were not on that train bound for Tiflis.[16] Where before I might have been still somewhat uncertain, then I was completely sure. In the twenty days following M's departure, there was no voice to listen to but my own.

M. was to live with Lydia,[17] but that plan has been changed since my decision

---

15. A port city approximately 1200 miles southeast of Moscow on the Caspian Sea.
16. Tiflis, also known as Tbilisi, is 900 miles south of Moscow and 300 miles west of Baku.
17. Lydia Myrtseva was the group's interpreter.

to remain in Moscow. Lang, her *feeling* for me is deep and sincere. I cannot wound her in any way. It's enough that I love you. I can't flaunt it in her face. And I am as fond of her as I ever have been. It is simply that this is the first time I have had the stamina to admit to myself that I do not, and I do not now remember when I did, want her as she wants me.

So, Lang, it's better for me to go. There's no other out. For economic reasons, if for no other, we would live together if I stay. And I could not torture her or myself by my nearness. I want so fiercely to belong to you. I don't want anyone to share me. I am already constant in spirit. I have such a poor best to give you, and yet I implore you to take it.

I'm going to Paris. I'll leave around the ninth. They say you are coming in the Spring. I will wait. Lang, I don't feel any embarrassment writing you in this vein. I love you. That's all I can feel. It's exalting.

Will you write me before I leave? As soon as you get this letter. But think, and think straight, for a long time, because I am not very worthy, and because I love you, it need not follow that you must return that love.

I'm so glad to get this all off my chest. It's been trembling on my lips for so long. Didn't you sometimes read them a little?

Dear dear Lamb

Dot

From: Dorothy West, Meschrabpom Film Corporation, Moscow, USSR
To: Rachel West, 23 Worthington Street, Boston
[Sunday] March 5, 1933

Mummy dearest darling,

How are you today? It is night here but we are seven hours ahead of you so it is possibly two or three at home. Does Daughter still have the radio?[18] Is it like old times again? I hope the flat is bigger than 470. And by the way, what did poor proud Annie do when English was sent to jail?[19] And how are they managing in that big house? Has anyone rented that dilapidated flat?

A group of comsomols[20] across the hall are singing the Russian Red Army songs. Russian voices are glorious. Our dear maid opens our door so we can hear them better. Then we go and look in their room and Mildred sings with them.

18. Helene Johnson's mother, Ella Benson Johnson (the eldest girl in her family), was called "Daughter."
19. In an earlier letter Rachel had reported that Mr. English Laughlin was "in trouble again—selling dope."
20. Communist youth league poets; usually spelled "komsomols."

I may come straight home and not go by way of China. If I can't get a return visa to Russia, I'll make preparations to leave and come straightaway by London and the Atlantic.

March 6th

It is Rest Day. Russia has five work days and one day of rest. Mildred stayed down here last night because she has a bad cold and Boris' house is like a barn in winter. So this morning I got up early and went to the drug store and got her some aspirin [ . . . ] . I stopped once and bought the Moscow Daily News, the only newspaper in English here, wherein I read all the banks had closed, and America was in a terrible state—I reached home, woke Mildred up made cocoa and toast for her, made tea for myself—I have got so used to drinking tea with milk now—and I had bread and butter and caviar, then I called the maid and she cleaned the room and put fresh sheets on the bed, and then I took a bath, and when I came out of the bath, I found Lang in my room and he and Mil had been talking about the depression in America, and how in the world would we see our way clear to go home by way of China because it is such an expensive trip. I'm all for trusting to luck and just going but Lang and Mil are cautious, so it is still unsettled, and I'll let you know more later. Well then Lang went and I cooked pork and potatoes for dinner, and made tea, and opened some plums and I ate some more caviar, because I love it, then Boris Pilnyak came to see how Mildred is, and he's coming back tonight to take her home in his little Ford he bought while he was in America. He likes Mildred because she's beautiful I guess, and he asked her to marry him, but she wants to go back to Harlem. She isn't studying him. He's a nice old guy though, and speaks terrible English and kisses your hand and carries on like all Russians. Russians are like colored folks, slightly crazy.

By the way I got the $2 Dollie sent me.[21] I wrote her a nice letter and thanked her. Perhaps by now she's got it. And by now you ought to have two letters from me, and one that I posted yesterday, and then, of course, the cable.

My father's death is not hard for me. Perhaps because I am so far away and it does not quite seem real. When I return to New York, and he is not there, I may be hard hit. Then, too, he is a month or so dead. Hysterical grief would be almost ridiculous. And too for the first time I am realizing my father was an old man. He must have been past seventy.[22] Wasn't he wonderful? He neither looked it nor acted it. And now with things the way they are in America I am glad he is not there ever to experience hunger or cold or want of any kind. There would inevitably have come a time when he would have been jobless and that would have killed him.

---

21. Dollie (also called "Doll") was Dorothy West's aunt Carrie Benson.
22. According to U.S. census records, he was seventy-two.

1:30

Lang came and he and I went to visit Sylvia Chinn.[23] She is one of the better known dancers here. She belongs to the new school of the dance, of course, and is thought very clever. She is half Chinese and half West Indian Negro. Her features are somewhat Negroid, but her hair is beautiful and slightly curly. She has nothing of the American Negro in her and talks with a very English accent. There are four Chinese here. I met her sister tonight. She looks more Negroid, but her hair is also straight. She is married to a director, and he was there tonight. They seem to adore each other. Prejudice is quite unknown here. Well Lang came at ten, and I was already[?] to my hat and overshoes, and we went and danced and drank tea and ate cake and candy. It was a pleasant evening, because Sylvia is very interesting, though she shows off a little.

Well back home again, and Mil is awake reading, so while my water is getting hot I am finishing my letter to you.

[ . . . ] You know, Mums, don't think I mind buckling down. Don't think I mind coming back to work hard for the first time in my life. Because I've had enough joy and fun this past year to last me the rest of my life, and if I take this trip to China my cup will overflow. And even if I do not, I will still have had infinitely more than the average person has from birth to death. I knew, as I know so many things, I would never be so carefree again as I have been since I've been here. My life has been one long hour[?] of continuous blessed joy. The trip I've had has been unbelievably beautiful. I am rich with experience. Life can give me nothing now except a child. I am really ready to settle down. All I want in life is to work hard for a few comforts for you and college for Virginia, and marry within a year and start to make a baby. That is my fortune that was told in the cards long ago for me by that woman who saw everything that has happened, my coming here, my father's death, and my knowing of it through a letter. I wish I could remember everything she said. But she, too, is dead now.

March 7

It is afternoon and a glorious day. Mildred is up and much better. She is typing now some poems for Lang, some translations he has made from Chinese and Russian. We've had our breakfast of fruit and eggs and tea with milk.

23. Sylvia Chen (correct spelling) was the daughter of Eugene Chen, a Chinese immigrant to Trinidad who at one time was English secretary to Sun Yat-sen and a prominent left-wing member of the Kuomintang. Sylvia, who grew up in Trinidad and England, was interested in radical politics and the dance of choreographer Isadora Duncan. After Chiang Kai-shek came to power, the family moved to Moscow, where Sylvia studied choreography with Fokine and specialized in ethnic dances of the Soviet Union. West was unaware of her relationship with Hughes, who said Chen was "the girl I was in love with that winter" (qtd. in Rampersad 265).

[ . . . ] In a day or two I will know more definitely about Riga.[24] I'll write again.

Lots of love, darling. Keep a stiff upper lip. And like Clinton[25] said to Grandpa, lean on me, and I don't a bit care how hard you lean. I can carry you.

Dot

From: Helene Johnson, 1890 Seventh Avenue, Apt. 2A, NYC
To: Dorothy West, Meschrabpom Film Corporation, Moscow, USSR
April 24, 1933
Monday

Dearest Dimpsie,

Darling little cousin, Tommy is sending you this $5 for your birthday[26] and she sends with it all her good wishes and all her love. She is very good to me, darling Dimp, and she is your really and truly fine friend.

I cabled you to come home against my own wishes, dear, but because the family wants you back so. You've been away so long, darling, and they are worried about you and I'm afraid to have you stay over there so far from home or my responsibility. I love you and want you to stay and work hard and make good, things are so terrible over here, but you know how families are.

Of course you stay with me Dot when you return. Ray wants you to live at Inez' but I think you and I would have lots of fun together here and Tommy and Lloyd and Olivia[27] and Al Thayer[28] and all your own particular and dearest friends want you back here. They all miss you so. Geo. Bernard Shaw's been over here since you've been gone. We can go to Oak Bluffs too after the crowd goes or after they're there. Darling, you'll be the catch of the season.

It will be wonderful, seeing you again, Dot dear. Take good care of yourself and do as you think best about returning. I wish they'd just give you a return ticket. The family wants you back awfully bad. We all miss you and love you.

Love to you, always and always, your own Big Cousin,

Helene

24. Riga, Latvia.
25. West's first cousin Clinton Johnson.
26. West turned twenty-six on June 2, 1933.
27. Edna (Tommy) Thomas and Olivia Wyndham (1897–1968) were longtime companions. They owned a farm in Sandy Hook, Connecticut, and they also shared an apartment in Harlem (and later in Brooklyn) with Thomas's husband, Lloyd.
28. In a WPA interview on Harlem nightlife, Alonzo "Al" Thayer recalled that life was a constant party for a handsome, talented young man like himself, but he also described the violence and corruption just beneath the surface and the Italian gangster who shot a woman in cold blood right in front of him. Thayer left Harlem for Los Angeles in the late 1930s to pursue a career as a model and actor.

From: Dorothy West, Meschrabpom Film Corporation, Moscow, USSR
To: Langston Hughes, Moscow, USSR
May 26, 1933

Lang, I love you. I'll never unsay those words as long as I live. For months I've wanted to tell you, but I am not very worthy, and I had to be sure of your feeling for me. You love me. I write that without boasting. But in wonder that this should happen to me. Why do you love me? Love someone who has more to give you. I have so little. Have no illusions about me.

But I have become so aware of your need of a woman. Let me be that woman. I am not ashamed to ask you. Let me give you the rest of my life. Let me make it rich.

I wrote you once before when you were in Ashkhabad.[29] The fates were against you getting my letter. I wanted us to go to Riga together.[30] The fates were against that, too. But I will be the strongest now. I will gird myself with my love and go after my love. Yes, circumstances forced me to this. We are both going away and going separately. I cannot lose you. I will not lose you. I was to go to Berlin with Mollie last November. But I wrote you that letter and waited. Mil, for more than a month, has been urging me to return to America with her, but until my telegram came, I was adamant. I have been waiting a very long time for you and me to be alone. Now I must go. Don't come with me. I want you to go to China. I want you to have adventures to the last of your life. Be forever a boy. I only want to be a woman somewhere waiting, without anxiety, Lang, my dear, and always with eagerness.

When my father died, it was then I was sure of my love. Because in my grief I did not feel wholly bereft. I even wrote my mother, I have lost my father but I am not alone. I am not lonely. If that seems premature, it is because I know your nature. You do not take women lightly. You have not taken me lightly. Your hug says more than another man's passionate kiss.

Then it was, with my father's death that I began to want a child. Let me say it, your child. Must we wait. We are both in full vigor. Now I have my best to give a baby. You who live so clean have too. Let me anticipate. Don't wait for money. And I won't wait to be wholly worthy of you. For months now I have cherished my body, eating as carefully as I could, sleeping regularly, exercising—toward this end, with you.

Must we be sensible about money? I have no dowry. I am sure you have very little in the bank. Does it matter? I shall write very much. You will write very much. You have a fine fearless brain to give a baby. I have an unusually strong body. That's sufficient heritage.

29. Ashkhabad, Turkmenistan.
30. Riga, Latvia.

While the child is in the making, I can live with my family, who will be happy to have me. Oh, I can see my mother! I shall be the first of us three[31] to give them a grandchild. It will be the proudest moment of my life. When I bear a dark son to you or a brown daughter.

Let's go to the British consul or to the Russian officials. With all my heart I want to cable Helene, Be glad for Lang and me, we are just married. Then when I know there is in me a seed, I shall go home so gladly, and wave you away to China and wait and wait, on your coming, or its coming.

The first of May[32] there comes on me a woman's sickness. Then we are both leaving so shortly after. Can we be married the 28th or 29th? It's so simple here. Without fuss and feathers. We've scarcely two weeks to be together.

Oh, Lang, I've not said all I wanted to say or what I wanted to say. This reads so baldly. But the time is so short. I can't wait! I love you. I think of nothing else. That night at the New Moscow I did so want to be mother to your four children. I humbly beg you to let me be. I post this tonight, we go to the theater tomorrow. Don't see me before then. I shall feel so shy.

—You've come in! I should stick this in your pocket. Oh, my dear. I do love you. Let me not be ashamed for bearing my heart.

Dot

Lang, I've not thought of this! After all I may have been fooled. Perhaps your feelings don't coincide with mine. If so, let me forever think you never received this letter, and let me go on cherishing my lost love.

D


From: Dorothy West, Oak Bluffs, MA [?]
To: Countee Cullen, Pleasantville, NJ
[Wednesday] September Sixth [1933]

Countee dear,

So many people tell me the wonders of Chicago that now I do envy a heap all of you who have gone. I had the thought it was a large-scale county fair for neighboring yokels, but the scientific marvels and all must be something to come miles to see. Thank you for thinking about me. That was like you.

Do you drink beer? I'm beginning to acquire a taste for it. Are there any charming beer houses in Harlem? Look here, I've never had beer out of a stein. We must find a place in the village when I come. But don't you go drinking much beer. It makes the stomach a very round o. And you are years away

31. Cousins Helene Johnson, Dorothy West, and Eugenia Rickson.
32. She probably means June.

September Sixth

Countee dear,

So many people tell me of the wonders of Chicago that now I do envy in a heap all of you who have gone. I had thought it was a large-scale county fair for neighboring yokels but the scientific marvels and all must be something to come miles to see. Thank you for thinking about me. That was like you.

Do you drink beer? I'm beginning to acquire a taste for it. Are there any charming beer houses in Harlem? Look here, I've never had beer out of a stein. We must find a place in the village when I come. But don't you go drinking much beer. It makes the stomach a very round O. And you are years away from being portly. Although that condition came upon Arna when he was yet a lad.

Autograph letter from Dorothy West to Countee Cullen, September 6, [1933]. (Countee Cullen Papers, Amistad Research Center, Tulane University.)

I am writing a good deal. I have got back
an old earnestness. There is very much I want
to do. I want to be a great Negro writer. And
there is Paris. These are steps to it. I am going
back to the short story, my best and favorite
form. I must do at least a half dozen this year.
And I can work hot in Boston. In New
York I would worry about eating and sleeping,
and perhaps I would want to go very much.
In Boston I will live quietly and work hard, and
go to New York on grand sprees. I will save up
so much of my nicest self for my coming.

Mollie writes me from Berlin. She
should be soon returning. In the early fall I
expect. How she does love Berlin. And Berlin
is almost my favorite city, too. I shall
always remember my first white night there
and myself in a trailing green gown.
I shall be here until nearly the first.
Write me. — My love always.
Dot —

from being portly. Although that condition came upon Arna when he was yet a lad.[33]

I am writing a good deal. I have got back an old earnestness. There is very much I want to do. I want to be a great Negro writer. And there is Paris. These are steps to it. I am going back to the short story, my best and favorite form. I must do at least a half dozen this year.

And I can work best in Boston. In New York I would worry about eating and sleeping, and perhaps I would want to go very much. In Boston I will live quietly and work hard, and go to New York on grand sprees. I will save up so much of my nicest self for my coming.

Mollie writes me from Berlin. She should be soon returning. In the early fall I expect. How she does love Berlin. And Berlin is almost my favorite city, too. I shall always remember my first white night there and myself in a trailing green gown.

I shall be here until nearly the first. Write me.

My love always,
Dot


From: Dorothy West, 23 Worthington Street, Roxbury, MA
To: James W. Johnson, Nashville, TN
October 23, 1933


Dear Mr. Johnson,[34]

First of all I warmly greet both you and Mrs. Johnson, and realize with sadness that the years have slipped away, and where I was a girl, now I am a woman, and there is behind me much lost loveliness.

So suddenly I am serious and entirely grown up, and I know that the promise we, the New Negroes, were so full of is enormously depleted. And now there are newer voices that are younger and sweeter. It occurred to me that I could make up from much I have wasted by some way finding a space for young dark throats to sing heard songs.

33. The Harlem Renaissance writer Arna Bontemps (1902–1973) published in several genres: poetry, drama, biography, short fiction, children's books, and novels. He collaborated with Countee Cullen (1903–1946) on the play St. Louis Woman. At his death, Bontemps was writer in residence at Fisk University. Cullen was one of the few Harlem Renaissance artists who actually grew up in Harlem. Educated at New York University and Harvard, he published six volumes of verse and won numerous fellowships and honors.
34. James Weldon Johnson (1871–1938) was a lawyer, diplomat, journalist, novelist, and poet. He authored the acclaimed novel The Autobiography of an Ex-Colored Man (1912), and the black national anthem, "Lift Every Voice and Sing." In 1930 he resigned his position as executive secretary of the NAACP, after fourteen years of service, to accept the Adam K. Spence Chair in Creative Literature at Fisk University.

I wrote to several Negro newspapers urging them to let me edit a weekly literary page. I wrote so many to insure answers from one or two anyway. But surprisingly all of them sent interested letters, although for the most part they avoided the mention of money, my stipulation, since I know nothing is more encouraging to the writer than a monetary reward. Some said that if this section caught on, then perhaps—

And now I have decided—since so many papers apparently want it—to syndicate this paper. With the ensuing advertising there may be some money in it for the contributors—and myself!—because I have already promised the various people I wrote to for material that only their first contribution would be gratis, that I hope the sections will be in a position to pay for all subsequent ones.

This is your part Mr. Johnson. There is no one else—and I have written many people for this thing and that—but it is you, the dean of Negro letters whom I very earnestly beg to write the introductory editorial.[35]

I hope the first section will be ready the first days of next month, so I will appreciate your manuscript as soon as you can possibly send it. It is not for myself alone that I ask this. But for the New Negroes that they may know a rebirth. And for the newer voices that we may light their literary way before a little.

Sincerely,
Dorothy West

From: Langston Hughes, P.O. Box 1582, Carmel, CA
To: Dorothy West, 23 Worthington, Street, Roxbury, MA
December 5, 1933

Dear Dottie,

Awfully glad to hear from you, and to hear of your plan to edit a syndicated page. When you wrote, I had nothing on hand to offer you, but since then have finished this little story which perhaps you can use. If you find that it isn't suitable, please send it back, and perhaps I can send you something else later.

What's news with you? How is your mother? Have you been to New York lately? How's Helene?

Nothing new with me except that I'm working hard on my book, and on raising

---

35. "It is a good thing that Dorothy West is doing in instituting a magazine through which the voices of younger Negro writers may be heard," proclaimed Johnson in the opening editorial.

funds for the Scottsboro defense. We've had several big meetings out here on the coast.[36]

Wouldn't you like to be back in Minninskaya eating some of that good old bread and gravy Mildred used to make and listening at the thirty being shot over in the Kremlin?[37]

So long, darlink,
Langston

P.S. This *Little Hound Dog* is going to be in my book of short stories.[38]


From: Dorothy West, 23 Worthington Street, Boston, MA
To: Langston Hughes, P.O. Box 1582, Carmel, CA
[February 2, 1934]

Dear Lang,

Under separate cover I am sending you a copy of the magazine 'Challenge' which is the final result of all my thought and plans and hopes these past months. Miraculously, I got a little money, and a magazine suits me better than a newspaper page.

I hope it will be the organ for the young Negro voice. I have done this first issue unaided. I am eager for your criticism. Be as harsh as you like. You may want to answer the article on Russia. Please do!

I particularly wanted your help in this venture, for we have fairly opposing views, and there would have been an interesting result. But I have learned— and I am very happy to hear it—that you have become associate Editor of the *New Masses*. And thank you for the sample copy. I read it with interest and profit. I daresay you are entirely too busy to lend a helping hand to me. But this magazine is going to many of the colleges. Here is our chance to reach young thinking Negroes. Many young teachers and students sent requests for the magazine. I want people like you, and Eugene Gordon, and Schuyler, and others as wide-awake to reach this audience.[39]

36. In a case that sparked international protests, nine black youths, ages thirteen to twenty-one, were accused of raping two white women on a freight train. In April 1931, an all-white jury in Scottsboro, Alabama, sentenced one to life imprisonment and the others to death. One of the women subsequently recanted, admitting that she had not been attacked, and a second trial was ordered. Charges were eventually dropped against four defendants, but the remaining five endured lengthy prison sentences.

37. The group left the Grand Hotel in the fall of 1932 and began lodging at the Minninskaya, a small hotel across from the Kremlin.

38. Hughes's "Little Dog" appeared in the inaugural issue of *Challenge*, in March 1934. It was reprinted in his short story collection *The Ways of White Folk* (1934).

39. Eugene Gordon wrote for the *Boston Post*. His short story "Game" won first prize in the 1927

And yes, Lang, your story pleased me immensely. Personally that is what I prefer from your pen. For who else comes to your height here? But I dare say you think an article does more good. But articles are contemporary. And stories can be immortal.

Lang, I want this magazine to be one of diverse opinions. I have promised myself to print anything that is sincerely written. And I could not go through that Russian experience without having some leaning toward communism. But I cannot reconcile myself to taking an equal interest in the white worker, or any interest in the white worker. On that point I need a little light. I want to be solely concerned with the black race. With Negro children in particular, that they may have a right to a full life.

With best wishes,
Dottie

From: Langston Hughes, Carmel, CA
To: Dorothy West, 23 Worthington Street, Roxbury, MA
February 22, 1934

Dear Dottie—

You've done a grand job on the magazine and uncovered some interesting new talent. I hope you'll have lots of readers. And it's swell to see Helene in print again. Give the kid my love. Somebody ought to bring out a book of hers.

Get something from Gwendolyn Bennett,[40] Zora, Wallie, a cover from Doug.[41] All the old timers aren't dead. If they're dozing, you ought to wake 'em up. The sight of a brave little girl like you putting out a magazine ought to stir 'em to a gallant aid and assistance.

We're having a big manuscript sale out here for Scottsboro. Almost all the first-rate American (and several English) writers and artists have sent things. At the pre-view Wednesday a page of Countee Cullen sold for $25! The public sale opens Monday at the Western Women's Club in Frisco. On the last day James Cagney of Hollywood will auction for us.

Where is Mil—a darling?

---

*Opportunity* contest. George Schuyler (1895–1977) was a journalist and satirist; he authored the 1931 novel *Black No More* and the controversial 1966 autobiography *Black and Conservative*.

40. Bennett (1902–1981) was a popular artist known for her poems, drawings, and *Opportunity* magazine column, "The Ebony Flute."

41. Aaron Douglas (1899–1979) was a painter, illustrator, and muralist. In 1937 he left Harlem to establish the art department at Fisk University, where he taught until his retirement in 1966.

Loren[42] is about to take the bar out here. Arna[43] is coming out to work with me this summer.

> More power to you, little Editor,
> Lang

From: Zora Neale Hurston, Bethune-Cookman College, Daytona Beach, FL
To: Dorothy West, 23 Worthington Street, Roxbury, MA [?]
March 24, 1934

Dearest Dot,

Yes, to all questions. I'm too delighted at your nerve in running a magazine not to help all I can. I *love* your audacity. You have learned at last the glorious lesson of living dangerously. Thats the stuff! Let the sun go down on you like little King Harold at the battle of Hastings—fighting gloriously. Maybe a loser, but what a loser! Greater in defeat than the Conqueror. Certainly not a coward that rusted out lurking in his tent—too afraid to cross your steel with fate.

If you do not like this un-Negro story, why not go to "Story" Magazine 20 East 57th St. and get permission to re-publish "The Gilded Six-Bits"? The story brought me a lot of recognition and I havent time to write anything good in so short a time. Anything hurried and shoddy would hurt you as a publisher and me as a writer.[44]

I'd love to be in the issue with R. Fisher.[45] He is greater than Negroes rate him generally. That is because he is too honest to pander to our inferiority complex and write "race" propaganda.

In a big hurry darling

> Yours indeed,
> Zora.

My novel "Jonah's Gourd Vine" is a May publication (Lippincotts.) It is recommended by the Book-of-the-Month Club for May.

My next book "Mules and Men" is for fall publication. Same publishers.

---

42. Loren Miller and his future wife, Juanita Lewis, traveled to Russia with West and Hughes in 1932. Miller enjoyed a distinguished career as a civil rights attorney and judge. He successfully argued *Shelley v. Kraemer*, the 1948 U.S. Supreme Court case that struck down race-based restrictive covenants in housing. Both the Washington affiliate of the National Bar Association and the State Bar of California's highest award are named in Miller's honor.
43. Hughes and Arna Bontemps collaborated on several works. West published Bontemps's short stories "Barrel Staves," "Saturday Night: Alabama Town," and "Dang Little Squirt" in *Challenge*.
44. Hurston published "The Gilded Six-Bits" in the August 1933 issue of *Story*. "The Fire and the Cloud" appeared in the second issue of *Challenge*, in September 1934.
45. Dr. Rudolph Fisher (1897–1934) was a graduate of Brown University and the Howard University Medical School. He published several well-received short stories and two novels, *The Walls of Jericho* (1928) and *The Conjure Man Dies* (1932).

Did you like Nancy Cunard's "Anthology"? I think it is great.

Perhaps it would be better to use the enclosed story than to re-print, but you are the editor.

From: Dorothy West, NYC
To: Langston Hughes, P.O. Box 1582, Carmel, CA
September 7, 1934

Challenge
A Literary Quarterly
233 West 138th Street

Dorothy West, Editor
Louis G. Sutherland
Bus. Manager

My blessed Lang,

Where are you? I hope this letter reaches you, but I hear you've been banished from Carmel. But you must know by now that you are our leader and our hope, and so long as you keep your chin up, we are not too despairing.

Lang, the long months in Moscow when life was good in the Minninskaya did not do for me and to me what my job as Home Relief investigator is. Lang, I have seen so much and learned so much. I have a first hand knowledge of hunger and sickness and despair. I have a head full of tragic stories. Sometimes I cannot bear it. And yet this is the way I must learn my lesson. I am becoming a thinking person. I will never be aggressive. And I am not a leader. And I shall always write stories rather than searching articles. But now I will write what I see, and Lang, my eyes are clear and wide.

There are other little magazines springing up. Claude McKay[46] is starting one, but they tell me it will be conservative, for he wants his citizenship papers. And yet it was Claude who was in Moscow long ago.

This issue of 'Challenge' is not even pink, because it was compiled some time ago, and it is only in the past month or two that I am not able to bear the poverty of the poor.

But, Lang, you must give me a courageous article. I read your article in the 'Crisis' and thought it was fine.[47] And by the way I am glad to know O'Brien

46. McKay (1889–1948) was a poet and novelist, and one of the most influential of the Harlem Renaissance writers. West said of him in 1988, "Countee was very fond of me. But if anybody influenced me, it was Claude" (qtd. in Dalsgård 32).
47. Hughes's "Going South in Russia" appeared in The Crisis 41.6 (June 1934): 270, 278.

chose your Cora Unashamed as one of the best short stories of the year.[48] I wish you'd have thought enough to send me an autographed copy. Mildred gloated over hers. People asked me if you'd sent me one. It isn't too late, you know. I shall always think 'Little Dog' is one of the grand things in literature.

Are you coming East soon? There is so much I would like to say to you that I cannot put in a letter. I want to talk at length about the things that are close to your heart. I do not expect to see them quite your way, but I would enjoy the exchange of ideas.

May I have that article, Lang, for the December issue? Rip my poor little magazine into pieces, if you like, though I would prefer a timely article like your Crisis thing.

At any rate write me soon that I may know this letter has reached you.

I am not at the above address. I am at 243 W. 145 St., apt. 11.

I should like my magazine to help as an organ in the East. Of course, I've a city job but I will do all I can.

Let me hear from you with your promise of an article.

As always,

Best wishes,

Dot

From: Dorothy West, 1890 Seventh Avenue, NYC
To: Claude McKay, 1835 Seventh Avenue, NYC
September 13, 1935
Friday

Claude, my dear,

I stopped by at seven this evening but you were out. I wanted to see if you were quite well again. I had dinner with Hikida[49] tonight, and he mentioned having seen you in the Library a day or so ago, and we both said very nice things about you.

Hikida bought my dinner for me, so here is my dinner money, and you must buy milk and bread and cheese, sustaining things. Wouldn't it be heavenly if we were in a garret in Paris, living on as little, and not minding? If that wretch hadn't

---

48. Beginning in 1922, Edward J. O'Brien (1890–1941) published an anthology of each year's "best short stories."

49. Hikida Yasuichi, formerly an instructor of English at Osaka's Kansai University, arrived in the United States in April 1920 at age thirty. He was, according to David Levering Lewis, "the point man for Japan's low-budget operation to influence black American public opinion." Following the Japanese attack on Pearl Harbor, he was arrested and interned on Ellis Island. In June 1942 he was deported to Japan. David Levering Lewis, *W. E. B. Du Bois: The Fight for Equality* (New York: Holt, 2000), 390–91.

walked off with my coat I would save my money toward Paris, for they say it is the nearest to heaven one ever gets on earth, but I must mind my pennies for a cloak.

When you finish your book I want you to write a play. Lang's play[50] has left a bad taste in my mouth, and I want you to erase it. You see, Claude, this is the way I grow fond of people. It isn't the way you like. But I am three fourths maternal, and I must go fussing about this and that. I love best the people who need me most. But I despise weakness. Nechevo! This is not a dissertation.

I may come to see you Sunday but I think not. Or Tuesday then, and if I don't come will you telephone me at nine or so? I want to ask you something about 'Challenge.' And Zora says you two are going to help me make the magazine really mean something. Oh, Claude, I am fond of you, and bless you, and go on writing on your novel, and know that I believe in your talent.

Dorothy

From: Claude McKay, 1835 Seventh Avenue, NYC
To: Dorothy West, 1890 Seventh Avenue, Apt. 2A, NYC
September 26, 1935

Dear Dorothy

I phoned around six (Thursday) to find out whether you would have liked to spend a little of the evening at the Hobby Horse which is always quiet[51] but you were out and I didn't care to leave a message. Maybe I shall call again tomorrow (I must go downtown in the afternoon to see if I can strike a bargain for the Grosz book).[52]

It's odd there's a full course, whenever you decide to come by—sometimes for 3 days there is no caller and then as one person pops up others follow as if there were some kind of natural telepathy at work. Carl Cowl and Grace Campbell[53] are friends of the Liberator days 14 years ago!

If I don't see you before, I shall expect you on Sunday Evening.

Sincerely<br>Claude

50. Hughes's Broadway play *Mulatto*.
51. The Hobby Horse bookstore, located at 205 West 136th Street, was a popular gathering place for young black writers.
52. The German expressionist painter George Grosz (1893–1959). "I do not know anything that has rendered so perfectly the atmosphere, temper and tempo of Berlin of that period than George Grosz's *Ecce Homo*," remarked McKay. "For me that book of drawings is a rare and iconoclastic monument of this closing era even as Rabelais is of the Renaissance." Claude McKay, *A Long Way from Home* (1937; reprint, New York: Arno, 1969), 240.
53. Carl Cowl (1902–1997) was a literary agent and McKay's literary executor; according to McKay in *A Long Way from Home*, Grace Campbell was "one of the pioneer Negro members of the Socialist Party" (109).

From: Claude McKay, 1835 Seventh Avenue, NYC
To: Dorothy West, 1890 Seventh Avenue, Apt. 2A, NYC
Wednesday October 2, 1935

Dear Dorothy

Thanks for the loan of the dollar, herewith returned, and it was a great help, for I have been broke for two weeks and just this morning got some money. It was very considerate of you to give it and also the drink for the party. The poor young man was rather shy at first, but that is his natural manner.

I have an invitation from James Weldon Johnson in the Village next Tuesday from 5 until 7 p.m. and I should like you to go along. Can you?

I shall call you tomorrow evening, I mean late afternoon to see if you want to go to that Hobby Horse place.

Sincerely<br>Claude

From: Dorothy West, NYC
To: Claude McKay, 1835 Seventh Avenue, NYC
[Postcard]
October 3, 1935

Claude, my dear

I hadn't meant for you to do that so soon—or ever—but thank you.

I should indeed like to go to that party in the Village. I can squeeze out of work at four.

Nowadays I am not at home until eight or half-past because I stop at Zora's for my dinner. So it is better not to call me until after nine.

And tonight I must go on an errand after dinner so shall we go to the Hobby Horse next Thursday. Dorothy

From: Dorothy West, 1925 Seventh Avenue, Apt. 3N, NYC
To: Rachel West
[October 3, 1935]
Thursday

Dear Mums,

Isn't it glorious weather? I feel very good. My hair keeps nice, and life is generally not bad.

I am eating with Zora now. She lives just across the street.[54] She is a better cook than Lloyd,[55] and I think we can manage cheaper than Lloyd and I did, for with Zora and me it is fifty-fifty, of course.

Countee has sent me his new book and in it is a beautiful poem dedicated to me.[56] Shall I send you the book soon, and incidentally I finally sent those squares to Grace,[57] and, yes, I would like you to knit me a sweater as soon as I can send you some yarn.

Langston Hughes is here on his way to Spain. He'll be here until around the last of the month for the opening of his play. He's as sweet as ever, still the same eager boy.

I am going to a party for James Weldon Johnson in the Village next Tuesday, so this evening I am going downtown to look for a dress. Claude is taking me. All of my friends are being so nice to me. And by the way, Mil whom I saw last night said I must always send much of her love to you. She is a nice kid, and I hope she wakes up soon.

The Watsons were delighted with Zora and Alfy, and they with them.[58] Next week I'm going to take Barbara and Mrs. Watson down to Barthe's studio,[59] and I should like to give a party at the Watsons' for Zora when her book comes out.[60] I wonder ought I to ask them.

Sorry I can't send more, but I'm getting a dress and there's my rent.

Bless you all,

Dot

---

54. Hurston was living at 1925 Seventh Avenue, apt. 2J.

55. Lloyd Thomas, Edna Thomas's spouse.

56. "To One Not There," a sonnet dedicated to "D.W.," appeared in Cullen's 1935 book *The Medea and Some Poems*.

57. Grace Turner, a Boston teacher and artist, designed the cover for the first issue of *Challenge*.

58. The Watsons (James, Violet, and their four children) were a prominent New York family who, like the Clayton Powells, summered in Oak Bluffs with the Wests. The father was the first black man elected to a judgeship in New York City; the children were Barbara (the first woman to become assistant secretary of state for security and consular affairs); Grace, who worked for the Department of Health, Education and Welfare; Douglas, an aeronautical engineer; and James, also a judge in the U.S. Customs Court. Alfy is the Trinidadian writer Alfred Mendes (1897–1991), best known for his novel *Pitch Lake*.

59. Richmond Barthé (1901–1989) was one of the twentieth century's most distinguished sculptors. In 1988 West remarked that her "beautiful friend" Richmond Barthé "did not live in Harlem with the rest of us because he wanted to live quietly and do his sculpting. He was another one like Zora. Always winning grants and prizes" (qtd. in Dalsgård 39).

60. *Mules and Men* was published in October 1935.

From: Claude McKay, 205 West 115th, NYC
To: Dorothy West, 43 West 66th Street, NYC
Tuesday January 21, 1936

Dear Dorothy

Got home at 10:30 and found your note. I was all day at the library getting my data right. You see I must just work and work like a horse for the next three months. My contract stipulates that my book must be delivered on the 15th of March. And it is only half done. So you must excuse my not being home. And please, Dorothy don't tell people that I won't go out and all that and make them say they would invite me but *you* said I won't go out and don't want anyone to have my address. Better let them approach me and find out things for themselves. I like very much congenial association when I have time.

And you ought to go and see Edna Thomas and invite her down. She is very sweet and says she loves you and you should not be pettish about a little situation that was very difficult for her.

Thanks for the dollar for the concert, but as I didn't go I am sending it back. I am not altogether broke. If I were I shouldn't hesitate to keep it. But I am not a chiseler and you are just a poor worker and need it as much as I. Some other time when I need it, I shall be happy to take it. If I keep it I shall spend it worthlessly and that is not fair.

I hope your cold will be better. Did you enjoy the party? Zora and I went home with some artists and stayed up until 5. If you are in my neighborhood any evening, drop in again. My love to Molly and Selma.[61]

Yours Sincerely
Claude McKay


From: Marian Minus, 6412 Langley Avenue, Chicago
To: Dorothy West, 43 West 66th Street, NYC
[Wednesday] October 21, 1936, 6 p.m.

[no greeting]

The American Student Union, Phoenix (the campus "lit and wit" magazine) and the Daily Maroon (the college paper) are sponsoring straw voting here.[62] Today is the second of the three, and Roosevelt is leading by a narrow margin.

61. Dr. Selma Burke (1900–1995) was a sculptor and educator. She received an M.F.A. from Columbia University and a doctorate from Livingston College in Salisbury, North Carolina. She is best known for her portrait of Franklin Delano Roosevelt on the dime.
62. Minus (1913–1972) was a graduate student in social anthropology at the University of Chicago.

There are too many wealthy students here for Landon not to receive a large number of votes. I voted for Earl Browder.[63] [ . . . ] the Socialists and Communists are battling verbally in every corner of the University.

Someone just rushed to me to tell me that Dick Wright[64] is a Trotskyite. If only you could have seen the horror in her face! I must talk to Dick because I think he's going through the same thing which I am just recovering from. The Party is, of course, embittered because Dick was the Communist flag[?] in literature as far as Negroes are concerned. Now he will write because writing is his life. He will always have a message because he has always been a proletarian. But thank heaven he won't be forced to type[?] out shibboleths just because he is a Communist. They should have seen long ago that he was beyond that stage and was crying to be allowed to let his mature work be born. They are so stupid.

I am about to freeze so I must move.

When five o'clock comes and if it is still raining, I shall turn my feet from the path they will think leads to the Partridge Inn and you.

My love to you. And please, Dorothy, take care of yourself. It is such nasty weather. Mother says that it is raining in New York.

By the way, she had to work Saturday to make up for Columbus Day,[65] and she said she was sorry to miss you.

Marian

From: Dorothy West, Oak Bluffs, MA
To: Harold Jackman, 50 Morningside Avenue, NYC
Tuesday [February 1948]

Dear Harold,

This wretched winter may soon be ending. I have never watched the calendar so hard in my life. We haven't had all your snow or all your cold. But we've had far too much for a place that is generally considered idyllic. I don't care whether March comes in like a lion or lamb. I only want it to come and bring the spring.

My mother is recovering beautifully. In another ten days she'll be as fit as a

---

63. Earl Browder (1891–1973) and Kansas governor Alfred Landon (1887–1987) were the Communist and Republican Party candidates, respectively, for the presidency in 1936. Franklin Roosevelt won, with 63 percent of the vote.

64. Novelist Richard Wright (1908–1960) migrated from his native Mississippi to Chicago, where he joined the Communist Party, and to New York City, where in 1937 he co-edited the first (and only) issue of *New Challenge* with West and Minus.

65. Minus's mother, Laura Druette Whitener Minus (1886–1975), worked for the WPA. She was originally from Newberry, South Carolina.

fiddle. The doctor has given her a complete new lease on life. And I can assure you she's very grateful.

It won't be too long now before my book is off the presses. Just last week I was sent the front flap and back jacket copy for my corrections. I think I've done about all there is for me to do except approve the front jacket. I doubt that I'll see that, for who am I to judge an artist's work.

Publication date is tentatively March. But March is almost on us, so I rather think it will be April. As soon as the date is definite, I'll let you know.[66]

Marian has written me that you two have been hanging around a little, and I know you've had fun, which I hope to share with you in not too long a time. But it seems a good while back that I was very young. I shall trip the fantastic but not too lightly. Like all my family I manage to look much younger than I feel. But I wouldn't trade the years of my knowing for my lost innocence.

Didn't mean to grow philosophical!

Love, Dorothy

From: Doubleday & Company, 575 Madison Avenue, NYC
To: Dorothy West, Box 404, Oak Bluffs, MA
April 2, 1951

Dear Miss West:

As you probably know, several of us here have read your book, *Where the Wild Grape Grows*, with great interest. There are so many things about this book that we like that it seems a shame that it is still not publishable. I am writing now to give you some of our ideas on this book and hope that you will be willing to do some more work on it.

First of all, don't you think that you really have two stories here instead of one? When you are writing about Bit and Bea and Jenny, you have a really unusual and pleasant way of handling them. This is true, too, I think, of Essie Carlson and Old Ma; but when you get started with Pierce and Carol Hunter, somehow the book seems to lose its drive and its originality. Pierce's story is really implausible and somewhat melodramatic, while the quiet yearnings of the old ladies ring true always. I think it might be wise to cut out Pierce and Carol completely and try to introduce a new conflict. For one thing, couldn't more be done with Bea's son? It might not be necessary to bring him back into the story, but it strikes me that some illuminating flashbacks would be helpful. He could be a more important reason for Bea's

---

66. Harold Jackman and Marian Minus hosted a book signing for West in Harlem on May 13, 1948, just as *The Living Is Easy* began rolling off the printing press.

and Jenny's neurotic refusal to face up to old age. And his problems could be contrasted much more effectively to those of the old folks than Pierce's childish rebellions.

It seems to me, too, that something more should be done with the white people who live on the island. Why don't Jenny and Bea ever have any dealings with them? I think here you have a chance to deepen the story and give it some interesting details.

I realize that these are all rather vague amorphous ideas, but I pass them along to you only as suggestions for a new plot line. It would be wise, I think, to do some intensive work in setting up a new conflict in place of the Pierce and Carol story. Otherwise the problems of the old ladies, which you handle so well, will be too slight for a novel and could probably be better used in a long short story.

I would like very much to hear from you about this and hope that you will want to do some more work on the book and show it to us again.

Sincerely yours,

Betty Arnoff

ba/jkh


From: Dorothy West, Oak Bluffs, MA [?]
To: Langston Hughes
January 10, 1966

Dear Lang,

How good to see your still familiar handwriting. I am happy to wish you the best that the season can bring.

Thank you for including me in your anthology of short stories by Negro writers. I look forward to its publication. I have great respect for Little, Brown.

I don't remember The Richer, the Poorer. Spoken like a writer! But I do remember the first story I wrote for the News, though, alas, not its title.[67]

At that time The News had a feature called Blue Ribbon Fiction. The story I wrote for them had distinctively Negro characters. I mean I identified them as Negroes.

I wish you would take a look at that story, though it may run longer than you want for your purposes. Blue Ribbon Fiction ran full length, 3 to 500 words. I think you will find it a moving story.

---

67. West published "The Richer, the Poorer" in the May 14, 1958, *New York Daily News*. Hughes included it in his 1967 collection *The Best Short Stories by Negro Writers: An Anthology from 1899 to the Present*.

I believe the News has American and Canadian rights to my stories, though I remember Canada buying one of my short stories, and no red tape with the News. But that was some time ago. Perhaps my memory dims.

In any case, I am giving this release, and you can check it with the News.

As you may know, I'm working on a book for Harper and Roe [sic]. But I'm such a slow writer! Just living, which includes cooking and cleaning, takes up so much valuable time.

My best to you, dear Lang, and thank you for your good wishes.[68]

Dorothy

68. Hughes died the following year, after a brief illness, on May 22, 1967.

# APPENDIX I. STORIES FROM THE *NEW YORK DAILY NEWS*

"Jack in the Pot," September 29, 1940

"The Roomer," March 31, 1941

"The Penny," June 25, 1941

"The Puppy," May 9, 1942

"Fluff and Mr. Ripley," August 9, 1944

"The Doll," 1945

"The Blind Spot," February 25, 1947

"Wives and Women," March 7, 1947

"The Letters," August 13, 1947

"Happiness," September 17, 1954

"The Long Wait," November 2, 1954

"The Lean and the Plenty," March 6, 1957

"Homecoming," April 16, 1957

"Summer Setting," May 21, 1957

"Babe," July 11, 1957

"The Maple Tree," August 23, 1957

"The Blue Room," December 28, 1957

"The Richer, the Poorer," May 14, 1958

"Interlude," June 5, 1958

"Summer of Wonderful Silence," August 2, 1958

"The Long Wait," November 2, 1959

"The Birthday Party," April 29, 1960

"Mrs. Creel," June 6, 1960

"The Birds," July 19, 1960

"The Fun Ball," February 10, 1961

"The Stairs," December 11, 1961

"The Bent Twig," March 17, 1962

"The Dinner Party," July 5, 1962

"Nothing Lasts Forever," July 23, 1963

"The Bird Like No Other," August 24, 1964

# APPENDIX II. FAMILY TREE

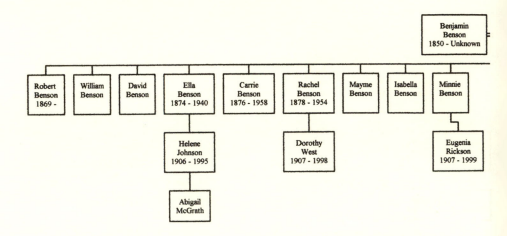

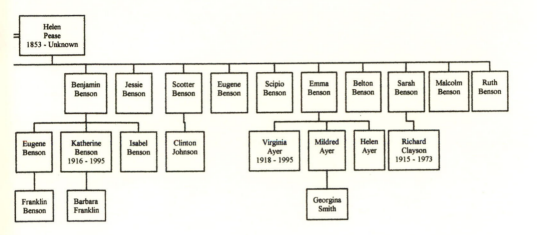

# NAME INDEX

VERNER D. MITCHELL is assistant professor of English at the University of Memphis and editor of *This Waiting for Love: Helene Johnson, Poet of the Harlem Renaissance.* He is a graduate of the U.S. Air Force Academy and holds a Ph.D. in English from Rutgers University. He lives in Cordova, Tennessee, with his wife, Veronica, and their children, Jared and Courtney.

CYNTHIA DAVIS is associate professor and assistant chair of the Department of English at Barry University. Her writings include *Dynamic Communication for Engineers,* as well as numerous essays and book reviews on Caribbean and African American literatures. She holds degrees from Boston College and Georgetown University and received her Ph.D. from the University of Maryland at College Park. She and her husband, Robert Sbaschnig, have two children, Renee and Matthew, and reside in Boynton Beach, Florida.